British History in Perspective
General Editor: Jeremy Black

PUBLISHED TITLES

Rodney Barker *Politics, Peoples and Government*
C. J. Bartlett *British Foreign Policy in the Twentieth Century*
Eugenio Biagini *Gladstone*
Jeremy Black *Robert Walpole and the Nature of Politics in Early Eighteenth-Century Britain*
D. G. Boyce *The Irish Question and British Politics, 1868–1996 (2nd edn)*
Keith M. Brown *Kingdom or Province? Scotland and the Regal Union, 1603–1715*
A. D. Carr *Medieval Wales*
Eveline Cruickshanks *The Glorious Revolution*
Anne Curry *The Hundred Years War*
John W. Derry *British Politics in the Age of Fox, Pitt and Liverpool*
Susan Doran *England and Europe in the Sixteenth Century*
Seán Duffy *Ireland in the Middle Ages*
William Gibson *Church, State and Society, 1760–1850*
David Gladstone *The Twentieth-Century Welfare State*
Brian Golding *Conquest and Colonisation: the Normans in Britain, 1066–1100*
Sean Greenwood *Britain and the Cold War, 1945–1991*
S. J. Gunn *Early Tudor Government, 1485–1558*
J. Gwynfor Jones *Early Modern Wales, c. 1525–1640*
Richard Harding *The Evolution of the Sailing Navy, 1509–1815*
David Harkness *Ireland in the Twentieth Century: Divided Island*
Ann Hughes *The Causes of the English Civil War (2nd edn)*
Ronald Hutton *The British Republic, 1649–1660*
Kevin Jefferys *The Labour Party since 1945*
T. A. Jenkins *Disraeli and Victorian Conservatism*
T. A. Jenkins *Sir Robert Peel*
H. S. Jones *Victorian Political Thought*
D. E. Kennedy *The English Revolution, 1642–1649*
D. M. Loades *The Mid-Tudor Crisis, 1545–1565*
John F. McCaffrey *Scotland in the Nineteenth Century*
Diarmaid MacCulloch *The Later Reformation in England, 1547–1603*
W. David McIntyre *British Decolonization, 1946–1997: When, Why and How did the British Empire Fall?*
A. P. Martinich *Thomas Hobbes*
W. M. Ormrod *Political Life in Medieval England, 1300–1450*
Richie Ovendale *Anglo-American Relations in the Twentieth Century*
Ian Packer *Lloyd George*
Keith Perry *British Politics and the American Revolution*
Murray G. H. Pittock *Jacobitism*
A. J. Pollard *The Wars of the Roses*
David Powell *British Politics and the Labour Question, 1868–1990*
David Powell *The Edwardian Crisis*
Richard Rex *Henry VIII and the English Reformation*

1658**

Titles continued overleaf

List continued from previous page

G. R. Searle   *The Liberal Party: Triumph and Disintegration, 1886–1929*
Paul Seaward   *The Restoration, 1660–1668*
John Stuart Shaw   *The Political History of Eighteenth-Century Scotland*
W. M. Spellman   *John Locke*
William Stafford   *John Stuart Mill*
Robert Stewart   *Party and Politics, 1830–1852*
Bruce Webster   *Medieval Scotland*
Ann Williams   *Kingship and Government in Pre-Conquest England*
John W. Young   *Britain and European Unity, 1945–1999 (2nd edn)*
Michael B. Young   *Charles I*

Please note that a sister series, *Social History in Perspective*, is now available.
It covers the key topics in social, cultural and religious history.

British History in Perspective
Series Standing Order
ISBN 0–333–71356–7 hardcover
ISBN 0–333–69331–0 paperback
(outside North America only)

You can receive future titles in this series as they are published by placing a standing order. Please contact your bookseller or, in case of difficulty, write to us at the address below with your name and address, the title of the series and the ISBN quoted above.

Customer Services Department, Macmillan Distribution Ltd
Houndmills, Basingstoke, Hampshire RG21 6XS, England

BRITAIN AND EUROPEAN UNITY, 1945–1999

SECOND EDITION

John W. Young

First edition published in 1993
Second edition published in 2000 by
MACMILLAN PRESS LTD
Houndmills, Basingstoke, Hampshire RG21 6XS
and London
Companies and representatives throughout the world

A catalogue record for this book is available from the British Library.

ISBN: 0–333–74112–9 (PB)
0–333–74111–0 (HB)

First edition published in the United States of America 2000 by
ST. MARTIN'S PRESS, LLC,
Scholarly and Reference Division,
175 Fifth Avenue,
New York, N.Y. 10010

ISBN: 0–312–23123–7

Library of Congress Cataloging-in-Publication Data

Young, John W., 1957–
    Britain and European unity, 1945–1999 / John W. Young—2nd ed.
        p.   cm. — (British history in perspective)
    Rev. ed. of: Britain and European unity, 1945–1992, 1993.
    Includes bibliographical references (p.) and index.
    ISBN 0–312–23123–7 (cloth)
        1. Europe—Relations—Great Britain.   2. Great Britain—Relations—
    Europe.   3. Europe—Foreign relations—1945–   4. European
    Federation.   5. European Economic Community.   I. Young, John W.,
    1957– Britain and European unity, 1945–1992.   II. Title.   III. Series.

    D1065.G7 Y68   2000
    303.48′24104—dc21

                                                            99–054889

Printed in Hong Kong

CONTENTS

Contents

PREFACE

This book provides an historical survey of British policy towards the question of European unity from 1929 (when the issue first, if momentarily, became significant) to 1999 (when a single currency, the Euro, was launched in Europe). The main focus is on the development of policy at government level after 1945, but attention is also paid to pressure groups, the press and public opinion. As with other books in the series, the purpose is to introduce readers not only to the principal events in British relations with the European unity movement, but also to the debates on this subject between historians and political scientists. However, it is important to note at the outset that the nature of this debate changes as the book proceeds. This is mainly because European unity is a recent issue, mainly confined to the post-war period. For the years 1929–63 a considerable amount of work has now been done by historians, using government sources, the private papers of political figures and other archival material, so that an 'historical debate' can be said to exist. For the years 1963–8 government documents are available but they have not yet been digested and little genuine 'historical' research has been published. In this period therefore I have made use of my own primary research to supplement the books which have been written.

For the years 1957 to 1990 a number of very useful memoirs and diaries have been published, both by Labour politicians – notably the diaries of Richard Crossman, Barbara Castle and Tony Benn – and by Conservatives – in the early period there are several volumes of Harold Macmillan's memoirs; Edward Heath has now published a long-awaited autobiography which helps illuminate his ill-fated premiership; whilst on the Thatcher years there is now a plethora of memoirs, the most valuable being those of the ex-Prime Minister herself and two of her leading ministers, Geoffrey Howe and Nigel Lawson. All provide interesting material which, again, can be used to supplement the texts of political scientists on these years. After 1990 there is quite a lively debate among journalists and political scientists about the European policies of John Major, the negotiations of the Maastricht agreement and the growing rift over Europe within Conservative ranks. A number of works also touch, already, on the Blair government, mainly in the form of biographies of leading ministers.

Another point to make at the outset is that the terminology in the debate over European unity is often confusing. Words such as 'union', 'integration' and even 'federation' are used with little attention to their precise meaning. I have used 'federation' as the British themselves usually do, to apply to a situation where states surrender political decision-making to a central government institution. Such a European government may be the ultimate aim of some Euro-enthusiasts, but as yet the European Union is far removed from such a result. At the other extreme the term 'inter-governmental co-operation' is used to refer to a situation where states work together without surrendering any sovereignty to common institutions, though (as in the case of NATO) there may be an *implied* loss of independence. The terms 'functional' or 'sectoral' co-operation are used to refer to the co-ordination of policies in certain areas only – for example in the coal and steel industries, as in the 1950 Schuman Plan. 'Functional' co-operation need not lead to a diminution of sovereignty, though it did in the case of the Schuman Plan which created a 'supranational' institution, that is one which took over responsibility from governments for a 'sector' of activity. The term 'union' is, according to some dictionary definitions, the same as 'federation', but in the European unity debate it is much vaguer. The terms 'pooled sovereignty' and 'deeper integration' refer to the type of co-operation seen in the European Community, often called the 'Community method' whereby the member states have gradually handed certain powers to the European Commission and created a 'web' of co-operation between themselves. This goes beyond traditional types of co-operation between states, and it would be very difficult – but not impossible – for any member to withdraw from the 'web'; but principal decision-making power still resides with the member governments meeting in the Council of Ministers and, at leaders' level, in the European Council. The European Parliament possesses limited powers, and it is debatable how far the European Commission has independent 'supranational' power.

For the 1960s I have used the term European Economic Community (EEC) to refer to the 'common market' created by the Treaty of Rome, but 'common market' was always a more popular term in Britain, reflecting the country's obsession with trade issues. In the 1970s and 1980s 'European Community' became the usual way to refer to all the institutions created by the 1951 Treaty of Paris (Coal–Steel Community) and the 1957 Treaties of Rome (EEC and Atomic Energy Authority). All three institutions were in fact 'merged' in a treaty of 1968. After 1993, and the ratification of the Maastricht Treaty, I use the term European Union. I have referred to 'pro' and 'anti-Europeans' (or in the 1990s 'Euro-enthusiasts' and 'Eurosceptics') in a broad sense, but have tried to show that these terms are too crude to describe effectively the kind of debates which have occurred in Britain over the country's international role since 1945. Finally, I have sometimes bowed to the practice of referring to the EEC simply as 'Europe', because this is how it is referred to in many debates (thus, in the 1960s, there was considerable talk of 'going into Europe'). This is not the place to define the geographical, cultural or historical bounds of Europe but it is vital to say that the European Union still includes only a proportion of the countries and people of Europe. That 'Europe' has become coterminous with the integrated Western countries in many minds simply reflects the success of the Community (or Union) idea in practical and propaganda terms.

Numerous people have talked to me over the years about Britain and Europe. In particular John Kent and John Barnes of the London School of Economics and Geoffrey Warner have particularly influenced my thinking about the years 1945–63. It has also been useful to have a number of research students working in the area, including Alasdair Blair, Christopher Goldsmith and Gillian Staerck. But I must also thank Phil Taylor, David Dilks and Roy Bridge with whom I worked at Leeds University, Donald Watt, David Stevenson and Alan Sked, colleagues from the London School of Economics, Michael Goldsmith and Andrew Geddes of Salford University, and Geoffrey Berridge, Murray Forsyth, Philip Lynch, Jan Melissen, Joerg Monar, Wyn Rees and Stuart Ball, colleagues from Leicester University, as well as Richard Aldrich, Oliver Daddow, Anne Deighton, Edmund Dell, Mike and Saki Dockrill, James Ellison, Sean Greenwood, Wolfram Kaiser, Michael Kandiah, Christopher Lord, Piers Ludlow, Daniel Mason, Spencer Mawby, Alan Milward, Constantine Pagedas, Gustav Schmidt and all those Masters students who have studied European integration with me over the years. Salford University research fund supported my work at the Public Record Office on the years 1955–61; I am deeply grateful to the British Academy and the Faculty of Social Sciences at the University of Leicester for funding similar research on the years 1964–7. My thanks also go to Jeremy Black and the staff at Macmillan for help in bringing the project to fruition; to Bob Borthwick for doing such a thorough job as my Deputy Head of Department, allowing me to preserve research time; and to Janet Smith for typing up the manuscript with her customary care and attention.

LIST OF ABBREVIATIONS

BOT	Board of Trade
CAP	Common Agricultural Policy
CFP	Common Fisheries Policy
CFSP	Common Foreign and Security Policy
EC	European Community
ECB	European Central Bank
ECSC	European Coal–Steel Community
ECU	European Currency Unit
EDC	European Defence Community
EEC	European Economic Community
EFTA	European Free Trade Association
EMS	European Monetary System
EMU	Economic and Monetary Union
EP	European Parliament
ERM	Exchange Rate Mechanism
EU	European Union
Euratom	European Atomic Energy Authority
DEA	Department of Economic Affairs
FO	Foreign Office (Foreign and Commonwealth Office from 1965)
FTA	Free Trade Area
GAAT	General Agreement on Tariffs and Trade
IGC	Inter-Governmental Conference
JHA	Justice and Home Affairs
MEP	Member of the European Parliament
NAFTA	North Atlantic Free Trade Area
NATO	North Atlantic Treaty Organisation
NEC	National Executive Committee of the Labour party
OECD	Organisation for Economic Co-operation and Development
OEEC	Organisation for European Economic Co-operation

PR	Proportional Representation
PRO	Public Record Office
QMV	Qualified Majority Voting
SDP	Social Democratic Party
SEA	Single European Act
TEU	Treaty on European Union
TUC	Trades Union Congress
UN	United Nations
VAT	Value-added Tax
WEU	Western European Union

1

THE BIRTH OF EUROPEAN UNITY, 1929–1949

On 13 August 1945 Ernest Bevin, Britain's new Foreign Secretary, held a meeting with Foreign Office (FO) officials to discuss future policy towards Western Europe. A few weeks earlier the Labour party had entered government with its first overall majority; the 'Big Three' powers – America, Britain and the Soviet Union – had just held their last wartime summit meeting; Japan was on the brink of unconditional surrender. In this situation Bevin could hope to reforge Britain's international relations and many in the FO wished to see West European co-operation become a cornerstone of post-war British policy. They did not leave the August meeting disappointed. During the session Bevin outlined a 'grand design' to build co-operation with the Continent at all levels: political, military and economic. The first step would be an alliance with France, a pre-war ally, a fellow colonial power, and the largest European democracy. On this basis links could be extended outwards to the Low Countries, Scandinavia, and Italy. Reading the accounts of this meeting it might seem that Britain was ready, in 1945, to undertake the close commitment to the Continent in peacetime from which it had historically shrunk.[1]

Twelve years later, in March 1957, the European Economic Community (EEC) was founded without British membership. Britain since 1945 had repeatedly distanced itself from efforts to create supranational institutions in Europe. Instead the country based its political and economic future, in the international sphere, on the American alliance and the Empire-Commonwealth. This approach was not seriously challenged until 1961 when Harold Macmillan's government made the first application to

1

enter the EEC. By then Britain's economy was performing badly relative to the rest of Western Europe, the Empire was disintegrating and the US had long ceased to treat Britain as an equal. In retrospect the failure to fulfil Bevin's 'grand design' of August 1945 seemed to point to major errors of judgement by British policy-makers. Many writers, beginning with Anthony Nutting and Nora Beloff in the early 1960s, have argued that the British government 'missed the bus' in Europe when they ought to have taken the lead in efforts at European integration.[2] The purpose of the first two chapters is to survey British government policy before the foundation of the EEC, in the light of newly opened archives, to see why Britain avoided early efforts to create supranational European institutions.

Antecedents

The question of Britain's attitude towards European unity was far from new in 1945. In a general sense Britain had been under pressure to interest itself more closely in events on the Continent since the end of the nineteenth century. Though its power has frequently been exaggerated, Britain then possessed the largest Empire the world had ever known, it had been the first major industrialised state, and its parliamentary democracy was remarkably stable compared to European regimes. But most would argue that British decline relative to new industrial competitors had already begun. New powers such as America, Germany and Japan were arising to challenge Britain's industrial, commercial, Imperial and naval pre-eminence. The Boer War revealed both military weaknesses and the danger of a European combination against Britain, calling into question the notion of 'splendid isolation'. In 1902 Britain entered into its first long-term security alliance in peacetime, though significantly it was not primarily concerned with Europe. The treaty was with Japan and was designed to protect Britain's position in the Far East. In 1904 and 1907 Britain settled its differences with France and Russia in *ententes* – although, again, these agreements principally involved Imperial issues. Only in 1914 did Britain finally commit itself to war against the Central Powers, Germany and Austria–Hungary, which involved a major land campaign in Europe, higher taxes and such restrictions on personal freedom as conscription. (Previously Britain lacked the large conscript armies of continental states.) Notwithstanding this dramatic change in policy, in the wake of the First World War Britain tried to distance itself from

Europe once more, extending its rule to new areas of the Middle East, rejecting a formal alliance with France, and refusing to give real authority to the new peace-keeping body, the League of Nations, which was based on the idea of 'collective security' against aggressors. When France occupied the Ruhr in 1923, to enforce reparations payments from Germany, Britain criticised the French, and tried to pose as an arbiter between the two continental states. It then helped to bring about the 1925 Locarno Pact which stabilised West European borders and allowed Britain to concentrate on Imperial problems. Thus, despite increasing pressures to involve itself in continental affairs, Britain preferred to support a balance of power in Europe from the outside, as the best way to preserve its liberal institutions, its world trade and its military security. Such a stance also allowed the country to safeguard its strength – which was not as great as many Britons liked to believe.

The first occasion on which the idea of a *federal* Europe was seriously suggested in practical politics was in 1929 when France's foreign minister Aristide Briand proposed such a scheme. There are many parallels between the story of the Briand Plan and developments after 1945 which make the episode worthy of attention. The Plan came after a decade of French retreat from the Treaty of Versailles, which had imposed a harsh peace on Germany. In 1924, after the failure of the Ruhr occupation, France accepted a reduction of reparations payments and thereafter tried to develop a policy of co-operation with Germany. In 1926 a steel cartel was formed between the industrialists of France, Germany and Belgium–Luxembourg, and in 1927 a Franco-German commercial treaty was signed. On the political level Briand worked closely with Germany's Gustav Stresemann. The Briand Plan was a French attempt to work with Germany on an equal basis, accepting German revival and a further reduction in reparations, whilst guaranteeing French security. It aimed to do this by embracing Germany in a *European* framework. At the same time a European 'federation' would break down barriers to trade in Europe and help the Continent stand up to American economic competition. However, British ministers showed little enthusiasm for the plan, for a number of reasons. On the economic side, as Robert Boyce has argued, they were opposed to regional trading blocs, preferring a liberal trade policy; they wished to preserve special commercial links to the Commonwealth; and they did not wish to argue with the Americans, who seemed likely to oppose a European trading bloc because it would restrict US exports. On the political side no one in the British government had shown any enthusiasm for the 'pan-European' ideas of individuals such as the Austrian Count Coudenhove-Kalergi which had grown in appeal after the appalling destruction of the First World War. In 1926 Sir William Tyrell, the Permanent Under-Secretary at the Foreign Office, dismissed Coudenhove-Kalergi as 'a thoroughly impractical theorist'. Yet Boyce has also shown that, by 1930, many British industrialists and politicians believed that the world could soon divide into continental-size economic blocs including, perhaps, a European one. In response to this Lord Beaverbrook and others advocated the consolidation of the British Empire. Ralph White has argued that London *was* interested in European co-operation to preserve the peace, but wished to achieve this via more traditional methods of balance of power diplomacy. However, it was not only British reticence which defeated the Briand Plan: few other countries liked the idea; Stresemann, who did welcome the scheme, died in October 1929; and Briand did not produce a detailed Plan until May 1930. Even then he was contradictory and vague about how exactly a 'federation' could be created.[3]

In the 1930s any hopes of a European federation receded with the economic slump, the move towards exclusive trading and economic blocs, and the aggressive nationalist policies of Germany, Italy and Japan. Faced by balance of payments deficits and the decline of traditional industries, Britain created an 'Imperial preference' system in trade, and developed the Sterling Area among countries which traded in Sterling, so as to protect its share of world trade. Some in Britain did however show an appreciation of the potential gains of European co-operation. One was Ernest Bevin, then a trade union leader, who after visiting the US in 1927 believed that a large, single market in Europe would improve trade and employment levels. He continued to show a fitful interest in European unity in the 1930s, whilst realising the problems of national differences. In 1940 he advocated a rather different idea, an Anglo-French imperial customs union.[4] There were also a number of influential British figures in 1938–9, who believed that, given the failure of the League of Nations to preserve the peace, states should surrender some of their sovereignty to a federal *world* government. Supporters of the 'Federal Union' movement included Archbishop William Temple and the Ambassador to Washington, Lord Lothian. They were inspired by *Union Now!* a book by an American journalist, C. K. Streit, published in 1938. Even Streit however, believed that a federation was only possible among the liberal democracies, and his scheme could not therefore have avoided war with the aggressor states, which broke out in September 1939. Nine months later France fell and later Britain found itself excluded from a very different vision of Europe's future: Hitler's Nazi-dominated 'New Order'. But the ideas developed by the British Federal Union movement had an important impact on the wartime development of federalist ideas in Europe among Resistance movements determined that there would be no more destructive European wars. Therefore, as a study by Michael Burgess has demonstrated, there was a well-developed *British* tradition of federalism by 1940 – witnessed by proposals for an Imperial federation and for a federal solution to Britain's internal differences (between England, Scotland, Wales and Ireland) as well as by the ideas of the Federal Union.[5]

It is significant that, just before the Fall of France to the Nazis in June 1940, Britain offered its ally an 'indissoluble union', including common citizenship, Imperial unity and a single Cabinet. This was a radical proposal, drawn up by officials from both countries, most notably France's Jean Monnet. The 'indissoluble union' appealed to Britain's new Prime Minister, Churchill, and France's Under-Secretary of War, Charles de Gaulle, mainly as a way to keep the French Empire in the war. But the proposal was turned down by the French Cabinet, who feared a British attempt to take over the French Empire and were convinced of Germany's ultimate victory. The indissoluble union was quickly forgotten, and Britain was left to fight on alone.[6]

Consideration of European co-operation only revived after 1941, when Britain was joined by two new, powerful allies, the USSR and the United States, neither of which had been closely involved in European diplomacy in the inter-war years. The support of both was vital to defeat Germany, Italy and Japan, but both the US and the Soviet Union posed a threat to Britain's world standing. True, Britain and America were bound together by language, culture and liberal political doctrine and worked closely together during the war. Some writers have seen a smooth transition from British leadership of the Western democracies before 1941 to that by the Americans thereafter; one has even discussed 'Anglo-America' in terms of a single 'power' when the war ended, by which time the Soviet Union was already emerging as a new menace to the West.[7] But the British and Americans were often divided over such issues as the future of colonialism and economic policy, with the Americans critical of the British Empire and its preferential trade system. However close the two were, they remained sovereign states, with distinct strategic interests, and it was not easy for Britain to adjust to a position of inferiority to the US by 1944.[8] As to the USSR, British relations with it were never as close as those with America. Churchill, despite his later claims to have foreseen the Soviet menace, hoped for a good working

relationship with Joseph Stalin even in 1945. But ideological differences
with the Soviets always ran deep and the Red Army's advance into Eastern Europe in 1944–5 created apprehension among certain elements in
Whitehall.[9] For some a Western European bloc was seen as a way to withstand Soviet strength.

The Western Bloc Proposal, 1941–6

Ironically, the idea of a British-led 'Western bloc' was first put forward by
Stalin himself, in talks with British Foreign Secretary Anthony Eden in
December 1941. Stalin saw British military bases in Western Europe as a
way to hold down Germany after the war, and also as a way to compensate Britain for Soviet predominance in Eastern Europe – the thing he
wanted above all.[10] But Western European politicians, whose governments had gone into exile in London, also favoured closer co-operation
under British leadership. Norway's Trygve Lie and Holland's Eelco van
Kleffens wanted a new European security system to prevent a repetition
of the German victories of 1939–40 and Belgium's Paul-Henri Spaak
pressed Britain to lead Western Europe towards greater political and
economic unity.[11] Influential figures such as Labour leader Clement
Attlee and South African premier General Smuts also believed that Britain
must work closely with Western European countries after the war and in
1944, with victory in sight, the Foreign Office began to consider such ideas
sympathetically. A Western bloc, the FO considered, would share the burden of containing Germany after the war, provide Britain with 'defence in
depth' on the Continent and would boost Britain's influence in the world
by making it the spokesman of Western Europe. Yet Eden and his officials did not want the Western bloc to upset the United States by detract-
ing from its 'one world' approach to the problems of peace, seen most
importantly in the creation of the United Nations. It was vital to keep
the US involved in world affairs. Neither did the FO want to develop
the Western bloc as an overtly anti-Soviet alliance for fear of a rapid
breakdown in relations with Moscow.

However, any attempt to achieve a Western bloc before the end of the
war was scotched by Churchill, who argued that Britain lacked the
resources to build up Western Europe into a strong, viable military alliance. At best Churchill hoped for a loose 'Council of Europe' as part of a
number of regional organisations under the UN.[12] Yet despite the Prime

Minister's opposition, support for a Western bloc remained strong in the Foreign Office. In early July 1945 Orme Sargent, soon to become Permanent Under-Secretary (civil service head) of the Foreign Office, wrote an important memorandum, 'Stocktaking after VE-day'. This pointed out that, as the weakest of the 'Big Three', Britain must make itself the leader of the West European countries as well as the Commonwealth in order 'to compel our two big partners to treat us as an equal'.[13] At the end of the war therefore the British government hoped to keep the Big Three united, to develop a world security system through the UN (which was established in June) and to hold down the defeated aggressor states, especially Germany. But there were already fears of Soviet-Communist expansion, the Americans were expected to withdraw their troops from post-war Europe, and Britain's own position was not strong. The war had drained the country of financial reserves, harmed its overseas trade, and decimated its merchant navy. If anything, peace *added* to these problems: apart from the need for demobilisation and to end wartime controls, the British people opted for costly social reforms and nationalisation by voting Labour in the July election, and pressures were mounting in India for decolonisation. Economic and financial problems, Imperial crises and Cold War tensions faced the new government with daunting challenges and would help to reshape Britain's foreign policy in new directions.

Bevin's meeting with the FO about Western Europe, on 13 August 1945, was clearly more than an isolated example of interest in continental co-operation. As writers like Sean Greenwood have shown, Bevin's enthusiasm for a Western bloc was in line with FO thinking at the end of the war. By emphasising the need for *economic* co-operation Bevin might be said to have gone beyond the Foreign Office, which hitherto had put the accent on military and political links. Bevin was also ready to consider Western European exploitation of the Ruhr industrial basin, Germany's economic powerhouse, which the French wanted to put under international control.[14] However, a number of difficulties dogged Bevin's attempts to create ties with Western Europe. One was the attitude of the two main economic ministries, the Treasury and the Board of Trade (BOT) to European co-operation. Their lukewarm view had been made clear at an inter-departmental meeting in July when Treasury and BOT representatives argued that Britain must preserve its economic independence, its world trading role and its ties to the Commonwealth, and believed that America would oppose a European trade bloc.[15] Expanding *world* trade would allow Britain to revive its exports and so pay for vital imports of food and raw materials. A second problem was the continuing reluctance of the FO to antagonise the Russians, who had begun to complain about plans for an 'anti-Soviet' bloc. Bevin gained a reputation as a man who stood up to the Soviets after 1945 but, like Eden before him, he was unwilling to enrage them wilfully, especially at a time when America was not committed to Europe's defence. In fact, in September 1945, Soviet foreign minister Vyacheslav Molotov said he had no objections to an Anglo-French alliance. But the Foreign Office continued to be sensitive about Soviet reaction to the Western bloc.[16]

Another reason for the delays to the Western bloc was poor British relations with France. France was always seen as an essential component of any West European defence arrangement, even if its armed forces had been eclipsed in 1940. The restoration of French power was one of Britain's main war aims and had some success in 1944–5 when France was made a member of the UN Security Council and given an occupation zone in Germany. But Churchill and de Gaulle, who became undisputed French leader after August 1944, had an intense love–hate relationship. De Gaulle, aloof and proud, was determined to restore France to greatness and had no wish to rely on British 'charity' to restore its fortunes. Neither did he wish to recreate the British-dominated *entente* of the 1930s, which had ended in disaster for France. And he resented British closeness to their fellow 'Anglo-Saxon' power, America.[17] In December 1944, partly to demonstrate his independence of the Anglo-Saxons, General de Gaulle had travelled to Moscow and signed an anti-German alliance with Stalin. The British, who already had their own (1942) treaty with the Soviets, suggested that a tripartite pact should be signed, including them. But de Gaulle rejected this and set out two important conditions for any Anglo-French alliance. First, Britain must support France's desire for a harsh peace settlement in Germany: following three German invasions since 1870, the French government wanted to sever the industrial Ruhr and the strategically important Rhineland from Germany. Second, Britain must respect France's 'special position' in Syria and Lebanon, two French possessions in the Middle East. In neither case, however, were the British ready to oblige. In early 1945 Whitehall officials were already concerned at the likely economic dislocation in Europe if Germany were treated too harshly, and also at the dangers of a German–Soviet alliance if the Western powers mistreated Germany. Furthermore, in the Middle East the British, the predominant power in the region, were unwilling to upset Arab nationalists by supporting French rule in Syria–Lebanon.[18] Indeed, at the end of May 1945, when fighting broke out between France and the Syrians, British forces intervened to separate the two sides. The episode was humiliating enough for de Gaulle to declare – a month after victory in Europe – that if France had had the necessary resources, it would have gone to war with Britain![19]

In August 1945 Bevin hoped to resolve differences with France on Germany and the Middle East quickly. But only in December did Britain and France agree on a mutual withdrawal from Syria and they soon fell out over how to fulfil this deal. It was only de Gaulle's sudden resignation as French leader in January 1946 that finally guaranteed an end to the French presence in Syria–Lebanon. De Gaulle, unable to get agreement with other politicians on a new French constitution – in which he hoped to become a strong President – evidently resigned in the hope of being recalled to power by popular demand. If so, he miscalculated. Instead France's three main political parties, the Communists, Socialists and Christian Democrats, shared power in a coalition. This in itself created a new problem for Franco-British relations, because Bevin had little liking for the Communists, who closely followed the Soviet line in foreign affairs. De Gaulle may have been difficult for Britain to deal with, but at least he had been able to control the Communists.[20]

Sean Greenwood has argued that the French alliance was redefined in the FO after de Gaulle's resignation 'as primarily a steadying influence upon French internal affairs rather than as the foundation for a larger European policy'. This view underestimates the continuing desire of the FO to pursue a Western bloc in the long term: on 21 December 1946, for example, a memorandum by Orme Sargent reaffirmed the need for a French alliance as a step towards general European co-operation, a way to strengthen Britain's diplomatic position worldwide, and as an anti-German security device.[21] But the Communist presence certainly complicated British policy enormously in 1946, whilst differences over Germany also remained a problem. In April 1946 – encouraged by France's premier, Felix Gouin, to believe that differences over Germany need *not* prevent a French treaty – Bevin sent one of his leading officials, Oliver Harvey, to Paris. The FO hoped that a Franco-British alliance would boost pro-Western elements in France, who were particularly strong in the Socialist party. However, when Harvey reached Paris, the Communists and Christian Democrats (the latter keen to win anti-German votes in the next election) united against the Socialist Gouin in the Cabinet. De Gaulle's harsh demands on Germany were confirmed as French policy and the British felt snubbed. Later that month the British Cabinet rejected the French plan to separate the Ruhr and Rhineland from Germany. This plan, the British felt, would rekindle nationalist feeling in Germany and

ruin its economy. A few months later, in July, financial pressures forced
the British to agree to merge their occupation zone in Germany with that
of the Americans. Since the Americans were also keen to keep the Ruhr in
Germany, and even wanted to revive the German economy, Franco-British
co-operation became even more difficult. By now the development of
Cold War tensions between America and Russia also had a detrimental
effect on Franco-British relations.[22] In October France's new premier,
Georges Bidault, complained to Bevin that whilst Britain seemed pro-
American, France, because of the Communists, seemed pro-Soviet. Bevin
had already told Bidault they could not 'carry on a conversation . . . with a
third Great Power in the cupboard' – a reference to Soviet influence in
Paris.[23] Thus in 1946 the Communist menace sometimes made Bevin eager
to make a treaty (as in April) but at other times made him more cautious.

The only real progress made in Franco-British relations in 1946 was
the formation of an Economic Committee, in September, accompanied
by a settlement of financial debts. Economic Committees, which held
regular meetings to discuss mutual problems, were created between Britain and many other West European countries. But Bevin's interest in
economic co-operation went beyond bilateral agreements. In September
he also pressed the British government to study a customs union with
Western Europe. This of course was an idea that had interested him
before the war, and was now seen as a way to strengthen the region
against the Soviets. The Treasury and BOT reaction was predictably
unfavourable. They insisted again on the need to preserve Commonwealth trade and to reach an agreement on *freer* world trade, from which
Britain had traditionally gained. But Bevin managed to get a customs
union study established in early 1947.[24] It is therefore difficult to accept
arguments that he did not interest himself seriously in European economic co-operation. But, as Alan Milward has argued, British interest in
a customs union did not spread much beyond Bevin and his immediate
advisers; and Frances Lynch has shown that, when discussions were held
in January 1947 about Anglo-French economic integration, 'neither
government was actually prepared to modify its policies in the light of
a greater understanding of the other government's plans'.[25]

The Rise of Western Union, 1947–8

In 1945–6 a host of problems had united to prevent a British-led Western bloc: the doubts of the economic ministries; fears of upsetting the

Americans and Soviets; and above all differences with France over the Middle East, Germany and the influence of the Communists. But 1947 began, quite unexpectedly, with successful talks on a Franco-British treaty. This largely came about because of a short-lived Socialist government in France led by a leading anglophile, Leon Blum. Blum was encouraged to believe a treaty was possible by British Ambassador Duff Cooper, who has been seen as an early advocate of European unity. (Cooper's biographer is critical of the Foreign Office for failing to pursue such a policy in the early post-war years. He ignores much of the evidence that Bevin *did* seek European co-operation.[26]) In January Blum and Bevin met in London and, amidst declarations of Socialist brotherhood, agreed to make an alliance. Despite Blum's subsequent loss of office, the treaty was signed in March 1947, at Dunkirk, where the previous Anglo-French alliance was broken in 1940. This treaty has been the centre of some historical debate, mainly thanks to an historiographical essay by Bert Zeeman, who compared three articles by academics on the treaty. None of these studies seemed entirely satisfactory in Zeeman's view, mainly because they approached the issue from different, but partial, perspectives. John Baylis, whose interest lay mainly in military planning (and who has since modified his approach), looked too far forward in seeing Dunkirk as a stepping stone to NATO; Sean Greenwood was concerned with the treaty as an anti-Communist device; Zeeman and his fellow Dutch historian, Cees Wiebes, were right to see Dunkirk as a potential base for wider West European co-operation but admitted to concentrating too narrowly on power political issues. In fact in its actual form – a 50-year alliance against German aggression – the Dunkirk treaty was no different to the alliance that had been planned by the FO in 1944. It marked, at last, a long-term British security commitment to the Continent, but was no more than a paper guarantee (there were no military staff talks to follow it up) and was soon overshadowed by other events.[27]

The Treaty of Dunkirk was signed despite continuing Franco-British differences over Germany and the presence of Communists in the French government. Both these factors, which had delayed a treaty in 1946, were soon to change. In March–April 1947 the four occupation powers in Germany (America, Russia, Britain and France) met in Moscow to discuss a German Peace Treaty and the French openly began to side with Britain and America, rather than with the Soviets. This was partly because of practical issues in Germany: Britain and America controlled the Ruhr and could guarantee vital coal supplies from there to France. It was probably inevitable that, when faced with a breakdown in

East–West relations, France – as a West European, liberal-democratic, colonial state – would align itself with the West. Soon afterwards, in May, after growing differences in the French government on economic and colonial policies, the Communists were expelled from the coalition government in Paris.[28]

Almost simultaneously with this, Bevin began talks with the Belgians about a possible treaty, based on the Dunkirk model. An extension of West European alliances beyond France was of course consistent with Bevin's declared aims in August 1945 and answered Belgian foreign minister Spaak's long-standing demands for a treaty with Britain. Bevin told a Foreign Office meeting on 7 May that, with the Americans pre-dominant in the Western hemisphere and with the Soviets dominant in Eastern Europe, Britain must organise the Western bloc.[29] This was strikingly similar to an argument he had used in December 1945: that the world was being divided into spheres of influence on the lines of 'three Monroe doctrines'.[30] However, talks on the Belgian treaty had not pro-gressed far when a new basis for European co-operation presented itself. On 5 June, American Secretary of State George Marshall offered to assist a European economic recovery programme. Although the Marshall Plan was supposedly open to all continental states, it was not surprising that the Soviets refused to accept capitalist aid. Instead, in July, Britain and France jointly organised a conference of 16 West European states in Paris. A revolution thereby occurred in the Continent's affairs. Europe was split down the middle, with the Soviets dominating the East. But unity in *Western* Europe could now be built with the assurance of Amer-ican support. Indeed, from this time onwards the Americans became keen advocates of West European unity.

There is general agreement among historians about the importance of the Marshall Plan, but recent studies have questioned whether it achieved many of its original aims. European economic recovery, for example, was already underway in 1947, and growth really 'took off' in the early 1950s because of the stimulus provided by the Korean War. The Marshall Plan had few details when it was launched. Certainly it forced Western Euro-pean states to work together to draw up a joint recovery programme, but Alan Milward and Michael Hogan have shown what resistance there was to US attempts to shape Europe in its own image into a large, single marketplace. Each European country was keen to protect its own inter-ests, not least the British, who were determined to preserve Imperial trade preference and their special financial position in the Sterling Area. Bevin refused to be treated as 'just another European country'.[31] It would be wrong to conclude from this that Britain was opposed to European co-operation. Bevin played a leading role in organising the Paris conference and the way he grasped Marshall Aid is seen as one of his greatest triumphs.[32] However, the Foreign Office had always wanted Western European co-operation as a way to *improve* Britain's international standing, a way to match the power of America and Russia – *not* as a step towards the loss of independence. It is only in this light that Bevin's policy can be understood.

It is now time to consider Bevin's ideas on European co-operation more fully. Many historians, including Bevin's official biographer, Lord Bullock, have seen little evidence of a commitment by Bevin to Western European unity and some refer to his desire for Britain to match the Soviets and Americans only in passing.[33] Anthony Adamthwaite dismisses talk of West European co-operation in 1947–8 as a 'flirtation'. Michael Howard sees the idea of a 'third force' as an important theme in Bevin's foreign policy, but believes the Foreign Secretary visualised this 'as existing within a general area dominated by American influence'.[34] It is easy, with the benefit of hindsight, to interpret Bevin's foreign policy from 1947 onwards as aiming at the Atlantic Pact, led by America, signed in April 1949. Klaus Larres argues that, once 'the United States became involved in providing for the security of Western Europe, Bevin's enthusiasm for setting up a genuine Western European bloc faded quickly', an argument echoed by Lord Beloff. Ritchie Ovendale even claims that Bevin's desire for an 'English-speaking alliance' can be traced back to February 1946.[35] However, whilst it is certainly true that Bevin needed US support to help European economic reconstruction and to stand up to the Soviet threat, it is not necessarily the case that this would result in an American-dominated alliance, in which Britain was Washington's subservient lieutenant. There is considerable evidence that, while forced to rely on the US in the short term, in the long term Bevin hoped to build a 'third force' independent of, and equal to, America, yet in the wider framework of an anti-Soviet alliance.

As early as 1952, in the first biography of Bevin, Francis Williams argued that Bevin had genuinely been interested in such a 'third force'.[36] More recently historians such as Avi Shlaim, Geoffrey Warner and John Baylis have insisted that Bevin's European policy was far more sophisticated than generally supposed. In a path-breaking 1978 work Shlaim argued that in 1947–8 Bevin's intention was to create a power base in Europe which would allow Britain to act as a superpower. Warner has argued that Bevin showed considerable vision in studying a European customs union and that he sought a 'partnership between equals' with the US. Baylis too believes that, while requiring American assistance to resist Soviet Communism, Bevin wanted to maintain British independence and pursue the leadership of Western European nations.[37] The American historian John Gaddis has noted that an equal US-European partnership would have been popular in the US State Department, where policy-makers wanted to create a confident, strong Western Europe which could soon stand on its own feet, free of US support.[38] Robert Holland, concentrating on Imperial policy, insists that Bevin 'consistently sought to promote . . . a Third Force'. It is the British historian John Kent who has gone furthest on these lines, arguing that Bevin tried to maintain British power and influence by organising a Euro-African bloc, linking together Western Europe, the African colonies and the British-dominated Middle East. This was what the Foreign Secretary called 'the middle of the planet' and he believed its manpower and economic resources could equal both the USSR and the USA. Britain would therefore be able to compete on a level with the US in a wider Western economic system. Kent does not see the creation of NATO in 1949 as a triumph for Bevin, but rather as a defeat for his original vision which proved impossible to realise. These arguments have since been echoed in a substantial study of post-war Anglo-French relations by Sean Greenwood, who concludes that Bevin's support for NATO, 'as opposed to the more flexible concept of a Western Union . . . may be judged to be not the successful outcome of impressive and dogged foresight but the ultimate admission of failure'.[39]

There is certainly abundant evidence that, between about August 1947 and April 1948, Bevin showed considerable interest in a third force. It is extraordinary that such a body of evidence should have been virtually ignored by many commentators in preference for the assumption that Bevin always aimed to create the Atlantic alliance. Far from leading to British co-operation with a predominant United States, the Marshall Plan was defined at the same time as the 1947 convertibility crisis, when Britain tried to make its currency freely convertible into Dollars for the first time since the war. This move proved disastrous, since Sterling was sold in huge quantities, and convertibility had to be ended. The crisis ended hopes for a freer global trade system and highlighted the weakness of Sterling in the face of the Dollar but it also increased Britain's desire for economic independence. The breakdown of relations between the Western powers and the USSR, which became complete in the second half of 1947, also forced Britain to try to safeguard its interests in the wider context of an anti-Soviet alliance. In early September Bevin, significantly, chose to devote his address to the Trades Union Congress to the need for a customs union between Britain, Western Europe *and* the Commonwealth.[40] Both these elements were needed to boost British power. Later that month he met French premier Paul Ramadier and proposed a union between their two Empires as a way to match US and Soviet power. Britain also joined a Customs Union Study Group, established by most of the countries which had entered the Marshall Plan talks.[41] Once again, the economic ministries resisted Bevin, now arguing that a customs union would be an irreversible step towards a full economic union with Europe which would destroy Britain's essential role as a *world* trading power. The BOT has been accused by Alan Milward of 'unthinking protectionism' in these debates; the Treasury was more sophisticated, favouring greater trade with Europe but insisting that this could be achieved simply by inter-government agreements on lower trade barriers and a stable currency system. The Colonial Office, committed to a more liberal form of imperial rule than the French, added to the pressures against Bevin in Whitehall by opposing any Euro-African link. There was a clear tension between Bevin's hopes for a European-Commonwealth customs union, supposedly tying together manufacturing countries and raw material producers, and his opponents' arguments that European links would undermine the Sterling Area and Commonwealth trade, by opening these to European competitors, and thus would destroy important bases for British power. Nonetheless, when these issues were discussed by the Cabinet's key Economic Policy Committee in November, Bevin insisted that Europe must move towards greater economic unity in order to stand up to America and Russia.[42]

Advocacy of a third force reached its height following the final diplomatic breakdown with the Soviets in December 1947, when another meeting with them about the future of Germany ended in deadlock. At this time the Foreign Secretary discussed future Western policy with his American and French colleagues, Marshall and Georges Bidault. Talks were agreed on the future of Western Germany and Bevin again put particular emphasis on the need for European co-operation. Writers such as Elisabeth Barker and Nora Beloff have argued that such European links were merely a staging post on the road to NATO and chiefly designed to please the United States: a 'sprat to catch a mackerel' as Bevin himself later said.[43] In fact there was no specific discussion of an Atlantic military alliance at this time and when Foreign Office views were put down in a memorandum they told a very different story. 'The First Aim of British Foreign Policy', circulated as a Cabinet paper in January, talked only of

'a Western Union' among *European* states, with the backing (not the participation) of America. Britain should seek through the Western Union
'to develop our own power and influence to equal that of the USA and the
USSR'.[44] In his New Year broadcast Prime Minister Clement Attlee gave
philosophical justification to such a third force, declaring:

> At ... one end of the scale are the Communist countries; at the other
> end the United States ... Great Britain ... is placed geographically and
> from the point of view of economic and political theory between these
> two great continental states ... Our task is to work out a system ... which
> combines individual freedom with a planned economy.[45]

This had a striking similarity to the views of the 'Keep Left' group of
Labour MPs, who are too often viewed as having been an ineffective
minority. (This is mainly because critics of the 'Keep Left' group look
only at their arguments with Bevin over his anti-Soviet policy.[46]) The FO
junior minister, Christopher Mayhew, had a particular role in encouraging a pro-European policy and was determined to base British overseas propaganda on the leadership of 'all the democratic elements in
Western Europe ... what one might call the "Third Force"'.[47] In the FO
several leading officials now wanted to study a full *political and economic
union* with Western Europe as a way to resist the USSR, contain the power
of a revived Germany and underpin British power.[48] Finally, on 22 January, Bevin made a lengthy speech to the House of Commons in which he
bluntly stated 'Britain cannot stand outside Europe' and announced new
talks on a security pact with Belgium, Holland and Luxembourg. The
announcement was welcomed by the Conservative opposition whose
foreign affairs spokesman Anthony Eden was, of course, a long-standing
advocate of a Western bloc.[49] The press too were part of the new enthusiasm for a British-led bloc: *The Times* hailed Bevin's speech as 'a challenge
and a call to action'.[50]

The Decline of Western Union, 1948–9

In view of the rise to favour of the 'third force' between January 1947 and
January 1948 the obvious question is how British policy, by late 1949,
came to be based on the Atlantic alliance and continued Commonwealth
links – with the 'third force' categorically ruled out in FO studies. In

spring 1948 Bevin still seemed firmly committed to the development of European unity. Belgium, Holland, and Luxembourg, which had already formed their own 'Benelux' customs union, were impressed by Bevin's Western Union speech, and joined Britain and France in signing the Brussels Pact on 17 March. Although this was primarily seen as a multilateral military alliance, it included promises of financial, cultural and social co-operation and established regular ministerial meetings in a 'Consultative Council', a practice later copied in NATO. In April 1948 it was followed by the creation of the Organisation for European Economic Cooperation (OEEC), a permanent body set up by West European countries to supervise the four-year Marshall Aid programme, which had just been approved by the US Congress. Then in June, after several months of talks, the British, French and Americans agreed to establish a West German government. Thus, by July 1948, when the Brussels Pact powers began talks with the US on an Atlantic Pact, several important steps had already been taken towards creating a Western political-economic system. Bevin himself evidently continued to believe that he could preserve Britain's independence of the US by creating a self-reliant Western Europe under British leadership. He said as much to the Commons in a speech in September.[51]

Behind the scenes of unity *vis-à-vis* the Soviet Union however, the Western alliance had many internal differences, and for numerous reasons British policy began to differ radically from that of its continental allies. Some of the problems were political and philosophical. In the Western Union speech Bevin had called for a 'practical programme' of co-operation and had condemned 'ambitious schemes' which tried to go too far, too fast. In part this reflected traditional British pragmatism: Bevin, for all his grandiose vision of a Western Union, believed in a hard-headed, step-by-step approach to policy. Far more important, Bevin saw the prime aim of European co-operation as being to *strengthen* Britain's role in the world. He was not therefore likely to agree to the *loss* of British power to any centralised European institutions. Already a number of federalist groups had begun to form in Europe stimulated, among others, by Winston Churchill, who had made a speech in Zurich in September 1946 advocating European union and who had formed a British 'United Europe' group to support this. Churchill, whose European interests were encouraged by his son-in-law Duncan Sandys, had begun talking of a 'United States of Europe' in Brussels in November 1945 but was vague about what this meant. Significantly Churchill did *not* say that Britain should surrender sovereignty to any European institution. At Zurich he talked of Britain as a 'sponsor' of a European federation; and he did not want European co-operation to upset the Anglo-American alliance. He seemed most interested in securing a Franco-German rapprochement which would strengthen the West and put an end to the destructive rivalry of these two nations. He also wanted 'Europe' to include East European states.[52]

However, the fact that the Leader of the Opposition adopted such ideas helped to ensure their rejection by the Labour party. Bevin's condemnation of European federalism is well known: 'When you open that Pandora's box you'll find it full of Trojan horses'.[53] FO officials too, whilst ready to study a political-economic union in Europe, wanted to proceed gradually, developing institutions in an evolutionary process, rather like the development of Britain's unwritten constitution. The problem with this approach was that Britain's constitutional experience was very different to that on the Continent, where the development of democracy had been more difficult and tenuous and where revolutions and foreign invasions had led to frequent changes of regime. In Western Europe many saw the Western Union speech as a call to create common institutions and to devise written constitutions which were the norm for them. Britain and the continentals were further divided by the recent experience of war, which had strengthened British faith in their own institutions, at the same time that it destroyed many European regimes. Britain, by escaping defeat and occupation, avoided the need to reform its constitution and the questioning of the nation state which took place in Germany, France, Italy and elsewhere. This division of experience has been called 'the price of victory' by Michael Charlton, although it was only one aspect of Anglo-continental separation after 1945.[54]

Bevin's fear of unrealistic, 'instant' schemes for European unity seemed well founded when federalist groups held a Congress in The Hague in May 1948, attended by Churchill and other British MPs, which called for the creation of a European parliament with effective powers over a political union. Given Europe's enormous differences of language, customs, political structure and social make-up, it seemed preposterous to suggest a federal state structure so soon. As Bevin told the Commons, 'I don't think it will work if we . . . put the roof on before we have built the building'.[55] But the Foreign Secretary thereby showed his continuing failure to provide clear leadership to the Europeans, who were still uncertain where his own plans were leading. The French and Belgian governments in contrast – though also unready to surrender real authority to a central parliament – believed that public enthusiasm for European co-operation should be encouraged. Their two governments recognised a European parliament to be an unrealistic aim in the short term, but in September they proposed to the Ministerial Council of the Brussels Pact that it should at least be studied. The support of the French government for European institutions was strengthened at this time by arguments similar to those which had earlier influenced Briand: first, the French hoped to improve their own economic performance by creating a wider European market and had already begun talks with Italy on a possible customs union; second, the French were fearful of German revival, having experienced three German invasions in living memory (1870, 1914, 1940) and believed that German independence could only be controlled in a wider, European framework. France's policy of rapprochement with Germany after mid 1948 was particularly identified with the new Foreign Minister, Robert Schuman, who had been raised on the Franco-German border, and who was ready to consider a loss of sovereignty to common institutions in order to control Germany. Britain, more removed from the German menace, could never fully share this particular French motive for seeking European unity. Indeed in 1948–9, though not as keen as the Americans to proceed with Germany's economic resuscitation, Britain advocated German revival more quickly than France liked, partly in order to hold down occupation costs in Germany and partly because British policy in the 'Bizone' had to be dovetailed with that of the Americans. This German factor was highly significant in the division between Britain and France over European integration which grew after 1948.[56]

Pressure from Schuman and Belgium's Paul-Henri Spaak forced a reluctant Bevin to agree in October to a Brussels Pact Committee of Inquiry into the European Assembly idea. However, the Council of Europe which resulted from the talks in May 1949 was far removed from the hopes of the Hague Congress. Bevin's opposition had helped to emasculate the original proposal, so that the European Assembly was only a consultative body, holding short, annual meetings and controlled by a ministerial committee. The Council also had a wide membership, including Scandinavian countries and others who shared Britain's aversion to any loss of sovereignty. Then again, the debates over the Assembly had had an important impact on British relations with Europe, highlighting Bevin's differences with an important group of countries – France, the Benelux states, and Italy – which *were* ready to consider a loss of sovereignty. It was during these debates that the French emerged as the leaders of this continental group. Previously the Belgians and Dutch had been fearful of French domination, and looked to Britain for leadership.[57] Bevin for his part was unapologetic. The Council of Europe experience, and his contempt for the lack of 'realism' on the Continent, made him doubtful about relying on France, Italy and others as allies. These doubts were reinforced by the political instability of France and Italy, the continued existence of large Communist parties in both countries and the danger of a Soviet invasion of continental Europe. Such considerations made Bevin and the Foreign Office less certain about building British security around Western Europe alone. A long-running political crisis in France, between July and September 1948, in which one weak coalition succeeded another, seems to have weakened Foreign Office faith in their continental neighbour, on whom so many earlier hopes had been based.[58]

British-continental differences were heightened by events in the economic, military and colonial spheres. It has already been seen how the Treasury and Board of Trade, whilst supporting freer trade and exchange in Europe, rejected more radical integration and preferred to develop world trade in the context of the General Agreement on Tariffs and Trade. In spring 1948 the arguments against any European-Commonwealth customs union were mounting. Such a union would lead to revolutionary changes in British economic and political practice. The most important point was that European access to Commonwealth markets would destroy Imperial trade preferences at a time when Europe took only a *quarter* of British trade, compared to the Sterling Area's *half*. Another vital point was that half of the trading and financial exchanges in the non-Communist world were carried out in Sterling. Investors in the City of London's financial markets, banking and insurance houses, had traditionally based their wealth on world trade and a strong, stable Pound. A change in such a long-standing system would be difficult to achieve, especially when it was defended by the Treasury, Board of Trade and Bank of England. Besides, members of the Sterling Area held financial reserves in Sterling: they too wanted a stable currency.

Furthermore, Western Europe's economies were *competitive*, not complementary, in what they produced and all had trading deficits with the USA. (It is a significant point, noted by Jeremy Black, that in this sphere Britain and Europe were driven apart by being, not too different, but too *similar*: in the Empire-Commonwealth the economic 'cement' rested on the differences between the parts, with the Dominions and Colonies exchanging primary produce for British manufactures; whereas Western Europe offered 'a union of competitors'.) The British economy was far stronger, in coal and steel production for example, than its European neighbours and there was great reluctance to work closely with these weaker economies. When the OEEC was established in April the British opposed American and French efforts to give it supranational powers. In August Bevin admitted to the Cabinet's Economic Policy Committee that a customs union had become an impossible idea. Finally, in January 1949, Bevin and the Chancellor of the Exchequer, Stafford Cripps, agreed on important principles for future co-operation with Europe, ending divisions between the FO and the Treasury. On the one hand, Britain should be ready to strengthen Europe by co-operating with the Continent as far as possible, but on the other, Britain must not carry this policy so far that it lost its independent economic viability. If Europe collapsed, in the face of Communist pressure, Britain must be able to rebuild itself with the support of America and the Commonwealth.[59]

The British were approached by Jean Monnet, the head of France's recovery programme, to discuss closer economic co-operation in spring 1949, and the British sent a small group of officials under Sir Edwin Plowden. These talks have been interpreted by some writers, including Monnet himself, as Britain's 'last chance' to co-operate with France in forging European unity. But this is evidently simply to justify Monnet's abandonment of his plans for British co-operation at the time. The British did not see the talks with him as vital and, indeed, the Cabinet's Economic Policy Committee had, in a meeting of 25 November 1948, decided that it could not risk integrating the British and French recovery programmes, because of doubts about France's economic viability. (Indeed, Roger Woodhouse has described this decision as 'the death-knell for an idea which had been in the air since 1946'.) In contrast to the Monnet–Plowden talks, the January 1949 principles on European co-operation, which were accepted by the Cabinet, have been seen by several writers as more important.[60] They marked in effect a British preference for preserving Commonwealth trade rather than taking more dramatic steps in Europe. In this British economic planners were influenced partly by traditional patterns of British trade and partly by contemporary conditions in world trade, where *primary materials* – food and raw materials, which the Sterling Area had in abundance – seemed vital as a source of economic recovery. Only in the 1950s would it become clear that, with post-war shortages overcome, *manufactured goods* were becoming more important in world trade and only in the late 1950s did British ministers become concerned over Britain's pattern of trade, and the poor performance of British manufacturing industry. Alan Milward has argued that, as early as 1949, manufactured trade in 'Little Europe', between France, Germany, Italy and the Benelux states, had begun to expand more rapidly than Britain's. By concentrating on primary products in the Sterling Area the British had not only taken an easy option in the short term, they had also doomed themselves in the long term to competing mainly in a less vigorous, less expanding trading environment.

Studies in the colonial field suggest that it would have been impossible to fuse together European colonial empires in Africa for many reasons. British colonial philosophy, with its fostering of self-rule, was very different to the centralising policies of the French; colonies already had access to the British market and would simply open themselves up to destructive competition in a wider common market with European states; and it would have taken impossible sums of money to develop African resources in an effective way. Such inter-imperial co-operation as there was between European powers in Africa was restricted to technical issues such as improvements in communications, crop development and tackling diseases.[61] Yet outside government circles the idea of a European-Commonwealth Union persisted for some time. It was seen in the so-called 'Strasbourg Plan', drawn up in the Council of Europe Assembly later in 1949, and supported by Churchill's Conservative delegation.[62]

America and the Commonwealth had always of course been vital to Bevin's Western Union. But, whereas in January 1948 they were supposed to *back* European co-operation, by summer 1949 the US and Commonwealth were viewed as more solid and reliable pillars on which to build British political and economic security. Since the war Britain had tried to maintain its special position with the US, with which it had a common language and culture. Despite strains (over the terms of the December 1945 American financial loan to Britain for example), Britain and America had often acted together to resist Soviet pressure, revive Western Germany and to create an anti-Soviet bastion in Western Europe. In mid-1948, with Western Europe still weak, and with the Soviets beginning the year-long Berlin blockade, Bevin decided that American support might be needed for a long time to come. A customs union, Euro-African links and a strong French alliance were impossible to realise and Bevin began to see the 'third force' as a threat to the cohesion of the anti-Soviet alliance. Britain lacked material resources, in any case, and could not act as 'paymaster' to a 'third force'. US assistance was needed economically to provide Marshall Aid, tackle the dollar gap and create a multilateral Western trade system. Militarily too US support seemed vital in 1948–9, since European countries were incapable of matching the power of the Red Army. Certainly Britain did not have the resources to defend the Continent: indeed British military planners in 1948 saw Europe as indefensible and wanted to concentrate their efforts on protecting the Middle East. This was not very impressive for a country which hoped to 'lead' Europe. It was partly because of these embarrassing inadequacies that Britain renewed its efforts in spring 1948 to get a US military commitment to Europe, efforts which were fully supported by the other European countries. However, when the North Atlantic Treaty was signed in April 1949, its effect was not so much to reinforce *European* unity, as to provide an alternative to this in the form of an *Atlantic* community, which the Foreign Office found increasingly attractive.[63]

Britain's rejection of the 'third force' was confirmed in a study by a new Foreign Office body, established by Bevin in February 1949 to look at long-term policy plans. The Permanent Under-Secretary's Committee, in a paper entitled 'Third World Power or Western Consolidation', finalised in May, argued that the British Commonwealth would depend on the US for defence and investment for the foreseeable future. Because of national differences, economic problems and Communist influence, it doubted the ability of a more united Europe to match the USSR. It argued that nationalism would eventually undermine attempts at European unity and feared that the Soviets could overrun the Continent if war broke out. Bevin circulated these views to the Cabinet later in the year, thus finally rejecting the idea of a Western European-Commonwealth union. In its place he now favoured a more general consolidation of Europe, the Commonwealth and America into a 'natural' unit, a scheme as imprecise and grandiose as the original Western Union, but with the US now playing a leading role. Britain would remain important, however, as the vital link between the three elements and would use Europe and the Commonwealth to limit American domination. This reworking of the vision of January 1948 was the beginning of the 'three circles' approach to British policy, which was developed further by Churchill.[64]

Britain's preference for co-operation with America rather than Europe was confirmed in September when Sterling was devalued. Triggered by a depression in the US, the devaluation was surprising because of its scale (the Pound fell from $4.03 to $2.80) and stunned European countries, which were given no warning, which had respected Britain as their economic leader and which were now forced into devaluations of their own. Arguably the British had no choice, either about devaluing, or about consulting with the US beforehand. In a sense the devaluation crisis marked a triumph for British diplomacy, in that the US recognised the importance of Sterling as an international currency and, in effect, abandoned pressures on the British to merge their economic future with the Continent. This suited the Treasury and BOT who, since 1947, had fought against greater economic integration into Europe, arguing that Sterling had a vital *world* role – not simply a European one. Now the US State Department had apparently come to accept this view. Despite the doubts of several US representatives in Europe, Secretary of State Dean Acheson now agreed that Britain's currency was vital to world trade and that its Empire included strategically vital areas in the struggle against Communism so that it must be treated as a special case. Yet, as has been pointed out by Scott Newton, in his studies of the devaluation crisis,[65] the apparent triumph for the British masked a number of problems. Britain's behaviour soured relations with other members of the OEEC, especially France, and highlighted the self-interested nature of British policy: Bevin is often portrayed as a far-sighted and enlightened leader, but his overall aim was always to maximise British power in a Western alliance system. Yet his behaviour in September 1949 helped to confirm that *France* was now the only possible leader of radical integration in Europe. Acheson indeed told Robert Schuman in October, 'Now is the time for French initiative to integrate the German Federal Republic . . . into Western Europe'.[66] This was the inevitable corollary of British reluctance to integrate into Europe, for the US and others were not going to abandon the idea of European unity, which alongside the British Commonwealth was seen as a vital factor in the struggle against Soviet Communism.

The devaluation crisis confirmed Britain's drive for expanded trade in the Commonwealth rather than Europe. Whilst establishing a close Sterling–Dollar link, it also confirmed Britain in the role of being a subsidiary partner of the US. At the same time Britain tried to maintain a position as a major trading power, with an important reserve currency, which remained well beyond its means. As the American historian Peter Weiler[67] has pointed out, in a review of British foreign policy under the post-war Labour governments, Britain succeeded under Bevin in encouraging an anti-Soviet alliance, maintaining the elements of a world role and building a partnership with the US, but its independence was nonetheless restricted, its resources were strained and it had chosen to distance itself from radical steps to European integration. In the light of recent research Bevin can be rescued from accusations from critics such as Anthony Nutting, Richard Mayne and Nora Beloff[68] that he did not consider European unity seriously as a policy option in the late 1940s, but he was often at the mercy of the complex forces at work in post-war Europe. His supposedly triumphant creation of an Atlantic alliance was neither as smooth as it is often made to appear, nor did it provide a basis for the maintenance of British greatness which was Bevin's main aim. The costs of this policy in Europe began to become clear as early as 1950.[69]

2
THE SCHUMAN PLAN, THE EUROPEAN ARMY AND THE TREATIES OF ROME, 1950–1957

The Schuman Plan, 1950

Given the limits set by the Cabinet in 1949 on European integration, it is easy to understand Britain's response to the first step towards the European Community, the Schuman Plan.[1] The plan, launched by the French foreign minister on 8 May 1950, was the product not of head-in-the-clouds idealism, such as the 1948 Hague Congress, but of a realistic appreciation of French national interests. It was devised by the head of the French reconstruction plan, Monnet, but his role in events has since been exaggerated. The Schuman Plan was actually based on ideas which had been circulating in Paris for some time. The idea of linking together the industrial basins of the Ruhr (Germany) and Lorraine (France) was an old one and in December 1948 foreign ministry officials had suggested 'a European steel pool, in which Germans and French would share equally' as a way to create a 'community of interests' with Western Germany and so steer the Germans away from nationalism and militarism.[2] By 1950 the French desire to control German independence had intensified because of the creation of a West German government the previous September, and the readiness of the American and British governments to relax the industrial limitations on Germany which had been introduced after the war. Since Germany was becoming part of the Western alliance it was impossible for France to control it by force.

Monnet's scheme was for a supranational 'High Authority' which would control the coal and steel industries. This meant a limited institution controlling only two sectors of industries; but the plan still had enormous significance because coal and steel were the backbone of any industrialised economy. The plan was open to France, Germany and any other country which wished to join. Monnet's scheme, if successful, would give France the initiative in Western relations with Germany, tie Germany securely to other continental democracies and make war between France and Germany unthinkable. It would also guarantee coal supplies to France, thus safeguarding the aims of Monnet's reconstruction plan. From a wider, European perspective the Schuman Plan would provide more rational policies for Europe's coal and steel industries without recourse to a cartel of businessmen, such as that which operated between the wars. It would also mark an important, but practical advance for European unity, and it offered an opportunity to act *outside* the Atlantic Alliance which, the French felt, was geared too much to Cold War considerations and had no economic role. Part of the attraction of the Schuman Plan therefore was its multiple aims – a point London underestimated.[3]

Three important points need to be noted at the outset about Britain's position when the Schuman Plan was launched. First, Monnet had now devised a scheme which did *not require* British membership. Previously it had been widely assumed, not least in Britain itself, that mutual antagonism between France and Germany was so great that only Britain could play the 'honest broker' between them. (This was a continuation of the British belief that they could play a 'balancing' role between antagonists on the Continent – a belief which was about to be fatally undermined.) It had also seemed that France was incapable of forming a continental customs union without a major industrial power like Britain: talks on a Franco-Italian customs union had come to nothing largely because their economies were too similar, in areas of production such as automobiles, wine and tomatoes, and attempts to draw in the Benelux states, to form a 'Fritalux' (French–Italian–Benelux) union had also failed in 1949. But the Schuman Plan showed that France and Germany could seek a rapprochement without Britain, and the plan offered to make Germany – not Britain – the industrial power which could balance the largely agricultural economies of France, Italy and Holland and so produce a meaningful customs union.

The second important point is that West Germany and others were ready to take up Schuman's initiative. Germany's position was obviously crucial. The German Chancellor, Konrad Adenauer, like Schuman, was a Christian Democrat from the Franco-German border. He was also keen

to co-operate with Paris. He was an ardent opponent of Nazism and militarism, eager to tie his new Republic to other liberal democracies as a way
to avoid the nationalist excesses of the past. Furthermore, West Germany
could make practical gains from European integration, not least the end
of the Western occupation and of industrial controls. The Italian government was led by Alcide de Gasperi, another Christian Democrat from a
border region (Tyrolia). He hoped to rebuild Italy's international standing, develop its economy and safeguard its democracy via European
integration. The Dutch were more anxious to work with Britain, but
relied heavily on Germany for export trade and in practice followed the
Belgians, who were keen to create a large single European market to
boost economic growth. All these countries were ready to lose some
sovereignty in order to achieve vital national aims – a paradox which the
British were slow to grasp. The third point is that the US too remained
anxious to see European integration and, unlike Bevin, had no desire to
develop the Atlantic community as an alternative to it. Thus the British
faced a difficult situation in May 1950, when the French launched an
important, imaginative but realistic initiative, which was likely to appeal
to Germany and others and was welcomed by the US.

It was an indication of French priorities in early May that, although
both Adenauer and Acheson were told of the Schuman Plan before it was
launched, Bevin was not. Even the French Ambassador to London, René
Massigli, criticises his government for this, especially since Bevin had
earlier been assured that he would be forewarned of any French initiatives.[4] Bevin complained to Schuman and Acheson about the way he had
been treated when they arrived for talks in London about the future of
Germany on 11 May. Meanwhile, however, Prime Minister Attlee had
ordered studies to be made of the Schuman Plan and Whitehall departments soon saw merit in the French idea: the Ministry of Defence and
Foreign Office wanted a Franco-German rapprochement to ensure the
cohesion of the Western Alliance. Chancellor Stafford Cripps felt that
Britain must consider joining in, if only to 'steer' the proposal along lines
acceptable to London. It is regrettable that one of the fullest accounts of
European economic history at this time, that by Michael Hogan, is not
based on a full reading of the British archives at this point, but only on
American material and a few Cabinet papers. As a result Hogan underestimates Whitehall's interest in the plan.[5] This interest is confirmed in
a recent volume of diaries by Robert Hall, Director of the Economic
Section of the Cabinet Office. On 17 May he wrote that, while ministers
initially thought the Schuman Plan to be 'a plot' against Britain, the

Foreign Office and defence chiefs were more positive and, after a visit by Monnet to London, even economists had become favourable. Hall himself believed the plan could 'change the face of Europe'.[6] However, feeling in London was now firmly opposed to any 'third force' which might threaten the cohesion of the Atlantic alliance. Furthermore, on his visit to London, Monnet had made it clear that acceptance of the principle of supranationalism – the pooling of sovereignty in common institutions – was a non-negotiable basis for talks on the plan. From the French point of view this was entirely logical: in order to control German ambitions whilst treating Germany as an equal it was vital to ensure a loss of sovereignty by *all* who joined. But for the British it was to prove the main difficulty in joining the plan, threatening the limits set by the Cabinet on European co-operation in January 1949.

On 25 May, in order to win time to consider their position, the British suggested that they should be 'associated' with Franco-German talks on the Schuman Plan. But by coincidence, this proposal crossed with a French invitation to other Western European governments to discuss the plan in Paris. The Germans, Italians and Belgians soon agreed to attend a conference; the Dutch agreed to go on the understanding that they could leave if they disliked the result. Some in London felt that Britain should join on the Dutch terms. However, the important point was that Britain would still have to accept, as a basis for any talks, that any High Authority should involve a loss of sovereignty. The FO feared the British could become trapped if they joined the Paris talks, because they would then be on an irreversible 'slide' towards a fuller European federation. Furthermore if they joined in the talks, but later withdrew, they would be accused of inconsistency and bad faith. Intense negotiations over the following days tried to find a formula for Britain to join the talks on the plan whilst making clear its doubts about a loss of sovereignty. Such a formula proved difficult to find and on 1 June Schuman, anxious to proceed, gave the British a 24-hour deadline to accept the invitation to a conference. Again, from the French viewpoint, the desire to resolve matters was understandable, but to demand a one-day deadline for such an important decision was a questionable move.[7]

The economic historian Alan Milward feels that 'the French ... spared no effort ... to bring the United Kingdom into the proposed European framework', which is the view taken by Monnet and his sympathisers, including Anthony Nutting and Richard Mayne.[8] But other historians, and French Ambassador Massigli, have been more critical of Monnet and Schuman. Geoffrey Warner points out that the French always knew about

Britain's reluctance to surrender sovereignty, yet pressed the British hard on this point. The FO historian, Roger Bullen, in his introduction to the official volume of documents on the Schuman Plan, underlines the surprising nature of French tactics: after launching the scheme without warning, the French dawdled for more than two weeks before issuing invitations to a conference, and then expected Britain to decide its position at incredibly short notice. Warner and Bullen also reject criticisms, such as those of Sir Nicholas Henderson, a former British diplomat, that the British Cabinet decision of 2 June was taken hastily. It is true that the Cabinet was called together quickly, that Attlee and Cripps (hitherto well disposed to the Schuman Plan) were away on holiday and that Bevin was ill in hospital. But it was the French who faced the Labour government with a strict deadline and Bevin was consulted on the rejection of the latest French proposal.[9] An official committee, under the chairman of the Economic Planning Board, Sir Edwin Plowden, recommended rejection 'not because we necessarily preclude ... some surrender of sovereignty' in a *limited* sense, but because the French wanted an *open-ended* commitment by Britain to supranationalism, the precise implications of which it was impossible to judge. The Cabinet suggested ministerial talks with the French government to see if agreement could yet be reached.[10] But, in another display of determination, Schuman rejected this idea. He had already said that Britain might 'associate' with any European coal–steel institution in due course. At the time certain ministers, including Douglas Jay, a junior Treasury minister, believed that France deliberately 'excluded' Britain from the Schuman Plan in order to steal the leadership of Europe.[11]

Certainly, despite his reputation as an enlightened idealist, Monnet geared his proposal closely to French national interest. The idea of a French 'plot' goes too far, however. Rather it seems that British membership was not a priority for Monnet. Having got West Germany's commitment to the plan, he and Schuman were not willing to put supranationalism at risk in order to please the British. The account by Ambassador René Massigli, who desperately tried to involve Britain in the plan, certainly suggests this. Peter Calvocoressi has argued that it is not necessary to decide between the thesis that 'France excluded Britain' from the Schuman Plan and the thesis that 'Britain rejected the Plan': the two views are not mutually exclusive.[12] There were economic arguments against Britain joining the plan: its coal and steel industries were the largest in Europe and faced different market conditions to the continentals. But some accounts suggest that the Labour government's lack of imagination was to blame for this particular example of 'missing the European bus'.

An oft-quoted remark from Herbert Morrison, who chaired the 2 June Cabinet, was that 'It's no good, we cannot do it, the Durham miners won't wear it'. This reflected Labour fears of 'surrendering' their key national-ised industries to European control, at a time when continental Europe seemed dominated by capitalist Christian Democrat governments. To an extent too, Britain and France seemed to 'talk past' each other in June 1950, especially on the principle of losing sovereignty. Some argue that this was due to different ways of thinking: the British, unlike the French, could not talk in terms of principles without knowing their actual effect.

Yet it is clear that the decision to avoid involvement in the Schuman Plan was based on more than doctrinaire or philosophical narrow-mindedness. It was the logical culmination of the evolution in British policy since January 1948. As Roger Woodhouse has argued, 'the Schuman Plan, rather than precipitating Britain's rejection of a role in Europe, was symptomatic of a divergence which had already occurred'. Britain could never share France's obsession with Germany and saw no need to accept a potentially far-reaching surrender of sovereignty. But this still leaves plenty of scope to criticise what, in retrospect, proved a fateful decision. Two full-length studies of London's reaction to the Schuman Plan, by Edmund Dell and Christopher Lord, argue that there was a catalogue of errors and weaknesses in British policy. Dell points out that: given France's long-running concern with the German problem, Whitehall ought to have predicted a Schuman-type initiative; that more serious thought should have been given to French needs over previous years; that the chances of the Schuman Plan succeeding – and succeeding with-out Britain – were woefully underestimated; and that entering the talks on the same terms as the Dutch would have been a sensible option. Arrogance, a lack of imagination and the tiredness of leading ministers led to what Dell calls 'Britain's unnecessary self-exclusion' from the Schuman Plan. Lord underlines the fact that Britain's ability to influence developments in Europe was now much reduced: it was no longer required as an arbitrator between France and Germany; it now found France to be a genuine rival as the political leader of Western Europe; the US was likely to treat the nascent European community as a second 'special' partner in Europe; and Britain ran the risk of growing further and further apart from the Schuman Plan states as time went on. In fact, officials noted many of these problems at an early date but 'they were rarely brought together in one overall assessment' and for the moment they were outweighed by exaggerated fears of the loss of sovereignty implied by a supranational commitment.[13]

Ernest Bevin believed that the Schuman Plan would fail, allowing Britain to come forward with its own 'realistic' plan. But events over the following months did not move this way. In mid-June Labour policy on Europe was clarified in a pamphlet entitled *European Unity*. Work on this had actually begun some months before, but references to the Schuman Plan had been added to it. It rejected European federalism, made much of Britain's links to America and the Commonwealth and was critical of laissez-faire economics on the Continent. Unsurprisingly, outside observers generally saw it as evidence of the deep rift that had opened between Britain and the powers, now known as 'the Six', who had entered talks on the Schuman Plan. In late June the government easily survived a parliamentary debate on the Schuman Plan. 'If we go down on this', remarked the Lord Chancellor, Jowitt, 'I can't think of any better issue to go to the country on.' Europe was not yet a major party political issue and, although Churchill had used meetings of the Council of Europe Assembly to criticise Labour, and believed the government *could* have entered talks on the Schuman Plan, he had no wish to surrender British sovereignty. In July there was more embarrassment when the Secretary of State for War, John Strachey, made a rabidly anti-European speech which talked of a 'plot' to overthrow the Labour government. Schuman announced on 25 July that the Six were in agreement on all major issues with regard to a supranational authority for coal and steel. This put an end to Bevin's hopes of stepping forward with a 'realistic', non-supranational British plan (which Whitehall officials had now drawn up). A short time later two Conservative MPs, Harold Macmillan and David Eccles, fancying themselves more 'pro-European' than Labour, publicised their own plan for a non-supranational coal–steel institution. Monnet reacted to this with astonishing exaggeration, telling Schuman 'the British are waging a skilful campaign to sabotage our plan'. In fact Macmillan and Eccles were simply misguided. The last thing the Foreign Office wanted to be accused of was 'sabotage', for this would upset not only the Six, but also the Americans. Instead, after August, London's policy was to wait for the Six to establish a coal–steel community, and then to seek an association agreement with it.[14]

The European Defence Community, 1950–4

As work on the Schuman Plan proceeded public attention shifted to a new problem, which was to dominate the European unity debate for four years: German rearmament. Several historians, including, most recently, Saki Dockrill, have analysed this problem and the main elements of British policy seem clear. In June 1950 the Korean War broke out, provoking fears of Communist military action elsewhere, and leading US military chiefs to consider ways to strengthen the West's defences. Then in early September Secretary of State Acheson made a dramatic proposal to Bevin and Schuman, meeting in New York, that a West German army should be created. With NATO defences so weak, the US public unwilling to bear the burden of Western defence alone, and West Germany being revived as a loyal ally, this seemed an obvious step to Americans. However, to many Europeans the idea of recreating a German army, only five years after the defeat of Hitler's Reich, was appalling. Many Germans themselves were aghast at the idea, but the greatest opposition came from France. Predictably perhaps, Bevin, after some initial doubts, decided to support the American proposal. He argued that German rearmament would take time to achieve and could be carefully controlled; meanwhile the Americans had promised to send more troops to Europe if NATO agreed to German rearmament in principle. Schuman, however, strongly backed by his government, completely rejected Acheson's proposal and the New York meetings became deadlocked. NATO, despite the challenge of the Korean War, became completely divided. (It is significant that in these debates the British were ready to accept the *principle* of German rearmament, whilst the French wanted to know its precise effect. This was in contrast to each country's attitude towards the principle of supranationalism in the Schuman Plan, and gives the lie to arguments that the British cannot accept a principle in isolation from its result.) France's all too evident fear of Germany also threatened to put Franco-German co-operation in the Schuman Plan at risk. Yet this very fact goaded the French to devise a possible solution to the military problem. On 24 October premier René Pleven proposed that German troops could be rearmed, but only as part of a supranational European army, under a single European defence minister. The 'Pleven Plan', actually drawn up by Monnet, offered to give the Americans what they wanted – German rearmament – without giving the Germans any military independence. The most significant point was that there would be no German General Staff.[15]

After their rejection of the Schuman Plan, there was never any chance that the British would sign up for Pleven's European army. Apart from the deep aversion among the chiefs of staff to any loss of control over British forces, the Pleven Plan was viewed as militarily ridiculous. Monnet, who knew nothing of military affairs, had devised it as a *political* solution to the problems in NATO. Bevin saw it as further evidence of France's desire to control Germany and its supposed desire to be 'leader' of Europe. He believed the proposal would delay Western rearmament efforts and, more importantly, threaten the cohesion of NATO. In November Bevin even suggested to the Defence Committee of the Cabinet that it would be better to seek 'an Atlantic Federal or Confederate Force' which would control German rearmament without creating 'a continental bloc, under French leadership'. His virulent condemnation of any 'third force' highlighted how far he had moved since the launch of Western Union in 1948. Other ministers, however, believed that Bevin's own extraordinary plan would also delay German rearmament and felt it best to let the French proceed. In December the NATO Council meeting in Brussels also accepted this course: German rearmament was accepted 'in principle'; the US agreed to appoint a US Supreme Commander for NATO (General Dwight Eisenhower); and the French invited other countries to a conference in Paris on a European army, of which German troops would be members. West Germany, Italy, Belgium and Luxembourg agreed to attend. The Dutch took part after some delay. Britain, in common with other NATO states, merely sent an observer to the talks, which opened in February 1951.[16]

It took several months before Britain fully endorsed the European army as the only acceptable route to German rearmament. This came from Bevin's successor Herbert Morrison, whose short tenure of the FO has often been criticised as a failure but who, according to his biographers, improved relations with the continentals. Morrison even pleased members of the Council of Europe Assembly (which he had condemned in 1949 as a 'talk shop') by his readiness to expand its powers.[17] Under Morrison a review of policy towards Europe was carried out by the FO's Permanent Under-Secretary's Committee which accepted that certain countries wished to move towards supranationalism and advocated a positive statement of British policy, in order to please the Americans and so establish a 'bridge' between 'Atlanticists' and 'Europeanists'.[18] It was this study which led Morrison to issue a joint declaration with Schuman and Acheson when they met in September 1951 in Washington, which aimed at 'the inclusion of a democratic Germany ... in a Continental European Community, which itself will form part of a constantly developing Atlantic Community'. Thus the aims of the three major Western allies on German rearmament and European unity were publicly reconciled, and Morrison added the commitment that Britain 'desires to establish the closest possible association with the European continental community at all stages in its development'.[19] So positive was the European reaction to this, that the following month, when Churchill won a general election, there were inflated expectations of a new British policy towards the Continent.

The failure of the 1951 government to take a more positive view of European co-operation has been seen as another 'missed opportunity' for post-war British policy towards Europe. This view was most seriously held by the Conservative backbencher Robert Boothby, one of the 'Tory Strasbourgers' who attended the Council of Europe.[20] Two Cabinet members, Housing Minister Harold Macmillan and Home Secretary David Maxwell-Fyfe (later Lord Kilmuir), also believed it was possible to follow a more 'pro-European' policy than Labour, and that Britain could take the leadership of Europe once more. In their memoirs Boothby, Macmillan and Maxwell-Fyfe were all critical of remarks by the Foreign Secretary, Anthony Eden, on 28 November 1951, when he said Britain could never join the European army. Yet Eden always strongly denied that he was crudely 'anti-European' and it is significant that none of his three critics themselves advocated a surrender of British sovereignty at this time.[21] Instead they seem to have imagined that some 'middle way' could be found between the inter-governmental co-operation followed by Labour and the supranationalism of Monnet, but they were unable to put this into concrete form. Indeed a speech by Maxwell-Fyfe to the Council of Europe in November went no further than Morrison had done in September in expressing the desire to associate with the Six, and was condemned by Belgium's Paul-Henri Spaak as 'disappointing' and 'derisory'.[22] Those historians, such as Saki Dockrill and Anthony Seldon, who have looked at events under the Conservatives in late 1951, have seen no real opportunity to join supranational organisations in Europe.[23] There was no enthusiasm for this either from ministers, officials, businessmen or the public. What seems to have concerned the 'Tory Strasbourgers' most of all was, not any idealistic commitment to European integration, but a fear of British exclusion from a group which could become dominated by Germany. Had Churchill been genuinely interested in a full British share in European unity, as he seemed to be in Opposition, it might have made a difference. However, he told the Cabinet: 'I have never thought that Britain should become an integral part of a European Federation'; he asserted its importance as a *world* power, and expressed his preference for the country to act as a link between the Commonwealth, America and the Continent, in terms reminiscent of

Bevin.[24] Churchill (who in 1950 had been an early advocate of a European army) also criticised the EDC as a 'sludgy amalgam'. He would have preferred a European force made up of *national* armies. Churchill and Boothby hoped the EDC would fail – again in order to allow Britain to regain the lead in Europe. But the Cabinet was persuaded by Eden that the EDC was the only way to achieve German rearmament without breaking NATO apart.[25] Thus, ironically, it was Eden, rather than the so-called 'pro-Europeans', who wished to protect co-operation amongst 'the Six' on EDC as a way to strengthen the West.

Eden's position, as argued by Roger Bullen, effectively meant following the FO line established under Morrison. This was to encourage the European army to fruition (as NATO required), to avoid any accusation that Britain wished to 'sabotage' the EDC (such as Churchill and Boothby were ready to consider) but also to avoid fusing Britain's future with the Continent. Eden's policy was summarised in an FO brief at the time: 'We are ready to play an active part in all plans for integration on an inter-governmental basis; defence considerations, our Commonwealth connections and the Sterling area inhibit us from subordinating ourselves ... to any European supranational authority; nevertheless we ... have assured [the Six] of our goodwill and our wish to be associated with their work, short of actual membership.' As David Dutton, one of several Eden biographers, has put it, 'Eden was in no sense narrowly anti-European. But he did stress the established props of Britain's great power status and feared that these were incompatible with full participation in an insular Europe.'[26] This policy can be described as one of *benevolence towards, but non-involvement in, supranationalism*. But despite its attractiveness it proved difficult to carry out. Eden himself, for example, sounded very negative in public on European unity, as in his January 1952 speech at Columbia University where he tried to end any hopes about a 'new' British policy by stating that Britain could not join a federal Europe because 'this is something which we know in our bones we cannot do'.[27] He had to steer a narrow course, supporting the EDC yet refusing to be part of it. In May 1952, when the Six signed a treaty in Paris to set up a European Defence Community (EDC), Eden agreed to sign a 50-year mutual security treaty with the new organisation. But the reluctant way in which he agreed to this was criticised on the Continent at the time and by historians such as David Carlton later.[28]

There were, however, some attempts to link Britain to the Six. In 1952 Eden launched a proposal to increase institutional ties between the supranational communities of the Six and the Council of Europe. This proposal, known as the 'Eden Plan', was again designed by the FO to build a 'bridge' between the Six and those European countries which preferred inter-governmental co-operation. A leading advocate was the junior FO minister, Anthony Nutting, later a determined critic of Britain's European policy. It should be remembered that in the 1950s the supranationalist countries were a minority group. The inter-governmentalists included not just Britain, but also the Scandinavian countries, Portugal, Switzerland, Austria and Greece. Macmillan (who actually considered resignation from the government at this time over European policy) was critical of the Eden Plan in Cabinet and it did not achieve much. It proposed very modest links between the Six and the Council of Europe such as joint meetings and the use of shared facilities. But Churchill's government had by now disappointed those who hoped for a more 'pro-European' policy and continentals like Monnet were too suspicious of British policy to show any liking for Eden's plan which achieved nothing.[29]

In May 1952 the government also decided not to pursue the 'Strasbourg Plan' for economic association between Europe and the Commonwealth; this was seen as likely to weaken Commonwealth unity. There was rather more success – eventually – with efforts to associate with the European Coal–Steel Community (ECSC), whose High Authority was formally established in Luxembourg, with Monnet as its President, in August 1952. A study by Ruggero Ranieri has shown that, in the early 1950s, there were certain civil servants in the Treasury, Board of Trade and elsewhere who were especially keen to achieve an association agreement between the steel industry and the ECSC, an approach which was supported by some in the steel industry. In 1953 it was even hoped that association might take the form of British membership of the ECSC's 'common market' in steel. This idea again shows that not all in Whitehall were blindly 'anti-European'. The plan would not mean a great loss of British independence, but it would mark a close commitment to the Six and it would have the important practical effect of forcing the British steel industry to face rigorous European competition. But at this point old doubts about supranationalism were revived in the economic ministries of Whitehall. On the whole, industrialists too, doubtful of the ECSC's effectiveness, were fearful of the upheaval a common market might bring: businessmen did not become well disposed to European integration until the late 1950s. Thus the Whitehall proposal for a steel common market did not go forward, and all that was agreed in December 1954 was an institutional link to the

Six through a 'Council of Association'. This was important in White-hall's eyes as a way of maintaining links with the Six, but hardly very dramatic.[30]

Meanwhile public attention and most diplomatic efforts in 1952–4 continued to focus on achieving a European army. Although the EDC treaty had been signed, it had to be ratified before it could go into effect. This proved a long, demoralising process. In Germany, ratification was delayed for months while it was decided whether rearmament was legal under the Constitution. However, the main difficulties lay with the French, the original proponents of the scheme, who now doubted the need for a European army, for numerous reasons. Some French politicians continued to oppose German rearmament in any form: these included the Communists, who slavishly followed the Soviet line. Some, especially Socialists, favoured pacifism or general disarmament. With the death of Stalin, in March 1953, and the end of the Korean War in July, many no longer saw the need for stronger Western defences and there seemed a strong possibility of East–West détente. (Churchill was at the forefront of those advocating a summit meeting with Stalin's successors and, indeed, in order to pave the way for an East–West settlement, was ready to contemplate a united but neutralised Germany. Once again, it was Eden who opposed this aim which, if achieved, would have killed Western European integration stone dead.[31]) There was also a consider-able body of French opinion, however, which opposed the 'surrender' of the French army to a European body for nationalist reasons. This last factor led to the replacement of Schuman as foreign minister at the end of 1952. The involvement of considerable French forces in the colonial war in Indo-China increased the danger that German forces would be the largest element in the EDC. One way to reassure the French about their security was to establish close links between Britain and the EDC. Britain was still a major military power, which could help France to control Germany. In April 1954, after long negotiations, Eden made a Treaty of Association with the EDC, which involved institutional links and the inclusion of a British army division in an EDC corps. But these British concessions failed to make much impression on the Continent and in August, when the EDC went before the French Assembly, it was defeated.

The death of the EDC was a stunning blow to the Western alliance and the cause of a supranational Europe. The French vote offended the Americans, who had been pressing for German rearmament since 1950, and Adenauer, who had based West German foreign policy on co-operation with France. Yet for the British it also seemed a vindication of their earlier doubts about the practicality of a European army. With the US at a loss what to do, the crisis came to Eden as an opportunity to point the Six back towards inter-governmental co-operation. Indeed he had long been ready to step forward with his own plan if the EDC failed. He toured the capitals of the Six and called an international conference in London in September. With no danger now of being accused of 'sabotage', he was able to put forward an FO scheme for European co-operation. He proposed to extend the 1948 Brussels Pact formed by Britain, France and the Benelux to West Germany and Italy. Thus it would become a seven-power body and would achieve the aim of tying Britain to the Six in a non-supranational body. It might also allow Britain to control future developments among the Six – a major prize.

Such was the blow to European morale that the demise of the EDC represented, that Eden's proposal was accepted at the London Conference. The expanded Brussels Pact became the Western European Union (WEU) in 1955. As to German rearmament, it was to be carried out under the auspices of NATO, and West Germany was to join NATO as a sovereign state. This was similar to the solution France had objected to so strongly in 1950 but Prime Minister Pierre Mendès-France was induced to accept it for a number of reasons: most important perhaps was the danger of French isolation, and of a US–British–German agreement to rearm Germany anyway; Adenauer promised that West Germany would not manufacture certain armaments, including atomic, bacteriological and chemical weapons; and a British commitment was made to keep a certain number of divisions and aircraft on the Continent. The last was a key concession by Britain, a country which had historically shrunk from any long-term promise to keep troops in Europe. But Eden convinced the Cabinet that it was essential as a once for all concession, in order to secure a settlement that was otherwise so attractive to Britain. Not surprisingly, Eden's official biographer, Robert Rhodes James, sees the London Conference as one of Eden's greatest triumphs; even the 'father of Europe' Spaak considered that Eden had 'saved the Western alliance'.[32] In contrast Monnet, wounded by the defeat of the EDC and offended by Mendès-France's policies, decided to resign the ECSC Presidency and support European unity as a private individual. Eden had successfully avoided either supranational involvements or accusations of 'sabotaging' European efforts; he had seen the EDC collapse under its own contradictions and had then devoted all his diplomatic skills to producing a European body to British tastes.

The European Economic Community, 1955–7

In retrospect, Eden's unexpected success of 1954 proved, as Richard Mayne said, 'a Pyrrhic victory', because it led the FO to underestimate the chances of 'the relaunch of Europe' the following year. As Anne Deighton has argued, Eden's very triumph in resolving the September 1954 crisis paved the way for a revival of supranational ambitions, because 'the way in which the Western bloc was completed in 1954–5 created an atmosphere of security in which continental integration efforts could successfully progress'.[33] The events of 1955 finally destroyed the policy of benevolence and non-involvement which Britain had pursued since 1951, and again demonstrated that London misunderstood the forces working for supranational integration on the Continent. Early in the year Mendès-France lost office, to be succeeded by the more pro-European Edgar Faure. Soon after, Churchill handed the premiership over to Eden. At this time France ratified the agreements on WEU and German rearmament, allowing West Germany into NATO in May. Yet whilst this could be seen as a success for British policy, its significance lay primarily in the military field and it also recreated the conditions for a Franco-German rapprochement. Furthermore, although the EDC had proved over-ambitious, the ECSC remained in existence and provided a potential basis for new economic co-operation among the Six.

In 1955, after the EDC failure, few European leaders were ready to use the word 'supranational' in public, most wanted to involve Britain in any new initiatives, and the US government was reluctant to identify itself publicly with new federalist schemes. But this did not mean that everyone had abandoned hopes for supranationalism. Spaak and Monnet considered extending co-operation, on ECSC lines, to new sectors of the European economy such as transport or atomic energy. These two 'fathers of Europe' were outdone however, by the Dutch foreign minister Jan Beyen, who argued that the 'sector approach', if it continued among the Six, must, sooner or later, face the need for a full-scale customs union. If this was the case, why not take the plunge into a full-scale common market now? The Benelux countries circulated a memorandum on these ideas, which was discussed by ECSC ministers at Messina, Sicily, in June. At Messina, still avoiding the emotive term 'supranational', the Six agreed to set up a committee in Brussels, under Spaak's chairmanship, to study both the 'sector approach' and Beyen's common market.

In July 1948, when the French had first proposed discussion of a European parliament and economic union by the Brussels Pact countries, one

FO official had minuted: 'It is hoped that this item will not occupy too much time'! Seven years later, with the heartening tale of the EDC behind them, British diplomats were equally overconfident. Gladwyn Jebb, the Ambassador to Paris and later an advocate of EEC membership, assured the FO that 'no very spectacular developments are to be expected as a result of the Messina conference'. (Contrary to what is claimed in certain studies, there was no British 'emissary' at Messina itself.[34]) At first the FO decided to follow its established policy: to stay outside the Messina process and 'associate' with any bodies which emerged. However, the Messina conferees put London in a difficult position because the Six decided to invite Britain, as an associate member of the ECSC and fellow member of the WEU, to join in the work of the Spaak Committee. There is no evidence that the Six expected Britain to *join* in any supranational bodies; rather they wanted Britain's blessing for their work after the EDC episode. In London the Messina invitation was treated differently from the invitation to discuss the Schuman Plan in 1950. This time the Six asked for no commitment in advance on the supranational principle, and the Conservative government, fresh from an election victory, was confident about its European policy.

The supposedly 'pro-European' Macmillan was now Foreign Secretary and it was decided by the Cabinet on 30 June (despite doubts from some ministers such as Chancellor 'Rab' Butler) to send a 'representative' to the Spaak Committee. In accepting the invitation to talks however, the Cabinet made clear that there was no 'prior commitment' to accept the results, and said that 'due account should be taken of . . . existing organisations such as the OEEC'. Furthermore, the representative chosen to go to Brussels was a mere Board of Trade official, Russell Bretherton. In this the Cabinet largely followed the recommendations of a key group of officials, the Mutual Aid Committee, which argued that 'by participating we shall give ourselves the opportunity to influence . . . the investigations along the most sensible lines'. The essential policy remained that of benevolence towards the Six whilst avoiding all federal commitments. But in contrast to Labour in 1950, the Conservatives joined in the deliberations of the Six in order to 'steer' them on acceptable lines. Thus Britain had abandoned the principle of non-involvement in discussions among the Six.

The perils of entering the Messina process in any form quickly became clear. Once the Spaak Committee began its work, on 9 July, it was apparent that the Six really had no intention of abandoning supranationalism. Though wounded by the failure of the EDC, which they had strongly supported, the Americans also encouraged the new efforts at co-operation among the Six. Spaak proved a businesslike chairman of the Brussels talks and one determined to establish new institutions, notably in the areas of atomic co-operation and a common market. London was taken aback by the strength of support for a common market, in the form of a full customs union, from West Germany. The FO believed that the Germans had little to gain from this policy and that their Economic Minister Ludwig Erhard would prefer to seek looser, free trade arrangements (the essential difference between a free trade area and a customs union is that, under the former, countries can maintain their own trade policies towards outsiders, whereas the latter demands a common external trade policy and, thus, greater co-ordination at the centre). But Chancellor Adenauer was still a keen Europeanist, and his determination to integrate the new Germany with other liberal democracies was strengthened in summer 1955 by the failure to progress towards détente with the Soviets. In contrast, in Whitehall, the Treasury and BOT, who dominated the key committees looking at European policy in 1955, were unenthusiastic about a European customs union. It was appreciated that this could lead to expanded trade, but the BOT preferred to keep to established policies based on freer world trade and Commonwealth preferences, whilst the Treasury feared losing control of the British economy and becoming susceptible to economic fluctuations on the Continent. Political considerations, such as influenced Adenauer, cut little ice with Britain's economic ministries. However, in one memorandum the Treasury also made the very worrying point that 'the interests of the UK would be adversely affected by the establishment of a common market in which we did not participate'. A special Working Group was set up under a Treasury official, Burke Trend, to look at the dangers of a customs union. One of its findings was that, even if Britain did enter a union its industrialists would probably lose out to the Germans in the main European markets. Such was Germany's competitive edge ten years after the war.[35]

Only a month after joining the Spaak Committee, Russell Bretherton pointed out the major problem facing Britain in the short term: 'If we take an active part in trying to guide the [Brussels talks] . . . it will be difficult to avoid the presumption that we are . . . committed to the result.'[36] To avoid too close an identification with the Six, Macmillan refused to attend an ECSC foreign ministers' conference in September, which reviewed the Spaak Committee's work. Macmillan, despite his 'pro-European' reputation, was preoccupied with other issues at this point, especially the future of Cyprus, and rarely intervened with much effect on the issue of the Spaak Committee. Other ministers, including Peter Thorneycroft at the BOT, Commonwealth Secretary Harry Crookshank and, most importantly, Chancellor 'Rab' Butler, now wanted to 'disengage' from the Spaak Committee. When interviewed by Michael Charlton about the Messina process Butler remarked he was 'bored' by it, adding that Eden was 'even more bored than I was'. Certainly there is very little evidence that Prime Minister Eden involved himself in the question in 1955.[37] So it was that Britain began to distance itself from the Spaak Committee. In November Bretherton asked Spaak to draw up his final report without any reference to Britain's position. Spaak took this as a British withdrawal from his committee's work; London did not quibble with his interpretation.

Yet withdrawal from the Spaak Committee, whose work had become embarrassing to London, did not solve Britain's long-term problem, the fact that a powerful customs union might now be formed on the Continent. London had completely failed to 'steer' the Messina process away from supranationalism, but the EDC failure was not far behind, Spaak's Committee was proceeding only slowly and Erhard's dislike of a common market was well known. In October, faced by these considerations, a Treasury official, Peter Nicholls, suggested abandoning the policy of benevolence towards the Six: 'If we do not want to see a common market set up, and if we want to avoid being blamed for its failure, it would suit us well to persuade the Germans to lean towards OEEC.'[38] The need to defend the role of the OEEC (originally set up to supervise Marshall Aid, but still in existence) was also strongly pressed by Sir Hugh Ellis-Rees, head of Britain's OEEC delegation. In late October the Mutual Aid Committee of officials, having completed its studies of a common market, recommended devising a British 'alternative' plan to tempt the Six away from a customs union. This was a dramatic turn of policy. As in 1950, many officials were confident that the efforts of the Six would fail anyway: unlike 1950, they were ready to take an initiative of their own, to forestall a continental trading bloc.

The proposal for a British 'alternative' to the common market was endorsed on 1 November by senior officials in the Economic Steering Committee. (At this meeting one official, Sir Frank Lee of the BOT, was a lone voice advocating membership of the common market.) The British alternative plan was approved on 11 November by ministers meeting in the Economic Policy Committee. The 'alternative' would be based on a free trade area rather than a customs union, but its exact details remained to be worked out. Ministers also rejected the idea of joining a European atomic energy organisation. They did not oppose this body as much as they opposed the EEC: indeed, nuclear co-operation with Europe could have brought commercial benefits as well as helping to strengthen relations with France. But membership of a European atomic agency could also have disrupted Britain's atomic weapons programme, upset the country's relationship with the US on nuclear matters and increased the dangers of nuclear proliferation. In order to slow down the work of the Six until a British free trade proposal was ready it was decided to put pressure on Bonn and Washington to abandon the idea of a common market and concentrate economic co-operation in the OEEC, working on inter-governmental lines.

The decisions of 11 November 1955 soon proved a major error of judgement, based on a misunderstanding of the forces behind the common market and overconfidence about the strength of Britain's position. The problems began as soon as approaches were made to Bonn and Washington. For it immediately became clear that neither West Germany nor the US wished to delay work on the common market. The British delegation to the OEEC then made a strong public statement about the need to avoid economic division in Western Europe. This, although not a formal rejection of Spaak's work, announced to the world that Britain was not happy with the Spaak Committee. It led Spaak and Holland's Beyen to fear British 'sabotage' of their efforts. Beyen was personally upset because he had recently visited London and was given no warning of a change of policy. Here, the British succeeded in alienating the most anglophile leader on the Continent. None of the Six wished to destroy the OEEC, but neither did they see it as an appropriate institution for the close integration they wished to achieve. The British themselves had taken little interest in the OEEC since Marshall Aid ended in 1952. At a meeting of the WEU Council on 14 December both Spaak and Beyen, fearing a collapse of all their work if France or Germany followed the British lead, launched an attack on Macmillan over British policy. Macmillan, evidently shocked by their strength of feeling, admitted that Britain's statement on the OEEC had been mistimed. Many British ambassadors were aghast at how badly British policy had been explained in November and FO officials were now keen to adopt an unprovocative policy until tempers cooled. This was not so easy however, because the genie of a 'new' British policy was now out of the bottle even if the details were not worked out.

Rather than the policy of 1951–4 based around benevolence and non-involvement, London now seemed opposed to the efforts of the Six and prepared to play an active role against them. The account by Elizabeth Kane emphasises that the fault lay in the *way* British policy was executed and argues that there was no real attempt at 'sabotage': rather than being 'hostile to the Six . . . they were attempting to pursue a policy which allowed the British to keep all options open'. However, Sean Greenwood has written that Britain's 'hope of influencing developments towards a free trade association easily slid into a deliberate attempt to wreck the customs union project . . . This was a most significant change' and James Ellison considers that the November episode 'was by far the most conspicuous and enduring evidence of Britain's potential hostility towards Six power unity' in the mid-1950s. It provoked enough concern for Spaak to write a personal letter to Eden, arguing that supranationalism was the only way to control Germany in future. In February Spaak visited London and put this point to Macmillan. The same month Eden was pressed by US Secretary of State Dulles not to upset the work on a Six-power customs union.[39]

At Venice in May 1956, ECSC ministers finally considered the Spaak Committee's report and decided to draw up two treaties, one for an atomic energy authority (Euratom), the other for an economic community (EEC). The process of devising these treaties was far from simple. Numerous issues divided the Six. From the first the French had preferred the Euratom proposal (which could bolster their own nuclear research programme) to the common market, which might harm French agricultural and industrial interests by opening them up to external (especially German) competition. Historically France had a high tariff 'wall' to protect itself from competitors, but the Germans and Dutch wanted to lower trade barriers rapidly within a common market. These divisions help to explain why the British were still confident that the Messina process would fail. At key points however, as H. J. Küsters has argued, the EEC cause was boosted by chance events.[40] One such was the French election of January 1956 which strengthened the pro-Europeans in the National Assembly and led to a strongly pro-common market government under Guy Mollet. Another coincidental factor, which drove France towards the EEC and helped destroy British hopes of avoiding such an institution, was the Suez crisis. This is not the place fully to discuss the Suez crisis, which dominated the second half of 1956. Initially the nationalisation of the Suez Canal served to draw Britain and France together against Egypt's President Nasser to the point that the Paris government even sounded out London on the possibility of joining the Commonwealth. In September France made a series of demands in the

Six-power talks in order to improve its own position in any customs union. (These demands included the harmonisation of social policies, to prevent France being at a competitive disadvantage because of its generous social legislation.) But in November, when the British decided to cease military action against Egypt, the French felt betrayed and abandoned close co-operation with Britain. Thereafter the pace of talks on the EEC quickened and the French became less determined to protect narrow national interests in the talks. The Euratom and EEC treaties were signed in Rome on 25 March 1957.

The British failed in 1956 to tempt other Europeans away from the common market. This was partly because London was slow to devise its 'alternative'. In contrast to the early post-war period, European policy was now dominated by the Treasury and Board of Trade, rather than the FO. In December 1955 Macmillan had become Chancellor of the Exchequer, with primary responsibility for devising a free trade proposal, but it was only in July that he and Thorneycroft put forward a plan. Worked out by officials of several departments, from a list of alternatives, 'Plan G' was based on a free trade area (FTA), created in stages, to be run via the OEEC and open to all OEEC members, which the Six could join as a single entity. This in itself however, was an admission that the Six would probably succeed in forming a common market anyway. Plan G was not therefore an *alternative* to the EEC, by the time it emerged; rather it sought to keep the Six and other OEEC states together, minimising the ill-effects on Britain of a continental customs union from which it was excluded.

Unlike the EEC, Plan G made no attempt at economic integration and, of course, it lacked strong central institutions. In her study of British relations with the EEC, Miriam Camps concludes that 'it was not maliciously conceived'. It was felt the Six would be attracted to it, and that Austria, Switzerland and Scandinavian states would be particularly interested in the proposal. A more recent account by Elizabeth Kane also argues that 'Plan G was . . . a genuine attempt to improve relations with Europe' but notes that it 'was a compromise policy, adopted only because there was no agreement in the Government as to whether to pursue a policy based on the Commonwealth and Europe as dynamic forces . . . or to base policy on Europe at the expense of the Commonwealth'. There were several aspects of Plan G which reflected the continuing overconfidence of the British government in dealing with Europe, and its determination to safeguard national interests. The British still believed Europe needed them more than they needed Europe, especially after the EDC failure.

Thus the proposed FTA would exclude foodstuffs 'in the interests of home agriculture policy and . . . the Commonwealth', and Britain would reserve the right to reimpose certain trade restrictions if necessary 'to protect sterling'. The Federation of British Industry strongly supported this approach: many businessmen now recognised the need for access to EEC markets, but ideally they wanted to achieve this without losing Commonwealth trade, on which many of the Federation's members were dependent. Britain also insisted 'that there should be no discrimination by the Messina Six . . . against us'.

The last condition was extremely important in the negotiations which followed because it implied that the Six must reduce their tariffs in the EEC at the same rate that tariffs were reduced in the wider FTA. This being the case, the British needed to press on quickly with the scheme so as to match the pace of the creation of the EEC. Yet several factors helped to delay a formal announcement of the plan after it was discussed by the Cabinet on 14 and 18 September. Preoccupation with Suez was one, but there was also the need to consult Commonwealth Finance Ministers (believed to be lukewarm on the FTA) and industrialists, and there was some resistance to the plan among ministers. (Significantly there was considerable press interest in the issue, the first time this occurred in a major way on European unity.) Divisions among the Six in the common market talks at this time probably contributed to the feeling of over-confidence in London. But the fact that Britain was now finalising its plan led Spaak to speed up discussions among the Six, fearing an attempt by Macmillan to 'sabotage' the common market. It was only on 26 November, after Commonwealth reactions proved better than expected, that Macmillan finally announced the intention to begin talks on an industrial FTA in the OEEC. By then the Suez expedition had ended in fiasco, relations with France were as bad as ever and the common market talks were about to take their last surge towards success. The Mollet government was even able to secure the inclusion of France's colonies under the terms of the common market, and to obtain promises of financial support for colonial development. This not only kept alive French hopes of a 'Eurafrican' combination which could boost French power but surprised the British, who had no desire to open their Empire to European competition or to include colonies in the FTA.

Macmillan's speech about the FTA on 26 November was notable for placing continued emphasis on the 'three circles' of British policy, with America and the Commonwealth as important as Europe. Furthermore, in the wake of Suez, Britain concentrated its diplomatic efforts on rebuilding links with Washington, which had been badly strained during the crisis. Macmillan himself became Prime Minister in January 1957 and saw his main success overseas in the early months as the Bermuda Summit with President Eisenhower in March. True, there were some positive points in Britain's European policy at this time. Most remarkably, just *before* Eden's resignation, the Foreign Secretary, Selwyn Lloyd – in terms reminiscent of Bevin in 1948 – suggested in Cabinet that, after the blow to British power at Suez, Britain might pool its 'resources with our European allies so that Western Europe as a whole might become a third nuclear power comparable with the United States and the Soviet Union'. This was strongly opposed by several ministers, however, who believed the main lesson of Suez was the need for a strong American alliance. When he became premier, Macmillan appointed two 'pro-European' ministers, Peter Thorneycroft and David Eccles, to the Treasury and BOT, and on 12–13 February the OEEC Council, after carrying out its own studies and seeing Plan G, agreed to begin talks on possible ways to create an FTA. However, there were predictable criticisms of the British plan, not least because of its exclusion of agricultural products, and from the start of the new talks the British were clearly in a vulnerable position.[41] For in March 1957 the FTA was only a paper proposal with controversial elements, whilst the Treaties of Rome had actually been signed.

Lost Opportunities?

Writing in 1960, Anthony Nutting considered the refusal to enter talks on the Schuman Plan as 'the most critical of the lost opportunities for Great Britain to lead Europe'. This argument has found support among later historians, such as Christopher Lord, who points out that Britain's absence from meetings of the Six, between 1950 and 1955, meant that it could not share in either their common working practices (which led to a close sense of co-operation) or in their mutual commitment to the Community project. However, in his biography of Ernest Bevin, Lord Bullock argues that if there was a 'missed opportunity for British relations with the supranational movement in Europe it came in 1955–7 not 1950'.[42] Bevin's policy did not result in a disastrous long-term rift with Europe and did not prevent Britain entering the Spaak Committee. Between 1950 and 1955 Britain aimed at non-involvement in supranational bodies but sought association with them. This allowed Britain to avoid any surrender of sovereignty and to preserve a world role whilst maintaining links to the Six and avoiding a deep division of Western Europe. Meanwhile, although the ECSC was successfully established, the EDC experience was hardly calculated to bind together France and its partners. Many have shared Anthony Nutting's belief that, after the war, 'Britain could have had the leadership of Europe on any terms she cared to name'. This was not just a later platitude: in July 1956 the 'pro-European' MP Boothby confidently told the Commons that if the Six 'really see that we are prepared to come in and take the lead they will virtually allow us to write our own ticket'. By the time Miriam Camps published her account of British relations with the EEC in 1964, it was readily assumed that the post-war decade was one of 'missed opportunities' in which the 'leadership of Europe was [Britain's] for the asking'.[43]

But there are several problems with such arguments. First, as is all too evident with Boothby, they are simply another version of the national arrogance seen among those who were obsessed with the need to maintain the Empire and a world presence. The assumption was that West Germany, France and the rest were sitting waiting for a British lead when in fact they were quite able to take their own initiatives. Second, such ideas were often based at the time, not on any real idealism about Europe, but on a particular view of British interests, especially a desire to prevent a German-dominated European bloc. Third, they hardly ever included a willingness to surrender sovereignty to common institutions: neither Boothby nor other 'Tory Strasbourgers' (like Maxwell-Fyfe and Macmillan) ever embraced supranationalism. Yet a pooling of sovereignty was the essence of the Schuman Plan and EDC, and was strongly supported by Spaak, Adenauer and others. This commitment to supranationalism was seldom appreciated in London, either by so-called 'pro-Europeans' or their critics. Boothby, in 1953, said he opposed all idea of a Six-power federation and advocated a 'wider, looser and more flexible European association, under British leadership'. The truth of the matter was seen when Britain *did* try to take a lead in Europe: Bevin tried to 'lead' Europe after 1948, but was unable to prevent the Schuman Plan; Eden tried to establish institutional co-operation with the Six through the 1952 'Eden Plan', but Nutting himself acknowledged 'our plan was a half-way house and Europe was in a "whole hog" mood'; and although the WEU was set up in 1955 it was quite clearly seen as inadequate by the Messina powers, who soon began a new project.[44] The fact is that Britain could not have had the leadership of Europe *on its own terms* because Britain saw no need to abandon its sovereignty to common institutions, whereas the Six saw this as vital. Britain could only have played a leading role in European integration, paradoxically, *if* it had accepted the continentals' terms and embraced supranationalism, but very few people advocated this before 1957.

The failure of the EDC in August 1954 seemed to confirm British doubts about the practicality of supranationalism for a time and made the Six anxious to have British approval for the 'Messina process' after June 1955. But the demise of the EDC also led Whitehall to underestimate the continued potential of far-reaching integration in the economic field, and made London overconfident about the strength of its position *vis-à-vis* the Six. Then again, it is fair to ask whether the Conservative government should have been more alive to the opportunities and dangers of Messina. After all, in both the decision to enter the Spaak Committee talks and in the decision to launch the FTA, the British showed that they did realise the potential of a continental bloc. Official studies in 1955–6 recognised the declining value of Commonwealth trade preferences and noted that, if the Six created a customs union, 'the disadvantages of abstaining would, *in the long run*, outweigh the advantages for Britain'.[45] The dangers of a Soviet invasion of Western Europe had receded since 1950 and hopes of Britain matching the superpowers had faded, so that conditions were already very different to Bevin's day. What is more, the Six had already suffered enough setbacks to show that the 'unity' they aimed at was a long-term affair; indeed, it might not be too far removed from Bevin's earlier hopes of 'evolutionary' progress on European co-operation. Arguably Britain had exaggerated the menace of 'federalism' since it first raised its head in May 1948. The governments of the Six clearly had no intention of forming a 'federation' in the near future, with the loss of sovereignty to a central government. Rather, at least in the ECSC, they were ready to pool their sovereignty in a limited 'sector' of the economy. The EEC was weaker than the ECSC in the loss of sovereignty from member states: indeed alongside a (potentially supranational) executive, called the Commission, it had very strong national representation in a Council of Ministers, which made the key policy decisions.

Why did the Conservatives not launch a major reconsideration of their European policy in 1955–6 as Bevin had done in 1948–9? In part the answer is that the policy established by Bevin had not yet broken down – at least until Suez. British involvement in the common market would, it was felt, destroy the Sterling Area, create long-term tensions in NATO and take the country 'further along the road of political federation than we would wish'.[46] Until November 1956 the 'three circles' concept was intact, many Britons had great faith in the Empire-Commonwealth and the Six still seemed divided. Furthermore the Six themselves did not expect Britain to join their new institutions: people such as Spaak and Beyen simply wanted London's blessing. Suez did have a great effect on British confidence in its world role, and confirmed that America would not treat Britain as a 'special' partner in world affairs. But, astonishingly, it did not lead to a major rethinking about foreign policy: in the short term, as noted by Geoffrey Warner, London responded by shoring up the American alliance whilst France moved more firmly towards the EEC.[47] Thus policy in late 1956 and early 1957 tended to push Britain further away from Europe. Only the next few years would reveal the problems of this course, as the Americans refused to treat Britain as an equal, the EEC proved a success and most British colonies gained their independence.

In part too there was a lack of vision in Britain, especially from leading ministers. Eden took no real interest in Messina and his memoirs have no details on the issue. Neither do Butler's, who was dismissive of Spaak's efforts. Macmillan seemed confused over what he wanted in Europe, beyond trying to limit German power. John Barnes has argued that 'Eden, Butler and Macmillan were all part of a broad consensus in Whitehall which recognised the growing importance of Europe . . . but . . . was not yet ready to narrow its horizons to Europe alone'. There was no appreciation of the costs of remaining outside the EEC which seem so obvious in retrospect. 'In refusing to join', Alan Milward has written, 'British governments were weakening the nation more than defending its sovereignty . . . and the consequences for manufacturing industry were immediate. Economically and politically Britain's role became increasingly peripheral.'[48] This is not to say that there were no changes in Britain's European policy. In fact, the common market forced Britain to diverge from the tactics of 'benevolence and non-involvement pursued' in 1950–4. First, in contrast to Bevin in 1950, the Conservatives decided to involve themselves in the Spaak Committee discussions. Second, having realised their error in taking this course, they tried to distance themselves from the Six by making a vain approach to West Germany to abandon supranationalism. Spaak and Beyen, with some justification, then feared a British policy of 'sabotage' and progress on the FTA scheme simply led the Six to quicken the pace of their own decisions. Certainly there were arguments among the Six but the clumsiness of British diplomacy did little to exploit these. The final error was the treatment France received over Suez and the British obsession with pleasing

America over the following months. The most damning overall criticism of British policy is that, whatever the excuses, the vital opportunity was lost to join the EEC at the outset, at a time when official British studies *did* comprehend the possibilities of the common market. The FTA proposal was another attempt to keep all Britain's options open: to preserve Commonwealth trade, avoid common market membership and yet maintain links to Europe and expand continental trade. But the distrust built up in 1955–6 already made its success problematic.

3

MACMILLAN, THE FREE TRADE AREA AND THE FIRST APPLICATION, 1957–1963

The Failure of the Free Trade Area, 1957–8

'What I chiefly fear' wrote Macmillan in April 1957, 'is the Common Market coming into being and the Free Trade Area never following.'[1] From the start the British attempt to create a Free Trade Area (FTA), via talks in the Organisation of European Economic Cooperation (OEEC), faced numerous difficulties. Once the Six had signed the Treaty of Rome they naturally wished to defend their hard-won creation, and they were already suspicious of Britain's attempts to disrupt their co-operation. The British had little interest in political integration in Europe. Neither did the FTA offer the Six much in economic terms. Even Paul Gore-Booth, Deputy Under-Secretary at the FO, acknowledged in his memoirs that an FTA for industrial goods, combined with Commonwealth trade preferences, meant that 'the Commonwealth could expose European goods coming into Britain to competition which British goods entering the Common Market would not suffer'. Thus, Britain would gain most. The government was also reluctant to make concessions on agricultural goods because of the strong anti-EEC views of the National Farmers' Union, whose support was vital to many Conservative MPs. In his study of British pressure groups and the EEC, Robert Lieber concluded that the farmers contributed to major delays in the FTA talks, and to the situation whereby 'Britain overplayed her . . . bargaining position in the negotiations'. A more recent study, by Wolfram Kaiser, confirms that,

53

while British industry and the Trades Union Congress were quite positive about the FTA and made few demands on the government, the farming lobby was able 'to delay concessions on agriculture'.[2]

Although the Six found it very difficult to begin work on their own Common Agricultural Policy, France, Holland and Italy were bound to be upset by the omission of agricultural produce from the FTA. French experts saw the FTA as moulded to British interests – opening European markets to British industry whilst preserving Commonwealth trade and protecting British agriculture. In Paris there was concern that a successful FTA would destroy the EEC. France had only accepted the EEC with ornate safeguards and in peculiar circumstances and, as Miriam Camps wrote in her seminal account of the FTA, it was difficult to see why the French should accept new trade arrangements without similar guarantees. More recent, archivally based studies suggest that, while British policy aimed to be constructive in 1957–8, it was too much locked into traditional attitudes, failed to show a deep commitment to a European future, never resolved its own internal contradictions and was probably doomed to failure at an early date. Richard Lamb has written that the British spent the years 1956–8 trying to escape a basic incompatibility between the FTA and the EEC, which was obvious virtually from the outset: 'if Britain was to keep down her labour costs by cheap food from the Commonwealth the Six would never allow her into their customs union'.[3]

The need for Britain to escape this contradiction and achieve an FTA was strengthened by the country's economic position. Already, by 1957, Britain faced balance of payment problems and lower growth than its neighbours. The country continued to rely on world trade, with a strong currency to satisfy the countries of the Sterling Area and investors in the City. But overseas liabilities restricted growth at home, and Britain's share of world trade fell in 1950–5 from 25 to 20 per cent. This was compensated by the fact that the total *volume* of trade was rising; nonetheless, in 1958 West Germany overtook Britain as an exporter of manufactured goods. This poor performance was not entirely new, of course, but it began a long-running debate about the country's economic failure. To some extent the post-war decline of growth rates and trade relative to other powers was inevitable: countries like Germany and Japan were bound to recover from defeat. To a large extent problems were internally generated: British investment was low, consumer spending too high, and wages were rising much faster than output. But, as George Peden has argued, overseas liabilities and changing trade patterns also seemed part of the problem and the FTA showed 'the extent to which Britain felt her interests to be bound up with Europe'. This echoes Miriam Camps' view that, whatever its inadequacies, the FTA 'represented a real and substantial shift in the British government's attitude towards Europe'. British ministers knew that Commonwealth states were beginning to develop other export markets, and looked to America for development aid, so that the value of Commonwealth trade preferences was declining. The British were slow to adapt to this. They had, arguably, good excuses in that the Commonwealth still took 43 per cent of national trade and represented a market of 600 million people. Britain was still a leading coal and steel producer, with (in 1957) higher living standards than the Six. Furthermore (helped by a return to freely convertible currencies) the City's banking and finance houses revived strongly in the later 1950s. A full review of British policy in July 1958 accepted that Britain's international aims were 'suffering from lack of resources', but the priorities for the future were to preserve the Commonwealth, the American alliance and the Sterling Area. At this time British policy-makers continued to believe they were in a strong bargaining position *vis-à-vis* the Six. And, although he was well aware of the EEC's political significance, Macmillan's prime concern (at least until 1960) was to prevent a closed *economic* bloc being formed which could harm British trade.[4]

In April 1957, Britain's Minister of Defence, Duncan Sandys, published a White Paper which, in the wake of Suez and the possession of a British hydrogen bomb, planned to rely for future defence on nuclear weapons. This meant cuts in Britain's Army of the Rhine, despite the 1954 undertaking to maintain force levels in Europe. The decision was widely criticised in Western Europe and in order to improve Britain's standing, Selwyn Lloyd launched an improved version of the 1952 'Eden Plan'. Ambitiously retitling this as 'The Grand Design' Lloyd proposed to tie together the Six and other European states via institutional links between the EEC, WEU, and the Council of Europe, including a new parliamentary assembly. It is important to note that this was an attempt to put forward a new political initiative; British ministers were not, as is often claimed, narrowly obsessed about economic questions at this time. But the assembly would be a purely consultative body and no one else showed much interest in the scheme. Despite Lloyd's protestations to the contrary, the Six saw it as another attempt to disrupt the EEC.[5] Even British ambassadors, like Gladwyn Jebb in Paris, saw little value in the 'Grand Design'. Jebb even felt the FTA to be a questionable step, because it might not prevent the EEC becoming a political-economic group (perhaps dominated by Germany), which would be more powerful than Britain and could create a 'third force' independent of NATO. Jebb, still unwill-ing to advocate membership of the EEC, suggested that the best way to influence developments among the Six would be to include agricultural concessions in the FTA and – as a political concession – to accept *weighted* voting in European bodies. The latter step might prove dramatic enough to restore Britain's reputation, and Macmillan showed some interest in it.[6] However, despite private talk of such concessions, in pub-lic the British took a hard line on the need to create an industrial FTA. This was especially clear in speeches by David Eccles, President of the Board of Trade, who voiced British fears of an inward-looking, German-dominated EEC.

A Cabinet meeting on 2 May showed the government to be fully aware of the EEC's economic menace (as a discriminatory trade bloc) and a political threat (if it led to a 'third force'). But, under pressure from France and Germany, Macmillan agreed to delay progress on the FTA until after the Treaty of Rome was ratified. This concession was probably inescap-able but, apart from several months' delay, it meant that once ratification took place, the common market would begin to be created (with reduc-tions of tariffs and trade quotas) on 1 January 1959: this created a tight deadline for the FTA talks. Only in August did Macmillan appoint Regi-nald Maudling, the Paymaster-General, to take charge of the talks for Britain. Maudling was an intelligent, cool-headed and likeable young minister but he lacked international experience and had little sympathy for supranational approaches to European co-operation. He was assisted in his new work by an inter-departmental staff (with the Board of Trade and the Treasury pre-eminent) and reported to a special Cabinet Com-mittee. Macmillan hoped that Maudling, especially if he had German and American sympathy, could galvanise members of the OEEC to create an FTA. Otherwise the Prime Minister was prepared to be tough, telling the Chancellor of the Exchequer, Peter Thorneycroft, that 'We must take the lead, either in widening [the EEC] or, if they will not cooperate with us, in opposing it'.[7] As yet there were no outward signs of French hostil-ity, and Macmillan's greatest problem over the summer came at the Com-monwealth leaders' conference where the new Canadian premier, John Diefenbaker, pressed for the expansion of *Commonwealth* trade. This was bound to rekindle suspicion among the Six about Britain's Common-wealth links. Meanwhile the OEEC set up a number of working parties to look at the FTA.

The OEEC ministerial council finally met to begin work in earnest on the FTA on 16–17 October 1957. An Inter-Governmental Committee,

representing all members, was established under Maudling's chairmanship to study the FTA in detail, but several countries pressed for the
inclusion of agricultural produce in the talks and the French made clear
they would require complex safeguards before entering any agreement.
One of the most vital issues which needed to be resolved concerned so-
called 'trade deflection', a highly technical subject but vital to an understanding of what followed. 'Trade deflection' arose because, unlike the
common market, which had a common *external* tariff on imports from
outside, the FTA would allow members to pursue their own trade policies
with the rest of the world. (This was the principal difference between an
FTA and a customs union, and was vital to the British to preserve Commonwealth trade.) It meant that imports from countries outside the FTA
might be able to enter a member state with low external tariffs, but could
then be traded freely within the FTA. For high-tariff states like France
and Italy this was unacceptable, since it would open their markets to
extensive competition, and the Maudling Committee set up a special
subcommittee to look at the problem.

   This led on to the problem of 'origin controls': to minimise 'trade
deflection' the OEEC tried to establish a list of goods which would be
included in the FTA, and which were mainly produced by member states.
But, whereas France, Italy and Belgium wanted a restricted list, Britain
and Germany wanted to include all goods which were 50 per cent made
in the FTA. Another problem was how to avoid discrimination between
the EEC and FTA. If the EEC were to reduce tariffs among themselves
more quickly than they did with FTA members, or if the EEC reduced
tariffs on a wider range of products than did the FTA, that would effectively mean trade discrimination between the two groups. Discrimination between the EEC and the rest of the OEEC was precisely what
Britain hoped to avoid, yet the French government saw no point in offering all the commercial benefits of the EEC to the FTA – otherwise, why
had the Six accepted all the political obligations of the Treaty of Rome?
Other complex issues included the harmonisation of commercial laws,
defining rules for competition, and the movement of capital and labour.
Talks dragged on for months. Britain gradually began to make concessions, but without much effect: a January 1958 offer to reduce protective
measures on agricultural products was not far-reaching enough; and a
scheme to set up a complaints procedure to deal with 'trade deflection'
seemed inadequate. More dramatic was a British offer to accept majority
voting in any complaints procedure, but this was soon overtaken by other
events.

On 1 January 1958 the EEC was formally created. Its central executive body was the Brussels-based Commission, originally presided over by Germany's Walter Hallstein, who joined the Maudling Committee. Not surprisingly the Commission defended the separate existence of the EEC and did not want the FTA to delay co-operation among the Six. The Community also had a non-elected Assembly, to provide a democratic element, and a Court to settle disputes. However, the Assembly had limited powers, whilst the Commission could only act with the approval of the Council of Ministers, which represented member governments. Thus, it was the governments who continued to dominate the debate over the FTA which took place among the Six in early 1958. In February the French line stiffened, with a memorandum to the Six which proposed a quicker move towards free trade within the EEC than in the FTA; and which wanted trade between the EEC and the rest of the OEEC to be freed only on a restrictive basis. Details of the memorandum soon leaked and upset the British, who began talks with Sweden, Denmark, Norway, Switzerland and Austria (known as 'the other Six') on possible action if the FTA collapsed.

With Adenauer apparently ready to back the French, the dangers of a split in the OEEC between the Six and the rest were now clear, leading the Italian finance minister, Gudo Carli, in March, to suggest a compromise. The Carli Plan proposed that external tariffs in the FTA should be kept within a certain 'band', thus minimising trade deflection. Miriam Camps has argued that the British should have tried to develop this plan. But it still demanded a large amount of tariff harmonisation, which could harm British trade with the Commonwealth, and it did not deal with the problem of trade *quotas* on imports of goods (quotas, which put limits on the volume of trade in individual products, were still the main barrier to European trade at this time). Richard Lamb has described the Carli Plan as 'too complicated to be practical'. In any case, as Robert Lieber has shown, Britain's ability to make concessions to the EEC was still severely restricted by the views of farmers and industrialists, who were determined to protect Commonwealth trade. Pressure groups like the National Farmers' Union had considerable influence because of their links to the Conservative party and because the FTA talks primarily focused on economic needs.[8] Britain not only rejected the Carli Plan but Maudling openly warned of the dangers of retaliation against the Six if the FTA talks failed.

It is quite clear therefore that the FTA talks were in trouble *before* the collapse of the French Fourth Republic in May 1958, a victim of the colonial war in Algeria. Indeed, in April many observers concluded that it was impossible to establish the FTA before the first cuts in EEC tariffs due in January. However, the return to power of General de Gaulle was bound to make French policy more forthright. True, de Gaulle, the defender of French *grandeur*, faced daunting problems at home and in Algeria; in the past, he had opposed European integration and, initially, he aroused suspicion from Chancellor Adenauer. But, whilst French sources suggest that the General lacked strong views of his own on the FTA,[9] he soon came to appreciate the value of the EEC to the French economy, he was anxious to use the EEC to limit German independence, and he was influenced by the views of his officials and industrialists, who feared opening French markets to other OEEC states. When Macmillan pressed de Gaulle, in June, to approve the FTA and avoid the economic division of Western Europe, the General sent a noncommittal reply.[10] British desperation was reflected in the fact that they now bowed to the French request to resolve trade problems between the EEC and OEEC on an industry-by-industry basis. Macmillan for a time considered threatening to withdraw British troops from Europe[11] but had no wish to risk further instability in France or to alienate de Gaulle by taking a tough line. Neither did it seem sensible for Britain itself to break off the FTA talks, especially since it seemed Germany might yet press the French to compromise.

Instead of a compromise, it did not take long before de Gaulle began to assert himself more strongly than the leaders of the Fourth Republic. In September he pressed Macmillan and Eisenhower to establish an American–British–French 'directorate' over the Western alliance, so as to give France a leading role in Western counsels. The same month, EEC ministers, meeting in Venice, agreed that there should be unanimous agreement between them about any decisions on the FTA. This agreement confirmed that France could effectively 'veto' the FTA, and reflected Adenauer's desire to keep close to the French in 'building Europe'. France and Germany were too powerful for the rest of the Six to oppose them with success. In October, the EEC published its own Ockrent Report on FTA. The Ockrent Report was not exhaustive but it showed a predictable desire to preserve the EEC and tended to reflect French doubts on such issues as 'trade deflection' and the right to question Commonwealth trade preferences. The Report was an excellent example of a phenomenon noted by Miriam Camps: the FTA talks forced the EEC to define its own policies more fully, and indeed speeded up integration among the Six; at the same time this made it more difficult to achieve agreement with Britain. French representatives on the Maudling Committee went beyond the Ockrent Report at this point and began to press for the FTA to have a common external trade policy, like the EEC. This highlighted the contrast between the French desire for a customs union in Europe, with protection for French industry from high tariffs, and the British desire for a more open system, with low tariffs and without ornate controls, in which Britain could maintain its access to world markets. Macmillan now believed: 'The French are determined to exclude the UK. De Gaulle is bidding high for the hegemony of Europe.' Britain itself might have to call off the FTA talks, British ministers felt. In early November therefore, Macmillan warned de Gaulle that there was the danger of a deep cleavage in Western Europe.[12]

Not for the first time on the question of European economic co-operation, London and Paris were talking past each other. Each felt that the policy of the other was a threat to them. Britain feared exclusion from a politico-economic bloc on the Continent, which would harm British trade and could become the 'third power' in world affairs, perhaps destroying the OEEC and NATO, and perhaps dominated by Germany. The French feared that the EEC, carefully constructed to protect French political and economic interests and to limit German power, would dissolve in a wider FTA; they did not believe that Britain was committed to a European future, and did not see why Britain should be given access to EEC markets without paying a price. Arguments over trade deflection, agriculture and social policies reflected this wider disagreement. It is not even clear that Britain could have improved the FTA's chances with more timely concessions. Although the British initially overestimated their negotiating strength, they did make concessions, but even the offer of majority voting in some FTA decisions, which seemed a substantial step, now failed to impress. This was because the French now preferred *unanimous* decisions so as to preserve their own freedom to veto action in the FTA.

Given these positions, it was no surprise that France killed off the FTA. The problems had existed from the start and talks had probably only gone on so long because of the indecisiveness of Fourth Republican governments. Nonetheless, witnesses were taken aback by the bluntness of de Gaulle's Information Minister, Jacques Soustelle, when he told the Maudling Committee on 14 November, that an FTA was impossible – unless it included a common external tariff. The only realistic alternative to this virtual carbon copy of the EEC seemed to be an FTA which satisfied France by having little meaning at all: neither alternative was acceptable to Britain. Initially the British hoped that Germany and the Benelux countries would put pressure on France to compromise, but de Gaulle soon visited Adenauer and persuaded him to abandon the FTA. In return France would put the EEC's first tariff reductions into full effect on 1 January. (There had been fears that the French would use 'escape clauses' in the Treaty of Rome to avoid this, because of persistent fears that French industry would fare badly in the common market.)

Once again Adenauer's commitment to European unity and Franco-German reconciliation won out over other considerations; the other EEC states were unwilling to oppose the Franco-German combination and the British were unable to drive a wedge between French protectionism and the more 'open' approach of Germany and Holland. The challenge now was to cope with the introduction of the common market on 1 January. On 15 December, at Britain's request, the OEEC Council met for Maud ling formally to report the FTA's failure. The British then pressed the EEC to avoid trade discrimination against other OEEC members, but the request – reasonable enough in itself – was couched in threatening terms by David Eccles, who talked of 'defensive measures' against the Six. The British had used similar, but veiled threats throughout the FTA talks. On this occasion however, such tactics led to bitter arguments, with France's Maurice Couve de Murville walking out of the Council at one point. A British official, Paul Gore-Booth, considered it 'unquestionably, the worst conference I have ever attended'. De Gaulle eased the tension somewhat by agreeing that EEC tariff cuts (but not quota reductions) should be extended to members of GATT, which included all the OEEC states. Macmillan considered this 'a great moral success for us',[13] but its main impact was to reduce the pressures on de Gaulle to compromise further. The common market was about to come into effect and the FTA had been killed off. Britain now had to devise a response.

EFTA and the Decision to Seek EEC Membership, 1959–61

Between December 1958 and February 1959, a new Cabinet Committee on European Economic Questions and a committee of officials under the Atlanticist head of the Treasury, Roger Makins, decided that Britain should pursue a form of FTA without the Six. There was concern that otherwise certain countries, such as Denmark, would seek EEC membership and British trade would be even more restricted. British entry to the EEC was ruled out because it would harm Commonwealth trade, damage

British agriculture and impede the country's independence, even if the EEC was not as supranational as Britain feared in 1955.[14] Sweden and Norway in particular were pressing for action. The British government did not want to antagonise the Six, but an EEC Commission report in February saw no basis for a revival of talks in the OEEC. The Federation of British Industry, despite some differences of opinion among its members about European co-operation, had already established contacts with industrialists in Scandinavia, Switzerland and Austria. So, on 21 February ministers of 'the Seven' (Britain, Sweden, Norway, Denmark, Austria, Switzerland and Portugal) met for the first time in Oslo. Another meeting in March was followed by a visit around all seven capitals by Sweden's Hubert de Besche, who took the lead in developing a mainly industrial FTA, without strong institutions. Britain was quite ready to see de Besche play this role, because his ideas were in line with London's and Macmillan did not want to be seen leading an anti-EEC group. Indeed, Macmillan's main reason for backing a Seven-power arrangement was to put Britain in a stronger position for *talks* with the Six who, it was believed, would wish to come to terms with a successful new trading bloc.

Once the Cabinet decided, on 7 May, to make a Seven-power FTA, progress was swift, largely because the countries involved had already agreed, in 1957–8, on what sort of structure they wanted. It was also easier to satisfy the Federation of British Industries and the National Farmers' Union. Officials devised a detailed scheme in Stockholm in June–July. The main problem for Britain was the need to include bacon, cheese, and some other agricultural products in the FTA to ensure Danish membership. This caused complaints from British farmers in an election year, but Macmillan persuaded the Cabinet that: 'The stakes in this affair are very high ... For if we cannot successfully organise the opposition ... then we shall ... be eaten up, one by one, by the Six.'[15] The Seven-power FTA also included limited provision for majority votes, an appeals procedure to deal with 'trade deflection', and certain escape clauses (to deal with balance of payments problems, for example). In October 1959 Macmillan was re-elected Prime Minister, and (after some concessions on British imports of fish, to please Norway) an agreement was signed in November.

The new body was called the European Free Trade Association (EFTA) but there was confusion over its purpose: although Macmillan and Maudling saw this as being to 'form a basis for negotiating a comprehensive European settlement', it also had to be defended as valuable in its own terms. Yet, whilst it proved a workable, resilient organisation, EFTA had a much smaller population than the EEC and it brought few economic advantages to Britain, which was by far the largest member. By lowering tariffs with the Seven, Britain opened its markets to greater competition. In the early 1960s British trade grew markedly faster with the EEC than with EFTA (and exports to the EEC also outstripped those to the Commonwealth). In May 1959, Gladwyn Jebb had warned the FO that Britain's negotiating position was weakening all the time, and that it would be better to concentrate on securing a deal with the EEC. Events in later 1959 bore this out. Far from leading to 'bridge-building' talks between the Six and the Seven, EFTA simply solidified the division of Western Europe into separate trading blocs. EFTA highlighted Britain's preference for trade agreements without political commitments or economic integration, and did nothing to induce the French to negotiate.

Furthermore the new organisation, because it lacked the economic and political integration of the EEC, was viewed in a poor light by the US: when Under-Secretary of State Douglas Dillon visited Europe in December, Britain had trouble persuading him that EFTA was not simply a discriminatory trade bloc, divisive in European terms, and harmful to American exporters. Ironically for the British – the supposed exponents of freer world trade – the Americans had even less liking for the idea of an EEC–EFTA trade deal because this too would be damaging to American exporters. British arguments that the EEC was itself discriminatory cut little ice with the US (which in any case had long been suspicious of Britain's preferential arrangements with the Commonwealth) because the US valued the EEC as both a solid economic and *political* barrier against Communism, and a means of achieving Franco-German reconciliation. Britain's case was not helped by the fact that America and France both believed that a GATT agreement on freer world trade, embracing the US and others, made more sense than an EEC–EFTA deal. Given Britain's reliance on the 'special relationship', this was a significant problem. A Cabinet meeting on 15 December 1959 decided that it was best to seek trade liberalisation under the auspices of GATT. It was hoped that this would also keep the Six and the Seven together.[16] Neither was Macmillan able to use 1959 to improve relations with Adenauer, the one man who might have been able to influence de Gaulle in favour of an FTA. Instead Macmillan gravely offended Adenauer by flying to meet Khrushchev in February 1959, when the latter was issuing threats against West Berlin. By the end of the year Macmillan considered Adenauer to be 'half crazy', whilst Adenauer felt Britain to be 'like a rich man who had lost all his property but does not realise it'.[17]

Even before EFTA was signed, in October 1959 Macmillan had asked Selwyn Lloyd to look at 'the sort of price it would be worth paying in order to be economically associated' with the EEC. This coincided with a report by the FO's 'Steering Committee' (a long-term planning body): EEC membership was not suggested yet, but EFTA was of limited use, the EEC was 'here to stay' and there was a danger of Britain being excluded 'from ... European policy'.[18] A new Cabinet Committee on European Economic Association was formed in October and, although there was no immediate sign of grave concern about relations with Europe (there was something of an economic 'boom', fuelled by the government to coincide with the election), it is possible to see at this time the beginnings of a move towards a British application to join the EEC.

There were numerous reasons for this. Macmillan was increasingly aware of the *political* significance of the Six and of Britain's declining position. The latter factor was made clear in late 1959 when Eisenhower met Khrushchev in the first US–Soviet summit, leaving Macmillan on the sidelines at a time when he had hoped to act as a 'go-between' for them. The Federation of British Industry too moved in favour of a deal with the EEC. Most industrialists would have preferred an FTA-type arrangement, but their prime need was for access to the largest continental markets and many feared that the EEC would prove a stronger magnet than Britain for trade and investment. The British government also feared that the EEC would continue to develop beyond London's control. True, under US pressure, the EEC agreed to extend its trade quota reductions, due on 1 January 1960, to all members of GATT. (West Germany and Holland especially were as loyal as Britain to the latter organisation.) But there was no sign that the Six were ready to deal with EFTA, which they treated as a virtual irrelevancy. Meanwhile on the political front, in November, EEC foreign ministers had agreed to hold quarterly meetings in future to discuss international affairs. The danger of a concerted Six-power foreign policy led the FO to try to rejuvenate the Western European Union (which had done little of importance since its creation in 1955). By now domestic political considerations were also having some influence, as the EEC began to enter the arena of political debate. In December, when the EFTA agreement was ratified, Labour abstained. But the Liberals, now identified as the most 'pro-European' party, argued that the government should have 'associated' itself with the EEC.

Macmillan was well aware that it would be difficult to win over de Gaulle to *any* deal with Britain. De Gaulle wanted to retain the leadership of the EEC, had won the sympathy of Adenauer and felt Britain was too reliant on the US. Then again, the General was opposed to a large loss of French sovereignty to the EEC Commission, he wanted a 'tripartite directorate' with Britain and America to run the Atlantic alliance, and he was anxious to join the select 'club' of nuclear powers. Such desires could be exploited by Britain to try to win his support while safeguarding the unity of the West in the face of Communism. At a meeting of Western leaders in December (to prepare for a possible summit with Khrushchev) Eisenhower expressed interest in de Gaulle's wish for a 'tripartite directorate'. Macmillan now felt that Britain could offer a leading position in NATO to France without upsetting the US.[19] However, the Western leaders' meeting was also significant because of its discussion of economic co-operation, during which the US, instead of supporting an EEC–EFTA deal, stated their preference for a more general agreement on freer trade under GATT. The US also wanted Europe to become more involved in aiding underdeveloped states. The result, after further talks in early 1960, was the decision to *replace* the OEEC with a new 'Organisation for Economic Cooperation and Development' (OECD), which included all the OEEC members, plus America and Canada. Like the OEEC, the OECD was an inter-governmental body, lacking strong institutions and geared principally to trade discussion. It did nothing to improve the chances of an EEC–EFTA deal. Britain gained little from it but, thanks to the special relationship, agreed to its creation.

By April 1960 Macmillan's government faced numerous difficulties. At home there was a growing sense of national malaise – of social divisions, economic failure and loss of purpose. Hopes of maintaining a genuinely independent nuclear deterrent ended with the cancellation of the 'Blue Streak' missile. In Europe the Franco-German combination was strong and the Six were growing more confident. In May their Council of Ministers confirmed a decision to accelerate the reduction of trade barriers between them, so that quotas on manufactured goods would end in December 1961. Once again, the US was quite happy with this decision to strengthen the EEC, but Macmillan saw it as introducing a significant element of discrimination against Britain and other European states. Such developments led a growing number of Whitehall officials to favour a new initiative in Europe. In particular Roger Makins was succeeded as Head of the Treasury by Sir Frank Lee, the one leading official who had supported EEC membership in 1955. The latter, as Chairman of the official Economic Steering (Europe) Committee, established in March 1960, carried out a number of studies on relations with the EEC, and Lee sent a detailed outline of his ideas to the Chancellor of the Exchequer on

22 April, which Jacqueline Tratt has described as 'the definitive document that was to set Britain on a new course' in Europe. Lee and the Committee believed EEC membership – however difficult it might be to achieve – could stimulate growth, attract US investment, allow larger-scale production and force industry to become competitive; politically, membership would promote political stability in Europe, strengthen the Franco-German link and bolster Britain's world position.[20]

The last point was especially important, given the danger that the US might soon treat the EEC as more vital than the UK. In February 1960 Selwyn Lloyd warned Macmillan that 'the Americans will think more and more of the Six as the group which they have to consult' in Europe, and according to one minister, Eisenhower himself warned Macmillan that the special relationship would decline if Britain did *not* join the EEC.[21] In March and again in April Macmillan and de Gaulle had met, and Macmillan had sensed that, if offered a closer Anglo-French relationship, de Gaulle might now be ready to resolve the EEC–EFTA problem.[22] Rumours grew that Britain was considering an approach to the EEC and in June *The Economist* joined the *Guardian* in supporting EEC membership, although there was strong opposition from the right-wing, pro-Commonwealth newspapers owned by Lord Beaverbrook. 1960 also saw the publication of Anthony Nutting's influential pro-European book *Europe Will Not Wait*. Another development which probably had a profound influence on Macmillan was the end of his hopes for playing the role of East–West peacemaker when, in May 1960, a summit between Western leaders and Khrushchev ended in failure.

In June 1960 the British made a cautious move towards the EEC when the junior FO minister, John Profumo, suggested that Britain might join Euratom and the Coal–Steel Community. But the Six treated this as a half-hearted approach, and on 13 July the Cabinet, though basing its discussion on the work of Lee's Economic Steering (Europe) Committee, refused to commit itself to an actual application to the EEC. One difficulty was the uncertain attitude of the French, whose leader seemed determined to dominate EEC institutions. Another problem was the need for debate among British industry, agriculture, politicians and people about the idea of EEC membership, as well as the need to consider reactions in the Commonwealth and EFTA. Jacqueline Tratt, in her detailed study of Macmillan's decision-making in 1959–61, has also argued that the Prime Minister badly mishandled the Cabinet, failing to prepare his colleagues adequately for such a significant debate or to chair the meeting with much determination. However cautious the decision, the British government was clearly aware that the EEC was there to stay, that EFTA was of limited use and that some arrangement might have to be made with the Six directly.

Richard Lamb is more positive than Tratt, judging that 'Macmillan . . . had broken the ice' on 13 July. The Chancellor of the Exchequer, Derek Heathcoat-Amory, told his colleagues that EEC membership would be 'a political act with economic consequences', not vice versa. But sceptics like Reginald Maudling were not yet prepared to make such a decision.[23] In a debate in the Commons on 25 July, on a government motion for 'suitable arrangements' to secure 'political and economic unity in Europe', Selwyn Lloyd ambiguously stated that the government would wish to protect the interests of the Commonwealth, EFTA and British agriculture in any deal but seemed to rule out early negotiations. Immediately afterwards, however, Macmillan prepared for further, positive moves by promoting ministers to the Cabinet who were well disposed to EEC membership. These included Edward Heath who, as Lord Privy Seal, was given special responsibility for Europe, attached to the FO, where the new Foreign Secretary was Lord Home.

In August, Macmillan visited Adenauer in Bonn, where the Germans agreed to an exchange of views with British officials on future progress in Europe. The French President was evidently put out by the success of the Macmillan–Adenauer meeting and, on 5 September, gave a press conference where he said that political and defence co-operation should be extended among the Six, but only under the control of Heads of Government, who should meet together regularly in a Council. His hopes for political and defence co-operation seemed designed to limit the power of NATO; his desire for inter-government co-operation confirmed his dislike of supranationalism; and his omission of any mention of Britain showed he wished to remain the leader of the Six. The press conference caused concern in Britain, America and Germany, because of the threat to NATO, and among supranationalists like Monnet and Spaak, because of the threat to European union. It began a debate on the political future of Europe which threatened to complicate Britain's move towards Europe. Pressure for Britain to move 'to Europe' kept mounting. The official exchanges with Germany during November confirmed that there was no 'half-way house' to EEC membership. In November too, the Federation of British Industry, fearing the decline of Commonwealth trade, moved more in favour of EEC membership, despite the continuing loyalty of some businesses to Commonwealth trade.

Over Christmas 1960 Macmillan was considering the future of British and Western policy in the light of current problems. John F. Kennedy was about to become US President and his views were bound to be vital on a range of issues. Macmillan wrote a memorandum, which was called the 'Grand Design'. It was a plan of action for the West, to secure unity against the Communist threat, but also to deal with Britain's economic and military decline, notably by maintaining Britain's nuclear deterrent. It reflected a growing sense of foreboding in Macmillan's government about the future at home and abroad. So far as European issues were concerned, Macmillan hoped to maintain the US alliance, and to draw the EEC and EFTA together, but he acknowledged the overriding need to win over de Gaulle; to do this he wanted Kennedy to answer de Gaulle's demands for closer US–British–French 'tripartite co-operation' at the head of NATO, including recognition of France's nuclear ambitions. The paper was discussed by leading ministers at Chequers in January and led to a series of exchanges with Kennedy in early 1961, in the hope that he would help win over de Gaulle to British membership of the EEC.[24] The main difficulty was that Kennedy, like Eisenhower, was reluctant to share nuclear secrets with countries other than Britain. Also, some of Kennedy's officials, notably Under-Secretary of State George Ball, were keen to develop supranationalism in Europe. They were critical of de Gaulle's attitudes *and* doubtful about Britain's commitment to the EEC. However, when Macmillan met de Gaulle at Rambouillet in January 1961 the British premier tried to tempt de Gaulle with tripartite talks and nuclear co-operation. Macmillan also said that Britain was ready to enter the EEC, on the right terms, and won de Gaulle's approval for an Anglo-French exchange of views on Europe (similar to the previous exchanges with Germany and Italy).[25] De Gaulle's positive approach at this point may also have been helped by Adenauer's agreement in February to discuss the idea of EEC political co-operation via an inter-government Council, as de Gaulle wanted.

In talks during February and March 1961 the French made it clear to the British that they must make a decision in principle about EEC membership before negotiations could start. But Macmillan was still uncertain about de Gaulle's policy and there remained the need to prepare the Commonwealth, EFTA, the Americans and the public. Heath had had an initial exchange of views with Commonwealth representatives in September 1960, when Canada, Australia and New Zealand were especially concerned about the future of trade preferences with Britain. The British would require special arrangements for Commonwealth exports to the EEC in any membership agreement. But a Commonwealth leaders' meeting in March 1961 was bitterly divided over the apartheid policies of

South Africa – further calling into question the value of the Common-wealth to Britain in future. Regarding EFTA, it seemed that some members (like Denmark and Norway) would wish to join the EEC with Britain but others (principally Sweden and Switzerland) were still keen to make EFTA succeed in its own terms. Britain would have to try to protect EFTA interests when it joined the EEC. In March and April, during meetings between Heath and America's George Ball, and then between Macmillan and Kennedy, it was clear that the Americans would back British membership. Indeed Kennedy's officials had conceived their own 'Grand Design' for a new US–European partnership, which should involve British membership of the EEC and might include a joint NATO nuclear force. Unfortunately this had little appeal to de Gaulle, who saw it as a reworking of US domination over NATO.

On the domestic front, public expectations of an application to 'enter Europe' began to mount during the spring, and the EEC issue became of prime political importance. The Conservative party was particularly con-cerned over the possible loss of support in rural areas, if the EEC's (still undefined) Common Agricultural Policy (CAP) damaged farmers' inter-ests. In addition, Tory nationalists, and many Labour MPs, opposed any loss of parliamentary sovereignty to the EEC, whilst others still had faith in the Commonwealth. It was clear that the EEC issue cut *across* party divisions. The Conservative and Labour parties both had their 'pro' and 'anti-marketeers'. The Labour leader, Hugh Gaitskell, had not yet taken a position on the EEC, but he could be expected to exploit any govern-ment problems over the application and was one of those who wished to safeguard the Commonwealth.

In spring 1961 Whitehall officials could see little future in relying on EFTA and the Commonwealth as sources of political prestige, and the British economy seemed likely to strengthen in the competitive environ-ment provided by the Community. Numerous studies had been completed by Lee's Economic Steering (Europe) Committee. If Britain wished to help in shaping the CAP and to join in the tariff reductions between the Six, it really needed to act quickly. Yet it was political considerations which dominated the Cabinet discussion on 20 April, when it was finally agreed in principle to explore EEC membership despite the continuing doubts of key figures such as Maudling. Even then, faced by conflicting pressures and the unpopularity of his government, Macmillan proceeded cautiously. Rather than call a Commonwealth meeting on the issue, the Cabinet decided in June to send individual ministers to consult particular Commonwealth states on British entry to the EEC. The Commonwealth countries could hardly oppose an application outright and some (such as Malaysia) welcomed it. It was argued in Whitehall that remaining *outside* the EEC could actually damage Commonwealth cohesion because the Community would become a more powerful politico-economic bloc than Britain, which would thereby lose its ability to protect Commonwealth interests. But many Commonwealth states expressed concern over their exports, and New Zealand (heavily reliant on the British market) was given particularly fulsome promises that its trade would be protected. In order to placate EFTA, the British also promised to maintain the ultimate aim of 'an integrated European market', embracing the Six and Seven.

These were important commitments, which limited Britain's freedom of manoeuvre in the talks which followed and which are easily criticised for that reason. Richard Lamb has argued that 'Macmillan was living in a dream world, blissfully ignoring the fact that the French would not consider allowing Britain to join the EEC unless she abandoned Commonwealth preference and her cheap food policy'. But as Lawrence Butler has pointed out, in the case of the Commonwealth, it was not at all clear to contemporaries that they should completely abandon old extra-European links in order to forge deeper European ones: Commonwealth trade was in decline but still accounted for a fifth of British exports; there was a strong 'Commonwealth lobby' in both major political parties; Britain was of central importance to the Commonwealth and still involved in 'decolonising' certain areas; the Commonwealth link was seen as a way of keeping its members from being absorbed into the Communist bloc; it was also seen as a means of convincing the US that Britain was valuable to Western security. Thus, in Butler's view, the government's aim was to retain the 'three circles' to overseas policy, with ties to Europe, the US and the Commonwealth – in the continuing belief that these were mutually reinforcing – while shifting the balance between them. Nevertheless there can be no doubt that, as Miriam Camps argues, the British attitude had 'evolved considerably' since the demise of the FTA. The British were as pragmatic as ever, but this very pragmatism now led them to accept that there was little alternative to membership of the EEC.[26]

The First Application, 1961–3

The Cabinet decision to apply for EEC membership was confirmed in late July, in two meetings.[27] Ministers were evidently swayed most by the political arguments in favour of entry. But Britain's economic problems had just been highlighted by Chancellor of the Exchequer Selwyn Lloyd's 'little budget' which increased interest rates and restrained wage increases. Significantly in 1961, for the first time, Britain exported more goods to Europe than to the Commonwealth. Still, according to his memoirs, Macmillan felt 'the chances are *against* an agreement, unless – on political grounds – de Gaulle changes his mind',[28] and the Prime Minister's announcement of the application to the Commons was surprisingly lacklustre, emphasising that Britain would not actually join until it knew the terms of entry. This may reflect the fact that he had come round to an application slowly and reluctantly, under the pressures of British economic problems, a lack of alternative policies, and American pressure. Aside from de Gaulle's views, Macmillan was worried by possible dissent in the Conservative party and did not plan to launch a public campaign for EEC entry until the negotiations had advanced. Nora Beloff emphasises that a number of leading ministers had doubts about the EEC, including 'Rab' Butler who, as pointed out by his biographer, was MP for a farming constituency and had particular worries over the CAP. Butler was put in charge of a new Cabinet Committee to oversee the application: this move was evidently designed to reduce his own doubts and placate the National Farmers' Union. However, Macmillan's press secretary, Harold Evans, says that Conservative Whips were sure the party would remain united on the issue,[29] and in the debate on the application in early August Macmillan was more confident. He emphasised the political advantages of entry, played down the danger of a loss of sovereignty and hoped for an 'outward-looking' Community – all points designed to appeal to British sensibilities.

The debate resulted in a clear government majority and the Six accepted the request for talks on 26 September. It is indicative of the lack of political debate on European issues prior to this that two-thirds of voters, tested in an opinion poll, did not know whether Britain was in the EEC or EFTA, or else gave incorrect responses when questioned![30] Whatever the doubts over agriculture, EFTA and the Commonwealth, the government had taken a major step for (as in the Spaak Committee of 1955), once Britain became committed to discussions the pressure would be on to enter the Community. Then again, the decision to apply was developed cautiously. There were doubts about the step in the Conservative and Labour parties, among farmers, and in newspapers such as Lord Beaverbrook's *Daily Express*. The government also, as in the FTA talks, believed it could take a tough negotiating stance. Deciding to apply for membership was far from a guarantee that Britain would enter the EEC.

The British established a strong negotiating team to assist Heath in carrying out the negotiations. According to Andrew Roth's study, Heath himself travelled over 100 000 miles as EEC negotiator. The first ministerial conference with the Six took place on 10 October when Heath said Britain was ready to accept all parts of the Treaty of Rome, but wanted special terms for Commonwealth access to EEC markets and the protection of EFTA's 'legitimate interests', and hoped to have some influence in shaping the CAP. Ministers from the Six agreed Heath had made an encouraging start,[31] and at a second meeting in early November a number of study groups were put to work on the major problems which required settlement. However, on a visit to Macmillan, de Gaulle remained sceptical about Britain's commitment to a European future, fearing that its Commonwealth and American links would upset the nature of the Community.[32] And in Brussels the negotiations proceeded only slowly. This was partly because the Six had to agree among themselves on any negotiating point, before they talked to the British; and partly it was because until spring 1962, the Six were working on two other issues: the CAP and political co-operation. Until January, at de Gaulle's insistence, they paid most attention to defining the basis of the CAP. Britain's hopes of influencing the CAP were dashed as the Six made a series of cumbersome compromises about agriculture which made Britain's position more difficult.

The CAP, largely based on French ideas, worked by restricting agricultural imports and setting a common 'target price' for agricultural produce, so as to guarantee farmers' incomes. The system would not come into full effect until 1 January 1970 and it was not yet decided how to fund it but, unless it could be altered, it presented the British with several problems: it threatened to restrict cheap agricultural imports from the Commonwealth (which historically had helped Britain to hold down its cost of living) and force Britain to buy more expensively from Europe; it would, as an inevitable result of the first point, weaken the cohesion of the Commonwealth; it would revolutionise Britain's system of farming support (based on 'deficiency payments' direct to farmers); it would be costly to fund; and it was unlikely to benefit Britain because the country's agricultural sector was small. Rather than trying to reform the CAP once inside the EEC, therefore, the British were determined to win reassurances about its operation *before* they entered the Community, even if this meant long delays in the entry talks. This policy was maintained despite the fact that the Ministry of Agriculture, under the pro-European Nicholas Soames, had increasingly come to feel that Britain's system of deficiency payments (itself too expensive in Treasury eyes) could be reformed without damaging farming income.

A British–EEC ministerial meeting in February confirmed agriculture and the linked issue of Commonwealth trade as key problems in the talks and, under pressure from Commonwealth leaders, Macmillan agreed there should be a special Commonwealth conference on the problem in September, before any final decision on entry. The difficulty was that, simultaneously, de Gaulle's confidence was growing. He now achieved a settlement of the colonial war in Algeria, which had dominated French politics since 1956, and he began to assert himself more in the talks among the Six on political co-operation. Britain – of course – disliked the idea of EEC co-operation on political and security issues, because this could upset NATO, but, as with the CAP, hoped to become involved in EEC talks on the subject *before* actually entering the organisation. Heath made the British position clear in a speech in early April. At the same time a rift opened among the Six about the whole subject. The Benelux states, Germany and Italy wished to preserve NATO, to develop supranational- ism in the EEC and to extend membership to Britain; but in a press con- ference on 15 May, de Gaulle restated his desire for independence from America, and his preference for a 'Europe of States' rather than supra- national bodies. His position on British membership was still ambiguous, and Macmillan hoped it might be possible to build co-operation with de Gaulle on the principle of a non-supranational Europe. Yet there were problems with adopting such a course because, paradoxically, it would alienate the very members of the Six who *did* want British entry. The deep divisions about political co-operation in the EEC Council of Min- isters hardly helped the British application. Then again, with the talks on political co-operation among the Six deadlocked, attention could now focus on Britain's position.

Detailed bargaining on the application began after 8 May 1962, when experts' reports on the key problems were available to Heath and EEC ministers. The reports showed a fair degree of agreement and the Six conceded that Britain should be allowed a reasonable 'transition' period for entry. Britain, anxious to see progress, made some important conces- sions at this time, most significantly by agreeing that industrial goods from developed Commonwealth countries should be subject to the EEC's Common External Tariff. Some now hoped that the negotiations could be completed before the special Commonwealth conference in September, but there were still many technical problems. One was that, while the EEC states accepted that the *Commonwealth* should receive some protection in the agricultural field, they did not see any particular need for a long transitional period for *British* farmers. In any case, Pierson Dixon, the British Ambassador to Paris, still feared de Gaulle would block British entry – though he would wait until after France's next general election to do this. Macmillan considered Dixon's views 'Interesting, but unbelievable' and on 1–2 June went to meet the French President at the Château de Champs, believing de Gaulle could yet be swayed. A third view on events was provided by Heath, who believed de Gaulle's tactics were to ensure the entry talks failed by negotiating toughly.[33]

It had long been clear that a key issue for British membership was the attitude of de Gaulle, and at Champs Macmillan felt he came closest to winning the General over. De Gaulle again expressed concern over Britain's links to America and the Commonwealth, but Macmillan said that, while Britain favoured NATO, it also wished to work with France and West Germany to balance American power. Macmillan exaggerated the success of the conference on his return home and in his memoirs admits to finding de Gaulle's views unfathomable. Couve de Murville and the head of the French foreign ministry, Hervé Alphand, both believed de Gaulle was impressed by what Macmillan had to say at the Champs meeting. What may have affected de Gaulle most, however, was the hope of co-operation with Britain on nuclear weapons – the surest way to boost France's international status. The British had recognised for some time of course, that the offer of nuclear co-operation would impress de Gaulle, and French officials later claimed that Macmillan made such an offer at Champs. However, Macmillan's memoirs deny that he went so far and it is still difficult to reconcile the British and French accounts, a fact that helps explain differences among historians about Champs: thus, while Piers Ludlow believes 'there was no significant change in the French stance as a result of the . . . meeting', Constantine Pagedas points out that official French statements became more positive about Britain and feels that some dramatic nuclear deal probably *was* discussed. Wolfram Kaiser thinks that de Gaulle was quite forthcoming on nuclear co-operation with Britain – but was never willing to tie this directly to what Macmillan wanted in return, the enlargement of the EEC.[34]

Whatever transpired at Champs, it did not lead to any relaxation in France's negotiating position in Brussels. In a series of intensive meetings during July Britain continued its gradual retreat, now abandoning any hope of securing 'comparable outlets' for Commonwealth agricultural produce in EEC markets to those the Commonwealth enjoyed in Britain. The Six were adamant that Commonwealth preferences must end after a 'transitional' period, although they were ready to offer trade agreements to certain Commonwealth states. As in the FTA talks, France took the lead in pressing a tough case but the rest of the Six tended, albeit reluctantly, to follow: in the last resort the unity of the EEC was more vital than British membership, and Adenauer was reluctant to fall out with de Gaulle. In early August the French suddenly intensified their pressure, by asking Britain to agree to pay all its earnings from trade tariffs to the EEC after membership – even though the EEC itself had not yet agreed to such an arrangement. For a time it seemed that de Gaulle was trying to cause a breakdown of the talks, but then the French backed off, and the negotiations recessed for the summer.[35] Britain's hopes of entering the Community were still alive, but there would be no rapid agreement, de Gaulle's position remained uncertain, and Macmillan now had to face a difficult Commonwealth conference.

At the Commonwealth premiers' conference, beginning on 10 September, Macmillan tried to focus, not on the detailed terms of British entry, but on Britain's changing world role. He argued Britain would be stronger, and better able to defend Commonwealth trade, from *within* the EEC. But premiers Diefenbaker (Canada), Menzies (Australia) and Holyoake (New Zealand) all feared for their future trade with Britain, and the Afro-Asian nations could see little benefit for them from the EEC. The conference agreed that Britain's application should proceed, but the doubts of most leaders were obvious and had a particular impact on Labour's Hugh Gaitskell, who was a supporter of the Commonwealth and lacked any commitment to the EEC. Within the Labour party there were some firm pro-marketeers, who believed the EEC could boost the British economy, and even some left-wingers who hoped to create a 'third force' that could stand up to the superpowers. But there were also anti-marketeers who saw the EEC as a capitalist 'club', dominated by Germany, which would destroy the Commonwealth. Most Labour members, and their trade union associates, had no strong feelings on the issue but they were keen to attack the government. In view of this, and with opinion in the party and country moving against the EEC, Gaitskell made a strong attack on Macmillan's probable entry terms at Labour's annual conference. In addition to defending the interests of the Commonwealth, EFTA and British agriculture (all of which the government wanted), Gaitskell said Britain must preserve its independent foreign policy and the ability to use national economic planning (a vital point for Socialists).

On paper these five conditions still left it possible to enter the EEC, but Gaitskell's tone was definitely opposed to membership which, he said, would 'end a thousand years of history'. The speech seemed to justify French criticisms of Britain's lack of readiness to 'enter Europe'. Labour pro-marketeers such as George Brown and Roy Jenkins were dismayed but, as Philip Williams argued in his biography of Gaitskell, the speech had to be wholehearted in order to be effective in uniting Labour against Macmillan. L. J. Robins, in his study of Labour and the EEC, concludes that Gaitskell's statements on Europe were 'short-term tactical moves to win unity' in the party. But Gaitskell had turned the EEC dramatically into a party political issue.[36]

According to his memoirs, Macmillan was pleased to survive the summer with his European policy intact.[37] Nevertheless, the lack of domestic consensus and the Commonwealth's worries meant there were considerable problems when negotiations resumed on 8 October. In December the talks, after painfully slow progress, became deadlocked over detailed agricultural issues. France and Britain blamed each other for the delays, but the fact was that – even more than ever – Britain could not afford to delay, whilst France could. In October de Gaulle's supporters had easily won the French general election, and Macmillan knew the French President would be more difficult to deal with, especially since he had now established a very close rapport with Adenauer and was able to influence the latter's views. According to George Ball, Adenauer now asked the Americans, 'You don't think for a moment that Harold Macmillan is . . . ready to enter Europe, do you?'[38] It may be that de Gaulle was already preparing to veto the British application.

Events now moved rapidly to a climax. Meeting the General at Rambouillet in mid-December, Macmillan again ran into problems over the nuclear issue. This was because de Gaulle supported genuinely independent nuclear forces in France and Britain, which America could not control; but Britain, unable to develop its own missile to carry nuclear warheads, had for some time planned to buy a US system. The Americans had just cancelled the missile Britain originally wanted, but there was an alternative in the submarine-based 'Polaris'. Macmillan was about to go to Nassau, in the West Indies, to meet President Kennedy and discuss the problem. As at Champs, British and French accounts of the Rambouillet meeting differ. But de Gaulle's attitude was far more negative than at the earlier meeting and, at the very least, he seems to have wanted to be kept informed about Britain's Polaris decision.[39] When he arrived in Nassau, Macmillan warned Kennedy that, without Polaris, the British government would 'sink'. Increasingly unpopular at home, faced by a divided Commonwealth and with the future of the EEC application uncertain, Macmillan desperately needed to retain the nuclear deterrent, or Britain would seem completely powerless. Ironically de Gaulle's reluctance to let Britain join the Six made it even more imperative for Macmillan to buy Polaris. There seemed no other way for Britain to maintain its international status. But when Kennedy, contrary to the advice of many US officials, agreed to help Macmillan, it effectively doomed the EEC application. Macmillan seems to have hoped this would not be the case, arguing that Britain had long planned to buy some kind of US system. Also, Kennedy agreed that France might buy Polaris missiles on 'similar' terms to Britain.[40]

But de Gaulle's dislike of ties to the US was also well known, and it was really no surprise that the Nassau Pact, about which he was not consulted, angered him. He saw it as confirmation that Britain was not independent, but US-dominated, a potential 'Trojan horse' for American influence in the EEC. The French Cabinet rejected a Polaris deal on 9 January 1963. Over the next few days there was no sign of any dramatic move in the entry talks, and Heath began a visit of EEC capitals. On the 14th however, de Gaulle declared his opposition to British membership in a press conference, saying it would change the nature of the Community. Initially the British decided to fight on but when Heath met EEC ministers, on 15–18 January, Couve de Murville refused to continue the talks. A final meeting was held on 28–29 January, but it simply saw mutual recriminations, with Couve de Murville blaming Britain for the slow pace of negotiations. Most other EEC representatives, notably Paul-Henri Spaak, blamed France for the breakdown but none would oppose the French outright. France was simply too important to the future of the EEC. A week later, Adenauer, without consulting Benelux or Italy, saved de Gaulle from isolation by agreeing to revive the Franco-German partnership in a new treaty of co-operation.[41]

After de Gaulle's veto Anglo-French relations were strained, but Macmillan took no counter-measures. Spaak considered the British negotiators 'surprisingly restrained', and in London, according to Harold Evans, there was 'relief that the uncertainty had at last been resolved'.[42] Nonetheless the public humiliation of a veto was a major blow to Britain's international standing, to Conservative confidence and to Macmillan's premiership – which came to an end nine months later. The EEC application was ultimately the victim of de Gaulle's vision of Europe. Macmillan told Kennedy that de Gaulle wanted 'a Napoleonic or Louis XIV hegemony' in Europe.[43] Though exaggerated, there was a kernel of truth in this. De Gaulle did not want to destroy the Western alliance, but he did want to maximise French independence of the US. He did not want to lose power to Community institutions either, but he believed that economic co-operation among the Six, together with a close Franco-German alliance, would provide the means to equal American power. Britain, however, could be a rival for the leadership of the EEC in a way that Germany – reluctant to assert itself in world affairs after Hitler – was not. Other Community members wanted British membership, but France was a vital component of the EEC and, especially if he maintained the close relationship with Adenauer, de Gaulle knew he could deliver a veto with little risk of a response from his Community partners. Pierson Dixon's argument, that de Gaulle had intended to deliver the veto for some time, has considerable weight. All de Gaulle required, according to this explanation, was an excuse – which Nassau provided – although he might have preferred the negotiations to break down unassisted. It is a thesis which has continued to find support among historians, notably Wolfram Kaiser. Then again, there are suggestions that de Gaulle, until December 1962, was in two minds as to whether Britain could fit into his vision of Europe, hence his willingness to let the talks drag on; and Edward Heath has argued that the mere suspicion that de Gaulle might wield his veto 'could not, of itself, be a reason for breaking off the negotiations'.[44]

If de Gaulle were uncertain about British entry it leads on to the question whether Britain could have done more to assure the application's success. The British certainly realised after the failure of the FTA, that to achieve any solution to the economic division of Europe they needed to win over de Gaulle and that this would involve *political* concessions: Macmillan hoped to convince the General that they could work together to match US power. British officials and ministers realised by 1960 that their own resources were strained, that Commonwealth links were weakening and that the Americans would not treat them as genuine partners. The British government also proved ready to accept the idea of joining in European economic integration. But the decision to apply for EEC membership was slow and in part the change of view came because the supranational element in the Community no longer seemed a threat, because of de Gaulle's views on the subject. This arguably made it more imperative to satisfy de Gaulle about Britain's intentions and here Macmillan simply could not deliver enough. Britain's political divisions over Europe and insistence on satisfying the Commonwealth's trading needs suggested a lack of commitment to Europe. The application talks became bogged

down in technical details and Macmillan was never ready to sell membership as an idealistic step, preferring instead to underline the continuity in
British policy: EEC membership was to prop up British power, revive
its economy, leave its sovereignty intact, and allow Britain to make the
Community 'open' to outside trade.

The dithering at the top in London was consistent and calls into question the blunt judgement of those like Rolf Steininger who believe that
'Britain's EEC failure was the work of one man, de Gaulle'. As Jacqueline
Tratt has argued, 'Macmillan . . . was no driving force on Europe'. 1959
was wasted with the attempt to force the EEC to come to terms with Britain by creating the rival EFTA trading bloc; and, in retrospect, his failure
to win the Cabinet over to an application in July 1960 can be seen as fatal:
for, if negotiations had been completed before late 1962, de Gaulle might
have found it impossible to wield his veto. Another recent study, based in
part on EEC archives, reinforces the argument that, notwithstanding de
Gaulle's ultimate significance, the British themselves could have handled
their application better, making it difficult for him to use the veto: indeed
Piers Ludlow believes that the focus of so many studies on the personal
diplomacy between Macmillan and the General, and on the idea of a nuclear deal (which never actually came close to fruition), is misguided; the
damning problems in Ludlow's view were the conditional nature of the
application, the terms of entry London initially requested, the failure of
the British to make timely concessions and the technical nature of the
Brussels talks in which Heath and his team became mired – all of which
allowed de Gaulle to slow down the pace of progress until he had secured
his political hold in Paris, established a close rapprochement with Adenauer and found a suitable excuse for a veto. These were errors for which
Macmillan himself ought to take the blame, rather than seeing de Gaulle
as the single villain of the piece.[45]

Historians differ on the precise motives which led Britain to seek
Community membership in 1961. Oliver Bange talks about the 'predominance of political considerations in the decision to join the Common
Market' and especially points to the thinking behind Macmillan's Christmas 1960 Grand Design memorandum as evidence of this. Jacqueline
Tratt believes that it was concern over Britain's trading position which
first provoked a crisis of confidence in London over its European policies
but agrees that, by 1961, political considerations – the need to preserve
Western unity in the face of Communism, to influence EEC decision-
making and to bolster Britain's declining international influence – were
in the ascendant. However, in looking at the *timing* of the application,

Wolfram Kaiser has a rather different list of political motives which influenced Macmillan. Believing that the Prime Minister always knew a veto was possible, Kaiser argues that it still made sense to pursue entry for two reasons: 'first, it would help to appease the United States government . . . and secondly, it would appease the different factions of the Conservative Party into uniting behind the Prime Minister . . . while at the same time deepening the ideological split in the Labour Party.' Indeed, Kaiser goes further and asserts that, even if the application ended in failure, it still achieved some of its main aims, not least by pleasing the Americans (who of course agreed to maintain Britain's nuclear deterrent).[46]

Yet Kaiser's interpretation, or rather its particular emphasis, is questionable: the Americans had long favoured a more positive British policy towards the European integration and the issue in 1961 is why Macmillan finally decided to give them this – a question which throws any analysis back into a debate about British perceptions of their relative decline; on a party political level, it is not at all obvious that Macmillan could rely on an EEC application as a vehicle to unite the Conservatives and the veto proved damaging to their domestic standing; also, it certainly did not divide Labour – if anything, Gaitskell was able to placate the Left with his attack on the EEC and heal recent party rifts. A far more convincing argument from Kaiser for the timing of the application, and one which deserves more emphasis, is that there was a growing perception in 1960–1, among civil servants, ministers, journalists, industrialists and other elite groups, that EEC membership was the only way forward if Britain was to remain a leading influence in world affairs. If there really was only one way forward, it had to be pressed regardless of de Gaulle's possible opposition, and its failure helps explain Macmillan's demoralisation in early 1963.

Among those who put greater emphasis on economic factors, Keith Middlemas has argued that the EEC application was part of a general attempt by Macmillan in 1960–1 to revive national economic fortunes, alongside an incomes policy and greater national planning. But this tended to take the form of shoring-up old policies rather than seeking fundamental changes. Thus the British would only join the EEC 'on their own terms . . . intent on competing while retaining their own specific interests and political identity'. A similar line was taken by Nora Beloff in 1963 when she criticised Britain for seeking EEC membership primarily as a way to gain access to European markets: Conservative and Labour leaders failed to see that supranationalism was a 'revolutionary' concept in international affairs, which could end the old power politics, guarantee liberal democracy and bring more rational economic policies. She also criticised de Gaulle for failing to make the mental adjustment to this new reality. But Beloff's argument is rather unfair to the British, who did come to accept such ideas as majority voting and (even if they did not like the details) a Common Agricultural Policy. Neither would her argument have solved the main problem facing Britain in January 1963. That problem was of course that de Gaulle was the man who held the key to British membership, so that greater interest in supranationalism would have done no good.

Macmillan might have been able to impress de Gaulle with a dramatic *political* concession that would boost French status, such as nuclear co-operation, but in December 1962, when faced with a choice between France and America, Macmillan put faith in his 'special relationship' with the White House. The choice was understandable, given that Britain (like France) wished to protect its nuclear status and had become heavily reliant on US support over a wide range of policy: as Anne Deighton points out, Macmillan, who dominated the debate over Britain's world position in 1957–63, had always been clear about the need for nuclear weapons and a close American alliance, but much less certain about what he wanted in Europe. Yet the events of December 1962–January 1963 left Britain without a viable wider policy for maintaining its international role. France had the EEC as a forum for economic and political activity, but Britain had already realised that the Commonwealth, EFTA and the US alliance – though useful – were insufficient bases for maintaining British power. Dean Acheson declared in 1962 that Britain had lost an Empire and was without a role. Alistair Horne, Macmillan's biographer, criticises his subject for not having a 'contingency plan' for failure on the EEC, but when Macmillan looked around for alternatives to membership he concluded, depressingly, that there were 'none'.[47]

4

WILSON'S ENTRY BID, 1964–1970

Pressure for a New Application, 1964–6

When Harold Wilson became Labour premier in October 1964, another application to 'enter Europe' seemed unlikely. The new government had a slim majority and could not last long, and even the Conservatives' election manifesto had judged that entry was impossible 'in existing circumstances'.[1] One of the leading 'pro-marketeers', Roy Jenkins, remained outside the Cabinet until December 1965 and the Foreign Secretary, Patrick Gordon-Walker, was a 'Commonwealth man', who believed 'we must base our policy on the alliance with the US' and wanted to treat the EEC simply as a 'neighbour . . . with whom we need good relations'. L. J. Robins, in his study of Labour and the EEC, noted that the 1964 government was 'riveted to [the] old doctrine which stressed Atlantic and Commonwealth ties, with Britain having an important military role to play East of Suez' and Robert Holland asserts that Labour 'had no intention' of seeking EEC entry.[2] One of the government's first actions was to offend all its trading partners, particularly the EFTA nations, by placing a surcharge on imports to deal with balance of payments problems. In January 1965 Gordon-Walker was replaced by Michael Stewart, who blandly believed that 'Britain was in the second rank, but . . . we could enhance our influence by active participation in . . . international groupings'.[3] When Wilson and Stewart made their first visit to Paris in April, Stewart was apparently not fully briefed on the possibility of entry into the EEC.[4]

It was about this time however, that pressures began to build up, which resulted in an application two years later. There were many reasons for such pressures. Britain's economic problems contrasted with the sustained growth rates of continental states, and the EEC continued to develop, notably with agreements on the Common Agricultural Policy (CAP). The five EEC members other than France, known as the 'Friendly Five', were keen to resolve relations with Britain, and Britain was eager to end the division of Western Europe into rival trading blocs. However, renewed discussions on 'bridge-building' between the EEC and EFTA failed to get far in 1965, mainly because, as in 1958, the EEC states would lose far more than they gained by allowing EFTA access to the common market. The failure to link the two organisations created a situation similar to that which existed in 1961, when many policy-makers conceded that British entry to the EEC was the only way forward. In Whitehall support for such a step was especially strong in the Foreign Office (FO) and the Department of Economic Affairs (DEA), a new ministry designed to direct national economic policy, headed by Labour's deputy leader, George Brown.

Brown, an outspoken figure on the Right of the party, had, according to his memoirs, hopes 'of creating a politically integrated Europe capable of standing up to the Russians and Americans'. He did not believe that the Commonwealth provided a strong base for British power nor was he interested in ideas (put forward by US Senator Jacob Javits in 1965) for an Anglo-American free trade zone, since this seemed like a scheme for the US to swallow Britain. Brown, with considerable confidence in British strength, insisted 'our role is to lead Europe' and then made the DEA the leading force in developing a pro-market policy in London, supported by his Permanent Under-Secretary, Sir Eric Roll.[5] They found support however, from Michael Stewart who became more pro-European as time went on, influenced by day-to-day dealings with the continent and – ironically – by Commonwealth pressures for access to EEC markets. According to Stewart's Permanent Under-Secretary, Paul Gore-Booth, in 1965 it 'was becoming clear that nothing short of a new attempt at membership of the EEC ... could break down the economic and political wall between Europe and ourselves'. The leading advocate of such a policy in the FO was Sir Con O'Neill, a brilliant, strong-willed individual, who had been Ambassador to the EEC in 1963–5.[6]

'Anti-market' ministers became concerned during 1965 that European policy was being developed by Brown and Stewart without the Cabinet being consulted. The Left's Barbara Castle was worried in March that this was the case and Douglas Jay, right-wing President of the Board of Trade, warned Castle in May that Brown and others wanted to join the

EEC.[7] Jay (said by Crossman to have become an 'anti-European' after suffering toothache on honeymoon in Vienna![8]) joined with the Agriculture Minister, Fred Peart, in mid-June in drafting a Cabinet memorandum which showed how EEC membership would increase food prices and damage Britain's balance of trade; but Wilson instructed that this should be kept 'in cold storage'. Stewart attempted, in December 1965, with Brown's support, to circulate a Cabinet paper urging entry to the EEC but this proposal was again opposed by the Prime Minister, who was evidently keen to avoid any Cabinet divisions on the subject. Then again, in January 1966, he did agree that the Stewart–Brown ideas for 'a move into Europe' should be discreetly studied by a group of officials under Roll.[9]

Wilson's attitude to EEC issues is clearly of enormous importance to historians. It is unfortunately surrounded by contradictions. The Prime Minister was a complex character: manipulative, secretive and lacking in idealism perhaps, but also a skilled political tactician, eager to prove his party's ability to govern. As his official biographer, Philip Ziegler, writes, Wilson's 'prime concern was that' the European issue 'should not be allowed to breach party unity'; and he tended to say one thing to 'anti-marketeers' and another to 'pro-marketeers'. He lacked strong views of his own on Europe and may have been interested only in party political issues. In 1962 he had supported Gaitskell in insisting that Britain could only enter the EEC if certain conditions were fulfilled. However, the most convincing interpretation of the evidence points to Wilson becoming more 'pro-European' in 1964–6. The reason he could not be more forthright on the issue was that he needed to keep the Cabinet united until a healthy majority was achieved. Exactly *why* he became better disposed to the EEC is even more difficult to assess and even the release of papers from his Downing Street office does not help resolve the question. He may have been influenced by the support of businessmen and Whitehall officials for membership, by the public opinion polls which consistently favoured a new application from 1965 to early 1967[10] and by the danger that the new Conservative leader, Edward Heath, an ardent pro-marketeer, could win votes on the issue. However, Wilson witnessed the Commonwealth being torn apart over the future of Rhodesia and, although he sought close relations with America, he knew that Britain was of secondary importance in US thinking. Thus Labour's initial foreign policy aims were undermined. 'As he sees it', wrote Crossman, 'the difficulties of staying outside Europe and surviving as an independent power are very great compared with entering on the right conditions.'[11]

However, Wilson seems to have been influenced by other considerations at this time. One was that, amongst other results, de Gaulle's nationalist policy had led the French to oppose great supranational authority being given to the EEC Commission in Brussels. Faced by plans to increase majority voting in the EEC, de Gaulle launched a boycott of EEC bodies in 1965 known as the 'empty chair' crisis which led in January 1966 to the 'Luxembourg Compromise'. By allowing members to veto decisions on 'very important issues' the Compromise seemed to safeguard member states against unwanted intrusions from Brussels. To Con O'Neill in the Foreign Office de Gaulle's behaviour was dangerous, threatening to destroy the EEC. To Wilson, however, the General's success was to be welcomed because one of the greatest objections in Britain to EEC membership of course was the danger of 'surrendering sovereignty'. For Wilson and others, membership of the common market was more palatable if supranationalism was reduced. Wilson believed he could work with de Gaulle and win the General over to British membership, since Britain and France together could hold the Commission down and build a 'Europe of States'. It is important to emphasise that Wilson's thinking on this point was *different* to that in the Foreign Office, where Stewart and O'Neill believed that Britain should avoid concessions to de Gaulle and instead rely on consistent pressure, and support from the Friendly Five, to help Britain into Europe. Wilson stuck to his preferred tactics after the election, telling newspaper owner Cecil King in April that 'the Foreign Office wants to support the Five against France' but that it was best 'not . . . to take sides particularly as the French are intent on maintaining a separate foreign and defence policy, which fits in best with British ideas'. Philip Ziegler and Ben Pimlott both see Wilson as having become better disposed to EEC entry by the middle of 1966; one of Wilson's other biographers, Austen Morgan, believes the Prime Minister came down in favour of entry at the start of that year; but John Dickie, in a study of the FO, says Wilson was privately committed to a European future before the 1964 election. [12]

Whatever Wilson's change of opinion by 1966, others in the government remained determinedly 'anti-market', believing that EEC membership would lead to dearer food, a rush of imports from Europe, lower living standards, a breach with the Commonwealth, a loss of national control over economic policy, the creation of a capitalist trading bloc and the surrender of parliamentary sovereignty to Brussels. Such strong views meant the Conservatives were hopeful of dividing Labour during the election campaign in March 1966. This danger was increased when a French representative, on 15 March, ambiguously suggested that France *would* favour the extension of the EEC to Britain. This statement may have been designed to placate de Gaulle's critics, one week after his latest controversial decision, to pull French armed forces from NATO – which marked a further assertion of Gaullist independence from America. Nevertheless, the apparent change of heart was welcomed by Heath and put Wilson in a difficult position for a speech in Bristol, on 18 March, which was intended as his key election statement about the EEC. As it transpired, however, the Prime Minister pulled off a remarkable coup. Though given a poor press, the Bristol speech succeeded in scoring a party political point and in satisfying both pro- and anti-marketeers. 'One encouraging gesture from the French Government', Wilson jibed, 'and the Conservative leader rolls on his back like a spaniel.' Heath, furious, denounced Wilson for 'nauseating, filthy insinuation', but the Conservative party decided not to tackle Wilson on Europe again. The speech was balanced between, on one side, statements about the potential benefits of EEC membership and, on the other, the conditions which Britain would demand as the price of entry, including cheap food imports, the protection of Commonwealth interests and independence in foreign policy. This even-handed approach was popular with voters and, as Austen Morgan writes, was consistent with Wilson's previous public utterances on the subject.[13]

The main lines of the Bristol speech were also consistent with the Labour manifesto which said Britain was ready to enter the EEC 'provided essential . . . interests are safeguarded'. Some had wanted a clearer pro-market statement and, as it stood, the manifesto was not much different to Gaitskell's line. Wilson was left free to choose his course: he could try for EEC membership, or he could argue that the right terms were not available. Once the election was won – by a handsome margin – the Prime Minister continued to appear even-handed. He gave Brown authority to concentrate his energies on the EEC, and created a 'Minister for Europe', George Thomson, but also appointed anti-marketeers Jay and Peart to a new Cabinet Committee, which was established 'to keep under comprehensive review . . . political, economic and military relations with Europe'. Yet it is important to note that, however even-handed its undertakings, the Prime Minister soon used the manifesto to outmanoeuvre the anti-marketeers. He did this by concentrating all future discussions on the *detailed* terms of EEC entry. After all, the manifesto (followed by the Queen's Speech) had said that Britain *would be ready to enter Europe* – the principle was effectively decided. The all-important condition was 'provided essential . . . interests were safeguarded' and this meant debating details, not principles. Anti-marketeers evidently did not, until too late, realise this highly important point.

The Cabinet Committee on Europe, chaired by Wilson, held its first meeting on 9 May 1966 when Brown presented a paper by Roll's group of officials on the 'pros' and 'cons' of Common Market membership which concluded that 'we should refrain from taking initiatives ourselves for the time being'. A covering note by Brown admitted 'it would be unrealistic to suppose that British membership could be brought about in the immediate future' since the French attitude was 'crucial, uncertain and most probably hostile' and Britain must improve its economic performance first, in order to enter. The Brown paper thus identified two major problems: a 'Non' from de Gaulle, like that of 1963, was highly possible and, if delivered, would be humiliating; and the question of British economic strength was very complex.[14] These two issues dominated developments in mid-1966.

In early July an opportunity to resolve the all-important difficulties with France came when the French premier Georges Pompidou visited London. By now the FO (including Wilson's foreign affairs adviser, Michael Palliser) was strongly pro-entry, but could see no signs of de Gaulle allowing this.[15] Unfortunately Pompidou's visit got off to a bad start when, a few days before, Britain's Defence Minister Denis Healey accused de Gaulle of being 'a bad ally' because of his withdrawal from NATO. Healey, who was also ill-disposed to the EEC, was forced to apologise before Parliament. Things got even worse when the French publicly stated that devaluation of Sterling might be necessary before Britain could join the EEC. The French were resentful of links between Sterling and the Dollar and critical of Sterling's role as a reserve currency (which could complicate British policy if it joined the EEC) and were currently advocating a return to a gold-based international currency system. This was not the first or last time that they showed a disregard for the stability of the British currency. When the discussions with Pompidou got underway however, Wilson's interest in getting into Europe could not have been clearer. He claimed to be fully independent of Washington, was confident the economy could withstand entry and said Britain would accept all the responsibilities of membership. Yet whilst Gore-Booth, official head of the FO, later wrote that Pompidou gave 'the impression of welcoming . . . an application by Britain', the head of the DEA, Eric Roll, had a different recollection: 'the French were as opposed as ever to our entry'. The official record is nearer to Roll's account: when pressed about British entry at lunch on 8 July, Pompidou refused to be drawn and

Couve de Murville, the French foreign minister, suggested that Britain should instead look to a form of association. This proposal was of little interest to Wilson however, because it would not give London an effective role in the EEC.[16]

Later in July more significant events took place on the economic front when, following a seamen's strike and another 'run' on Sterling measures were needed to tackle the country's trade problems. The new crisis found Wilson pitted against Brown and, to a lesser extent, the Chancellor of the Exchequer, James Callaghan. The latter two, though often rivals, felt that devaluation must be considered but the Prime Minister was firmly opposed to such a step. A Labour government had, of course, carried out the last devaluation in 1949 and lost votes at the next election. For a time Wilson feared an attempt to overthrow him and warned Castle, 'You know what the game is: devalue and get us into Europe. We've got to scotch it.'[17] This did not mean that Wilson opposed EEC membership; it meant that he hoped to achieve membership *without* a prior devaluation. However, he was able to exploit 'anti-market' sentiments to defeat Brown, and to persuade Callaghan – who was less enthusiastically pro-market – to avoid devaluation. Instead, a package of deflationary measures was announced on 20 July. Nevertheless the July crisis had a major effect on the EEC debate for several reasons. On one hand it exposed the weakness of the economy and justified French doubts about Britain's fitness for common market membership. But on the other hand, paradoxically, it strengthened arguments that Britain *must* enter Europe to resolve its long-term problems! The crisis also led Brown to threaten resignation so that, in August, Wilson offered him the coveted post of Foreign Secretary. The fact that Michael Stewart now took charge of the DEA meant that support for the EEC in the key departments remained strong.

The Second Application, 1966–7

In retrospect many commentators believed that Harold Wilson's commitment to EEC membership only developed *after* the 1966 Sterling crisis. In his memoirs, George Wigg, who advised the Prime Minister on security issues, compared Wilson's 'conversion' to the EEC to St Paul's on the road to Damascus with the difference 'that, judged by subsequent actions, Paul's conversion was sincere'.[18] Such judgements however may only reveal how well Wilson had disguised his intentions until July. After that he had many reasons to seek EEC membership: to placate Brown and the 'pro-marketeers' yes, but also to please the Americans (in October President Johnson spoke in favour of a united Europe as a partner in NATO), to shore up the British economy and provide the country with an international role. He also wanted to gain an influence over EEC policies, especially to support de Gaulle in weakening supranationalism and to control the future shape of the Common Agricultural Policy (CAP), the funding of which remained unsettled. Furthermore, as seen in numerous later declarations, Wilson hoped to use EEC membership to strengthen British technological developments, one of his major aims as premier (and he believed that Britain's strength on the technological side might tempt de Gaulle into allowing it EEC entry: after all, the General was keen to see Europe match America's technological prowess). Above all perhaps, Wilson wanted to outflank Heath and the Conservatives, who continuously advocated EEC entry. A difficult Commonwealth conference in September 1966 could only strengthen Wilson's desire to enter Europe. In order to minimise opposition and hold the Labour party together, Wilson proceeded carefully. He still wanted some concessions from the EEC on agriculture and the Commonwealth, and he differed from Brown in hoping for membership without a prior devaluation. Nevertheless, from now on the Prime Minister was more openly 'pro-market'. The tactical side of winning over the Cabinet and de Gaulle to British membership was now his major concern. The principle was decided.

By 22 October 1966 many studies on the EEC were complete and Wilson, under pressure from Brown, agreed that ministers should discuss them at a special weekend session at Chequers. Before the meeting even began however, Wilson suggested to Brown that it should be followed with a 'probe' by *both* of them to EEC capitals. According to Wilson a joint mission would allow him to sound out other leaders about 'doubts which were still troubling me'; according to Brown it was designed to prevent criticisms from anti-marketeers, who would believe that Wilson would protect their interests from the pro-market Foreign Secretary.[19] Wilson was careful to let anti-marketeers have their say but was embarrassed when Sir William Armstrong, the head of the Treasury, again said that devaluation might be necessary before entry. (It was recognised that a devaluation might be necessary once Britain was in the EEC, but Wilson did not want a devaluation *beforehand* because of the impact on public opinion; still less did he want two devaluations – one before entry, one after.) The ministerial discussion proper took place in the afternoon. The economic arguments (based on a presumed entry-date in 1968 before CAP funding was finalised) were well balanced, because it was so difficult to predict the impact of membership on growth, capital movements and Britain's independent economic planning. But political arguments for entry, presented by Brown and Stewart, significantly revolved around there being *no alternative* for Britain, if it wished to remain an important power. This was an astonishing admission of the country's decline in the world.

Wilson's summing-up of the discussion was another masterpiece of manipulation. He pleased the anti-marketeers by saying EEC membership was impossible in the immediate future, and by promising to study two political alternatives to the common market: Senator Javit's idea of a North Atlantic Free Trade Area (known as 'NAFTA') and the possibility of 'going it alone' (known as 'GITA'). However he also got informal agreement on a 'probing' visit by Brown and himself to EEC capitals and, although this need not have led to an application for membership, he pointed out that 'we had to make clear that the . . . visits had a serious purpose'.[20] Some anti-marketeers were very suspicious of this but only two, Richard Marsh (Minister of Power) and William Ross (at the Scottish Office), were ready to oppose a 'probe' outright. Yet this did not mean that the 'antis' had given up the fight. When Marsh (as recorded in his memoirs) complained to other ministers afterwards that Wilson wanted Britain in Europe, Crossman replied 'of course he does, but the General will save us from our own folly'. Healey too believed that de Gaulle would veto British membership anyway, so that there was no need to fall out with Wilson by opposing the attempt![21]

In early November the Cabinet, faced by mounting public expectation, formally approved the idea of a 'probe'. By now the bulk of the Parliamentary Labour Party was also ready, albeit without enthusiasm, to support a move on Europe. Many MPs elected in 1966 were pro-market, and many were impressed by Wilson's argument that European co-operation would provide a boost to British technology. But many anti-marketeers were quiescent too because they believed de Gaulle would veto any application. Wilson announced the probe to the Commons on 10 November. Brown assured friends that the 'juggernaut had started to roll and nothing could now stop it' and Gore-Booth believed that, even if Wilson's 'conversion' to Europe was less than genuine, there was no going back.[22] Yet still the Foreign Office had no evidence that de Gaulle's views on British membership had fundamentally altered since 1963. Indeed, when

Brown attended a NATO meeting in Paris before Christmas, he met the General and was presented with the latter's usual arguments against British entry: Britain was too close to Washington, with different trade patterns to the rest of the EEC and it would change the Community by entering it. The Ambassador to Paris, Patrick Reilly, saw this as further evidence that de Gaulle was 'extremely sceptical' about British entry and keen to discourage an early application.[23]

As Robert Lieber wrote in his 1970 study of Britain and European unity, 'for the Labour government, the progression towards Europe was a story of collapsing alternatives', but Wilson had the advantage over Macmillan in that the Commonwealth link and EFTA commitments were no longer seen as barriers to an application, and there was widespread consensus in support of such a step from the main political parties, the main newspapers (except the *Daily Express*), industrialists and the trade unions.[24] Yet whatever the consensus in Britain, the fate of the application ultimately rested with de Gaulle. For tactical reasons Wilson and Brown decided to visit France early in their probe. This was to avoid the impression that Britain was pitting the other five EEC states against France, a tactic which, of course, Wilson wished to avoid. Also, if de Gaulle was totally opposed to a British application, there was little point in visiting every capital. So as not to appear supplicants to de Gaulle, however, it was decided to visit one capital before Paris. The choice fell on Rome, because that was where the EEC treaty had been signed. When briefs for the visits were discussed by the ministerial Economic Steering Committee, Wilson said he would 'free-wheel'(!) in the discussions with the General, rather than try any particular line of persuasion – an astonishing display of overconfidence. The visit to Rome on 15–17 January set the pattern for the rest: in detailed talks Brown and Wilson gave reassurances about their good intentions about EEC entry and in turn sought reassurance about the terms they might obtain on agriculture (the worst problem), Commonwealth trade and other difficulties. Premier Aldo Moro confirmed, as London already knew, that whilst he wanted Britain in Europe, he could do little to overcome de Gaulle's doubts. After the 1963 veto, the 'empty chair' crisis and France's withdrawal from NATO, the Friendly Five were reluctant to provoke a crisis with de Gaulle over British membership. When reporting on the visit to the Cabinet however, Wilson remained confident, declaring 'Well, Paris will show'.[25]

On the vital visit to France on 24–25 January, Wilson made much of the 'technological community' in his opening talk with de Gaulle but, whilst the General had always shown an interest in the idea of Europe matching the superpowers, he seemed unimpressed by Wilson's ideas, pointing out that technological co-operation was already possible outside the scope of the EEC. Wilson's case may have been weakened by the fact that the best known example of Anglo-French technological co-operation in the 1960s, the Concorde airliner, was permanently troubled by British concern about its cost. Wilson's attempts to 'free-wheel' with the formidable de Gaulle came to nothing. Instead the General, who according to a French source felt that Wilson represented 'the archetypal politician he had fought so hard to displace in the Fourth Republic', turned the talks round to two other concerns: the conditions Britain would demand if it joined the EEC, and the fact that London was too close to Washington. De Gaulle was particularly anxious to safeguard the protection given to French agriculture in the CAP – the very thing Britain hoped to change – and criticised the link between Sterling and the Dollar. Nothing Wilson said can really have reassured de Gaulle about British proximity to Washington. The fact is that, in the fields which de Gaulle felt strongly about, such as nuclear weapons, NATO defence policy and finance, Wilson *was* close to America. He was never likely to adopt Gaullist policies of withdrawal from NATO, a fully independent nuclear deterrent and the abandonment of ties between Sterling and the Dollar. Despite these problems de Gaulle did not end the talks with a 'Non'. Instead he said France was willing to consider alternatives to Britain's full EEC membership such as 'associate' status. But Wilson was again unwilling to consider 'association', because it would involve new responsibilities without giving Britain a full role in Europe. He said he wanted full EEC membership or nothing. The French said they would study this.[26]

The fact that de Gaulle did not issue a resolute 'Non' at this moment was important because it gave Wilson greater confidence and allowed him to continue the probe with visits to Brussels, Bonn, The Hague and, on 7–8 March, Luxembourg. Wilson and Brown were able to reassure themselves on these visits that the adverse impact of EEC membership would be less severe than feared in some areas, such as regional policy, but more severe in others, especially the costs of the CAP. The latter problem however, evidently made it more vital to get into the EEC at an early date, because major questions about financing the CAP were due to be resolved soon and could make entry even more expensive for Britain. The visits also confirmed that no one, not even the West Germans, could persuade de Gaulle to concede British membership.[27] More worrying for the British if they had known about it, the Germans had reassured de Gaulle that they would not try to force his agreement.[28] This confirmed a growing problem for British policy in Europe after 1955. Traditionally Britain tried to maintain a balance of power on the Continent, and in the first half of the century had tried to balance France against Germany. But after the 1954 German rearmament crisis this ceased to be possible. Within the EEC, France and Germany formed a common unit – of which Britain was often the victim.

At the end of their 'probe' Wilson and Brown were determined to move on to an application and a voluminous account of all their European meetings was circulated to ministers. Wilson claimed in his memoirs that this showed his openness on the EEC issue but opponents of the EEC, like Jay, who later wrote a very full account of the issue, felt they were obstructed in circulating their views.[29] In Cabinet on 21 March Castle and Healey complained that, despite Wilson's confidence, the record of the talks with de Gaulle showed no real hope of his accepting British membership. However, it seemed that few ministers were likely to press their opposition to the EEC to the point of resignation; Brown was anxious at least to *try* to enter before the issue of CAP financing was settled, and Wilson was again careful to steer the discussions away from the principle of entry to the detailed terms.[30] He hoped for a decision before Parliament's Whitsuntide recess and held a series of Cabinet discussions during April to discuss the details of entry, with subjects ranging from regional policy and capital movements, to constitutional issues and the CAP. Wilson, now openly pro-EEC, minimised the problems and emphasised the gains of economic growth. Perhaps most significant however, was that all alternatives to EEC membership were ruled out. Brown and Stewart of course had already taken this line at the October 1966 Chequers meeting, but the Javits Plan (on Anglo-US co-operation) and 'Go It Alone' had now been fully studied, and both were dismissed. The Javits Plan meant US domination; GITA meant continuing British decline. This was highly important because, by implication (and despite Wilson's repeated stress on the importance of entry terms) it meant that Britain *had* to try to get into Europe – whatever the terms. Like Macmillan, Wilson had concluded there was 'no alternative' to EEC membership. Burke Trend, the Secretary to the Cabinet, even argued that if the EEC application were rejected, Britain must continue to press it, refusing to accept defeat. Such was the unenviable logic of the country's position *vis-à-vis* Europe. For the moment however, the Cabinet would not accept Trend's desperate tactics.[31]

At the end of April 1967 a special two-day ministerial conference was held to decide on a formal application. Anti-marketeers were becoming bored with the discussions, whilst pro-marketeers like Roy Jenkins and education minister Anthony Crosland brushed aside any economic problems over entry by questioning the validity of the figures. Chancellor Callaghan insisted that EEC entry was possible without devaluation and a majority were favourable to an attempt. Those in favour included Crossman (won over, it seems, because he *did* think entry would lead to devaluation! – which he wanted) and Tony Benn (later an ardent opponent of the EEC, won over by Wilson's ideas on technological development). The cabinet formally confirmed its decision to apply on 2 May. Anti-marketeers still consoled themselves with the belief that de Gaulle would veto the application and that, even if he did not, the final decision did not need to be made until the full entry terms were known.[32] At the end of the Commons debate about entry, held on 8–10 May, about 50 Labour MPs voted 'against' an application, but Wilson still won a sizeable, 400-plus majority since Conservatives and Liberals supported him. The Prime Minister acknowledged that EEC membership would cause some balance of payments problems, but said it would bring higher growth and give Europe a strong voice in the world, without involving too great a loss of independence for Britain. The accent therefore was again on keeping Britain a major international force, as it had been under Macmillan.

On 16 May General de Gaulle told a press conference that British membership would upset the EEC and that 'association' was to be preferred. He continued to avoid an actual veto of British membership, perhaps because he did not want to provoke a crisis, but many observers believed that the press conference amounted to a 'Non'. Nevertheless, Michael Palliser, Wilson's foreign policy adviser in Downing Street, advised the Prime Minister to 'bash on, regardless', arguing that de Gaulle's press conference was part of a 'war of nerves – to see whether your nerve is as strong as the General's'. At an EEC meeting in mid-June all members except France favoured British entry. Wilson, however, continued to bargain, not on using other EEC states to pressurise de Gaulle, but on persuading the General in personal talks to accept British membership.[33] The two met at Versailles on 19–20 June just after the Six-Day War in the Middle East. On the EEC however Wilson again made little impression. De Gaulle appeared unimpressed by Wilson's talk of creating a 'third force' to match the superpowers and again criticised British ties to America.[34] The Prime Minister still put on an optimistic face in Cabinet, but significantly, after the Versailles talks Wilson ended his reliance on direct talks with de Gaulle. In effect he switched to the tactics which he had earlier rejected – trying to force Britain into Europe through continuous pressure and the support of other EEC states.

In the second half of 1967 the Wilson bid to enter Europe stumbled to its predictable close, accompanied by some dubious diplomatic tactics and more evidence of Britain's decline as a major power. The Prime Minister's memoirs, full as they are on the EEC in earlier periods, have almost nothing to say on this period. In early July the British still faced the practical problem of tabling their application before the EEC Commission in the face of French opposition. To overcome this Brown attended a meeting of the Western European Union (which of course included the Six and Britain) and surprised the French by tabling the application there. Brown believed that French opposition was less important than the robust support of the other five EEC states. In August Wilson weakened the anti-marketeers by reshuffling the Cabinet to exclude Jay and a less vocal figure, Bert Bowden. Then in late September, the EEC Commission reported favourably on British membership. The junior FO minister, Alun Chalfont, known to be close to Wilson, declared in threatening tones in an off-the-record talk with journalists in late October, that Britain would not accept another 'Non', even suggesting that there would be a review of British military commitments in Europe if de Gaulle used his veto.[35]

All these efforts proved vain; the long-expected *coup de grâce* was finally delivered by de Gaulle in a press conference on 22 November 1967. By then the General had an excellent excuse to issue a veto because Britain had just finally been forced to devalue the Pound. The position of Sterling, not helped by the June Arab-Israeli war or by speculation about the EEC, had steadily worsened. In November Wilson finally bowed to the inevitable. At his press conference de Gaulle did not rule out British entry for evermore, but he attacked Wilson's 'extraordinary insistence and haste' in seeking entry now and believed that Britain only wanted membership as a way to compensate for its weaknesses, as revealed by the devaluation. Even then Brown insisted that the Cabinet should wait until the next EEC ministers' meeting in December to clarify the situation and in the interim considerable pressure was put on the Friendly Five to help Britain into Europe. Brown even pathetically complained to Willy Brandt, who was on a visit to Britain, 'Willy, you must get us in so we can take the lead in [the] EEC'.[36] Notwithstanding such naïve arrogance, EEC ministers agreed on 19 December that Britain's application could not be considered further.

British Policy in an Impasse, 1968–70

Labour's attempt to enter Europe had finally ended in disaster for Wilson. The man who had earlier opposed devaluation but hoped for EEC membership was forced to agree to devaluation and had the door to the EEC closed in his face. Wilson had been able to win over the Cabinet to an application but ultimately could not overcome de Gaulle, whose vision of Europe's future had no place for a British government which, whatever Wilson said, remained closely tied to America. Wilson vastly overestimated his abilities when he felt he could manipulate de Gaulle in the way he manipulated the British Cabinet, and de Gaulle never gave Wilson reason to believe that a membership application would succeed. In retrospect, even some of those close to the Prime Minister doubted the sincerity of his 'conversion' to Europe. George Wigg believed Wilson only took it up after July 1966 because he needed 'a device that looked and sounded like business' in tackling Britain's problems.[37] Even if one accepts that Wilson was interested in Europe before July 1966 it is unclear how genuine his interest was in the subject and he always knew de Gaulle could issue a veto. He was, evidently, a man who preferred tactics over strategy, never a 'Euro-fanatic', and could have had various reasons for his bid to enter Europe: to satisfy the Foreign Office and DEA, to please businessmen, perhaps above all to blunt Conservative attacks. Then again, in 1967 he threw himself fully behind the EEC, devoted a considerable proportion of government energies to it and staked a lot of his reputation on securing membership, all of which suggests a genuine attempt to achieve membership. He certainly paid a high price for failure in 1967–8 in declining public esteem.

If there is a fundamental reason why Labour turned towards EEC membership it is probably the fact that there seemed no viable alternative. The Commonwealth was bitterly divided over Rhodesia, US President Johnson showed no desire to treat Wilson as a real partner, and in 1967, by agreeing to abandon its bases 'East of Suez', the British government also accepted its demise as a world power. Some critics still believed that there were alternatives to EEC entry. Jay for example repeatedly insisted that the price of entry was too high and that Britain could survive by exploiting its links to America, the Commonwealth, UN and EFTA; whilst Barbara Castle had argued in the April 1967 Cabinet discussions that survival was possible if the government developed a broad alternative strategy to the Conservatives. Such a strategy would have included devaluation, import controls and a much-reduced international role, and would therefore have meant the end of 'consensus politics', which was never likely to appeal to Wilson.[38] The anti-marketeers in any case were divided and Wilson was able to manipulate them into a discussion about details. The principle had clearly been decided by Wilson in 1966 and it was that Britain must try to enter the EEC. Brown believed Britain could 'take the lead in the EEC', and Crossman judged that Labour adopted 'the Tory determination to get into the Common Market ... in order to keep Britain great'.[39] This explains why, in the wake of de Gaulle's veto, the British application remained, as Burke Trend had earlier recommended, 'on the table'. In early 1968, before his resignation (over Wilson's style of government) Brown continued to hope that the Friendly Five would force de Gaulle to change his mind.[40] But throughout the year no progress was possible. The anti-marketeers had indeed been 'saved by the General' and British public opinion polls were back to an 'anti' majority, as they had been following the 1963 veto. Furthermore, after the devaluation the British economy actually began to improve and this too reduced the urgency of EEC entry.

In early 1969 Anglo-French relations reached a new low, with the so-called 'Soames Affair'. De Gaulle was already upset at this time by efforts of Britain and the Friendly Five to consult on foreign policy through the Western European Union. Then, on 4 February, the General met the new British Ambassador Christopher Soames (a former Conservative minister) over lunch and, according to British sources, presented him with some dramatic ideas. Developing both his belief that Britain was too close to America and his dislike of supranationalism, de Gaulle suggested that Britain and France should work towards a European free trade area – such as Britain had wanted in 1956–8 but including agricultural produce – with an inner political association formed by France, Britain, West Germany and Italy. As a first step he suggested exploratory Franco-British talks. This was indeed a radical vision which fused de Gaulle's desire for independence of NATO, with British desire for a major role in Europe, freer trade and strictly limited supranationalism. But there were numerous problems with such a proposal. Michael Stewart, back at the FO after Brown's departure, saw de Gaulle's scheme as another attempt to distance Europe from America, and as a possible trap for Britain, which would betray the trust of the Friendly Five if it joined in bilateral talks with France. Wilson was due to visit German Chancellor Kurt Kiesinger on 12 February, and was now in an embarrassing position. Should he tell Kiesinger about de Gaulle's proposals? Or keep quiet and risk the Chancellor finding out later? In the end

Wilson decided to give the Germans a 'sanitised' version of the Soames interview. Things were made worse, however, by the fact that the FO also circulated a partial account of the Soames interview to Italy, the Benelux States and the US. Within days the story had begun to leak to the press and on 21 February the British decided to publish the full version of the interview. At every step the French grew more furious. They denied the British version of the talks and now rejected all idea of Anglo-French conversations. Most outsiders believed the British version of the Soames interview, but even the US, now led by Richard Nixon, was unwilling to criticise de Gaulle. On his first visit as President to Europe, Nixon admits he wanted to see de Gaulle more than any other leader![41] Britain was left facing de Gaulle's wrath alone: he had now withdrawn French representatives from the Western European Union thus ending its use as a 'bridge' between Britain and the EEC. The FO and Michael Stewart were unapologetic but were blamed by many for the crisis: Wilson's Press Secretary, Joe Haines, believed that the FO had deliberately tried to humiliate de Gaulle as revenge for his two vetoes.[42]

A few months later, in April, came the chance for a new start in Franco-British relations, with de Gaulle's sudden resignation. The occasion for this – defeat in an insignificant referendum – probably hid deeper reasons. A year earlier, in May 1968, the General had been stunned by student riots in Paris, followed by widespread strikes. These events weakened France's international position and led to pressures for a devaluation of the Franc. By resigning, de Gaulle left the devaluation decision to his successor, Georges Pompidou. De Gaulle's departure was bound to increase expectations about British entry to the EEC. It certainly led British 'anti-marketeers' to redouble their propaganda efforts.[43] As for Pompidou, he maintained his distance from NATO, but his foreign minister, Maurice Schumann, was keen to resolve the EEC's difficulties after the paralysis brought by de Gaulle.[44] French determination to strengthen the EEC may have been reinforced in September 1969 by the victory of the Social Democrats' Willy Brandt in the West German election. West Germany was already enormously powerful in economic terms and Brandt seemed likely to develop a more independent foreign policy, including more open relations with East Germany and other countries in the Eastern Bloc. Once again France needed stronger European institutions to help control Germany. It was Brandt who dominated the Hague Summit of 1–2 December which proved a great success. Here it was agreed to settle CAP finances (as France wanted), to extend the Community to Britain and others (as the Friendly Five wanted), and to discuss new co-operation in the fields of monetary and foreign policy. These steps promised to resolve existing problems (CAP), to widen the Community, and to make a further drive to deeper co-operation.

The Hague Summit was one of the most important in the history of the Community. Wilson's government could now begin the entry talks it had wanted in 1967. Yet the success was not all it seemed. Pompidou may have been overshadowed by Brandt at The Hague but the French agreed to consider British entry only after the CAP was adequately financed. This eventually proved very costly to the British in the long term, because as an industrial state they were unlikely to benefit from the CAP but, once inside the EEC, would have to help pay for it. Also, whilst de Gaulle's obstructionism had now ended, pressures for closer co-operation in the Community had grown, which were not necessarily popular in Britain. For example, disparities between Community currencies, especially the Franc and Mark, had led to talk at The Hague of full economic and monetary union which London was unlikely to welcome. Besides, the British economy was now performing better than for some years and some doubted the need to enter Europe. Interviewed on BBC's *Panorama* on 12 January 1970, Wilson adopted the same balanced tone he had used in 1966: entry would only be on the right terms, especially regarding agriculture, and there must be no 'great federal constitutions'. It was planned to begin full negotiations on entry in the summer but meanwhile Wilson was very cautious. The government published a White Paper in February which predicted that entry would increase food prices by up to 26 per cent and would have an adverse effect on balance of payments of, possibly, more than a billion Pounds. These pessimistic figures led some to accuse Wilson of becoming cool on Europe, but alternatively they could have been designed to strengthen Britain's negotiating position for tough bargaining with the Six. Wilson told Brandt that the paper was 'tactical but honest'.[45] Publicly the Prime Minister continued to contrast his own strategy, of negotiation only on the right terms, with Heath's supposed readiness to enter on any terms – an image which Heath himself tried to throw off. Philip Ziegler judges that Wilson 'was not yet retreating from his support for British entry, but he was placing on record the fact that a line of retreat existed'.[46] In late March he was bitterly upset when one Cabinet Minister, Peter Shore, used the White Paper figures to attack publicly the idea of entry.[47] But otherwise the government succeeded in maintaining its positive but cautious approach to the EEC until June, when Wilson lost power after a general election.

5

ENTRY, RENEGOTIATION AND THE REFERENDUM, 1970–1979

Heath and EEC Entry, 1970–3

There was never any doubt that Edward Heath would press for EEC membership with greater vigour than Wilson. The new premier believed that EEC entry would force British industry to become more competitive and, alongside a new industrial strategy and administrative reforms, would transform the country's economic future. Heath, according to one of his ministers, 'saw Britain in Europe as being the way back to being a Great Power' – a consistent theme, of course, from British leaders in the 1960s.[1] Unlike Wilson, Heath did not have such a divided party with which to contend, although a few MPs sympathised with the right-wing, nationalist Enoch Powell, a former Conservative minister (and supporter of entry in 1961), who had begun criticising European integration in 1969, first for economic reasons but later because of the threat to parliamentary sovereignty. As Christopher Lord points out, it was also the case that Conservative voters and constituency parties were unenthusiastic about Europe.[2] The new Cabinet was carefully chosen to support EEC membership, with a strong European Committee under the Foreign Secretary, Lord Home. Critics such as Norman Tebbit complained that the EEC was the only issue on which Heath maintained his initial business-like, determined manner.[3] In contrast to all other post-war British prime ministers, Heath's Europeanism led him to distance himself from the US. He even wished to avoid any use of the term 'special relationship'.[4] Such behaviour was designed, in part, to impress the French government which, as everyone now knew, had to be won over if Britain was to enter the EEC.

Britain was in a stronger position to pursue membership than in 1967. The position of Sterling, and the trade balance, had improved since the devaluation; few now believed in the future of the Commonwealth or saw it as a barrier to entry; all three main British political parties had backed EEC membership during the election; the National Farmers' Union (important in the Conservatives' rural constituencies) now recognised the potential gains of membership; and the Six themselves had agreed to open talks on wider membership. But Heath's greatest strength probably lay in the fact that Britain had retreated from earlier hopes of changing EEC policies fundamentally in entry talks. He was ready to accept the EEC as it stood, CAP and all. Nonetheless, France's position was uncertain. The French were increasingly fearful of German independence and their foreign minister Maurice Schumann seemed well disposed to widening the EEC. Furthermore, with the finance of the Common Agricultural Policy (CAP) settled, the French could more easily accept British membership, especially since Britain would contribute to the costs of CAP. The British could also be expected to help resist the loss of national powers to Brussels. Even in retirement, Charles de Gaulle might have spoken out against British membership; but this threat ended in November 1970 with his death. Nonetheless some *Gaullistes*, such as Jean-Marc Boegner, France's EEC representative, were sceptical about Britain's commitment to Europe. Neither, for domestic reasons, could Heath be seen to concede too much to achieve EEC membership. He planned to maintain NATO and said during the election that membership must only occur 'with the full-hearted consent of Parliament and people'.[5] The Labour opposition soon made use of the last promise to argue that there should be a popular vote before entry.

Whatever the Labour party's later criticisms of Heath, talks with the Six and three other applicants from EFTA (Ireland, Denmark and Norway) began with ministerial talks in Luxembourg on 30 June that had been planned under Wilson. Anthony Barber, the new 'Mr Europe' (as ministers with special responsibility for the EEC were called), used a draft statement prepared by the Labour government when he accepted existing EEC treaties, including CAP, and expressed particular support for developments among the Six which would benefit Britain, including regional aid and (to strengthen Britain's voice in the world) co-operation in foreign policy. Nonetheless, he said that special transitional arrangements must be made, safeguards for Commonwealth trade were needed and Britain was concerned about its likely 'net financial contribution' to the EEC. This last problem, which was to dog relations between Britain and the EEC until the mid-1980s, arose for two reasons. First, Britain would pay large amounts into the EEC under arrangements made in 1969. Payments, which became the EEC's 'own resources', came from 1 per cent of VAT receipts throughout the Community and from *all* tariffs on external trade, which in Britain's case was a large amount, since it was a major world trading power. Second, because Britain was an industrialised nation, it would receive very little back in CAP payments, which formed the bulk of the EEC budget. Instead British food prices were expected to rise sharply because of the way the CAP worked. The CAP was costly to run because it relied on intervention by the EEC in agricultural markets (often by buying up stocks of produce) to keep prices high and thus protect farmers' incomes. At Luxembourg the Six insisted that the EEC's 'own resources' were not for negotiation, and that transitional arrangements must be limited in scope and duration. The confidence of the Six was also emphasised by their continuing discussions about Economic and Monetary Union (EMU), following the 1969 Hague Summit, and by new ideas for a Common Fisheries Policy, to share out EEC fish stocks. A fisheries policy would have a particular impact on Britain and Norway, which had extensive fishing grounds. But by now such new EEC initiatives simply made Britain more anxious to achieve membership. Britain could no longer afford to let the protection of Commonwealth markets hinder the road to membership, although Sir Con O'Neill, who took charge of the talks as the official side, later complained that Commonwealth issues *did* take up too much attention: by pressing for special access to the EEC for New Zealand dairy products and West Indies sugar, Britain opened the way for the Six to press for concessions in other areas.[6]

The course of the negotiations has been thoroughly discussed in Simon Young's *Terms of Entry* and Uwe Kitzinger's *Diplomacy and Persuasion*. Both, however, were written close to the events they describe and a better understanding of Heath's policies is now provided by Christopher Lord's *British Entry to the European Community under the Heath Government*. As Lord argues, it is possible to take three views of the prospects for negotiation in 1970: that they were 'doomed to succeed', because Pompidou accepted the likeliness of British membership from the outset; that failure was still a real possibility; or – probably the best interpretation – that agreement was the most likely outcome, but that there were high stakes involved, therefore all the haggling was genuinely important.[7] Heath could draw on the services of such veteran Foreign Office pro-Europeans as Con O'Neill and Michael Palliser. The latter, who became head at the FO in 1975–82, was the son-in-law of Paul-Henri Spaak and previously adviser on foreign policy to Wilson. Although ministerial meetings were the decisive ones, most detailed talks were handled by experts' groups and working parties in Brussels. Many of these were put to work on 21 July 1970, after another long ministerial meeting. Frequent delays were caused by the need of the Six to agree a united position and an early change of personnel was forced on Heath when the Chancellor of the Exchequer, Iain Macleod, died. Barber was hastily moved to succeed him and Geoffrey Rippon, another Heath loyalist, became 'Mr Europe'. The FO hoped that the talks would be far enough advanced by spring 1971 to allow a deal to be cemented in an Anglo-French summit. Under Heath the British quickly abandoned any hope that the 'Friendly Five' would force Paris to accept British membership.

Whilst the experts' talks dragged on Heath ran into trouble at home. Opinion polls were strongly against membership in 1970–1 and Wilson decided to exploit the situation, never arguing against EEC membership in principle, yet criticising the terms that Heath was likely to secure. Heath's parliamentary majority was low enough to be threatened by a combination of Labour and anti-European Conservative MPs; and the situation grew worse thanks to by-election losses. In order to reassure nationalists in the Conservative party, Rippon's speech to the party conference in October argued that EEC membership would strengthen Britain's world role and allow greater aid to Commonwealth states. He met Powell's fears for parliamentary sovereignty by insisting that the EEC 'moves cautiously' and that there was 'no threat of instant federation'.[8] This speech had many of the weaknesses of pro-EEC speeches over the previous decade. It did not explain exactly how the EEC would improve Britain's economic competitiveness or why certain European countries like Austria, Sweden or Switzerland had achieved remarkable growth rates outside the Community. Neither could Rippon guarantee that the EEC would always avoid greater supranationalism: indeed, a week after the speech, the EEC's Werner Report was completed, by a group under Luxembourg's prime minister, recommending greater harmonisation of tax and budgetary policies with eventually, perhaps, a central EEC monetary institution, which could only mean a greater pooling of sovereignty in the Community.

By 27 October 1970 the 'fact-finding' stage of the membership talks was over and Rippon was able to strike deals with the Six on the association of British overseas dependencies with the EEC and market arrangements for milk, bacon and eggs. However, thorny issues, including special arrangements for New Zealand dairy products and West Indies sugar, as well as Britain's financial contribution, remained to be settled. In December, Britain proposed that its contribution should rise over a five-year period to a maximum 15 per cent of total contributions to the EEC, with provision for reviews if payments should become too high. At this point the French negotiating stance began to stiffen, with the insistence that Britain must, immediately after entry, pay its full contribution to the EEC, perhaps a fifth of total payments. For three months little progress was possible and the Germans feared Paris would again block British entry. Then, in March, France began to press for the talks to include the future of Sterling. As in 1967 the French government was concerned that the position of Sterling as a major trading currency would prevent Britain from adjusting the value of the Pound and becoming fully committed to EEC policies. As noted by Kitzinger, French behaviour could have three possible reasons: either they wanted the talks to fail, or they were still uncertain about British membership, or they wanted more concessions. Whatever the reason, the delays hardened anti-market sentiment in Britain, upset Heath's timetable for entry, and created new uncertainty over the country's economic future. Willy Brandt, to whom Heath paid a visit in April, believed Pompidou *would* allow British membership,[9] and Heath decided the time had come for a personal visit to Pompidou, to convince him personally of Britain's commitment to Europe.

Although many details remain unclear it is possible to reconstruct the main events that ensured the success of the Heath–Pompidou summit. The meeting was prepared in highly secret talks (unknown to the French foreign ministry and all but a few members of the Foreign Office) between British Ambassador Christopher Soames and the Secretary-General at the Elysée Palace, Michel Jobert. Heath's advisers were determined that the summit must not seem like a 'begging visit', and neither leader wanted the talks to end in embarrassment or failure. The agenda, largely set by the French, included the position of Sterling, relations with America and the philosophy of the Community – all major concerns in Paris. The Soames–Jobert talks were themselves able to iron out some detailed difficulties, so that a British-EEC ministerial meeting in mid-May confirmed the EEC's 'firm purpose' to safeguard Caribbean sugar producers, agreed terms for British membership of Euratom and also saw Britain formally accept EEC trade preferences in agriculture. This was the biggest advance in the talks for six months. Just prior to the summit, growing problems in world money markets led West Germany to 'float' the Deutschmark. This dramatic step, away from fixed exchange rates, took international focus off Sterling, called into question the whole idea of EMU (which relied on currency stability) and probably made Pompidou more cautious than ever about Germany's growing independence, all of which benefited Heath. Once the summit was underway, on 20–21 May 1971, Pompidou and Heath got on well. Their relationship was not a warm one, but both felt they could trust each other. After eleven hours of head-to-head talks, Pompidou professed to be happy about British undertakings to run down their Sterling liabilities, he confirmed that the interests of developing Commonwealth countries must be safeguarded and agreed, among other points, that member states would retain their national identity even if EMU did proceed. Critics might argue that Pompidou had not conceded much when he ended French opposition to Britain's EEC membership. Unlike 1961 and 1967 France now had the CAP in place and would benefit from British contributions to pay for it. Yet Pompidou had changed de Gaulle's veto policy despite Britain's continued reliance on Polaris, the importance of Sterling and the survival of the (much weakened) Commonwealth, and Heath had achieved what had eluded Macmillan and Wilson. Douglas Hurd, then Heath's political secretary, considered the summit 'the greatest single feat' of his premiership.[10]

The remaining problems for British membership, although often technically complex, were now dealt with speedily. At ministerial meetings in June Rippon finalised arrangements on British entry to EEC institutions; special arrangements were made to protect the markets of New Zealand dairy products during the early years of membership; and a compromise was reached whereby Britain's financial contribution to the EEC would increase annually until 1977, when it would be about 19 per cent of total contributions. This was of concern to the Treasury, but since the predicted size of the EEC budget had recently been revised downwards and world food prices were rising faster than those in the Community, it was not felt that the impact on Britain would be as adverse as originally feared. Besides Heath hoped that, once inside the EEC, he could gain money from the proposed Regional Aid Fund and, if real problems arose over the British contribution, it would always be possible to reopen the issue with the other members.[11] Although Heath was accused by Labour of getting poor terms for Britain, at the time they seemed reasonable enough, especially given the fact that Britain was a supplicant with two failed applications behind it.

With all the main problems resolved Heath was able to introduce a White Paper, on 7 July. The Paper conceded that the CAP would increase food prices and damage Commonwealth trade. But in presenting arguments in favour of entry, it included references to Wilson's arguments used in 1967, including technological gains, the strengthening of Britain's voice in the world and the lack of alternative strategies. The Paper strongly restated the belief that entry would improve Britain's economic performance (again without explaining how) and tried to answer the more common fears. Thus there was 'no question of any erosion of essential national sovereignty'; instead entry would allow Britain to influence EEC policies (on EMU for example) and to press for an 'outward looking' Community (including development aid to Commonwealth countries). This fitted Heath's own positive yet pragmatic approach to integration, which considered arguments about a loss of sovereignty to be 'at best a sterile debate and at worst a positive hindrance to European progress'. Despite accusations from his opponents that he was federalist in his view of Europe, Heath's public statements constantly reflected this more pragmatic outlook: thus, in 1970 he said that European unity simply meant 'the habit of working together to reach accepted goals' and in 1988 he wrote that the EC had 'developed *sui generis* and the final form of its political organisation will be *sui generis*'.[12]

Heath therefore tried to depict entry to the EC as being in line with established British policies. Traditional aims – security, growth, freer trade, independence – were simply to be achieved in a new forum. Yet he had also minimised potential problems in order to try to win over a sceptical public. Opinion polls at this time showed as few as one in four Britons in favour of entry. This was not as bad as it seemed. Polls on the EEC were always volatile from the early 1960s onwards, suggesting that the public did not have strong or well-informed views on the subject, and Heath's negotiating success in June soon led to an improvement in popular support. Industrialists, and much of the media, were pro-EC and a 'pro' campaign was launched by the well-financed European Movement. But the Prime Minister decided, in view of the difficulties, to delay any Commons vote until after the summer recess. Enoch Powell made a series of speeches in 1971 in which he insisted Britain's sovereignty *was* endangered, and up to 60 Conservative right-wingers were rumoured to be ready to oppose common market membership.[13] This was of concern to Heath because Harold Wilson became firmer in his position that Heath had failed to get good enough terms from the Six, so that Labour would vote against him.

Marcia Falkender, one of Wilson's closest advisers, believed the EEC 'to be the most difficult problem [he] had to handle' as Opposition leader, a view echoed by later analysts such as Ben Pimlott.[14] The events of November 1967, and Britain's subsequent economic improvement *outside* the common market, led many Labour MPs to return to their earlier scepticism about the EEC. Then came the 1970 election defeat in which George Brown, the leading advocate of entry, lost his seat. Many Labour MPs, as well as trade unionists and constituency activists, simply wished to oppose Heath's government on every issue; many shared the popular fears of higher prices, unemployment, the threat to sovereignty and the end of the Commonwealth; many saw the EEC as a capitalist, bureaucratic institution, supported only by elite groups in Britain but likely to harm working-class interests. One long-standing anti-marketeer, Douglas Jay, pressed in August 1970 for a referendum to be held before Britain entered the EEC.[15] The question of whether to hold a referendum on such a key constitutional issue soon took on a significance of its own. The idea was taken up by Tony Benn. As Benn's biographer, Jad Adams, points out, Benn was still a pro-marketeer in 1970, but was increasingly seen as a leader of the Left and became anti-market in 1971. He argued that a popular vote was needed on Europe and tried to use the common market issue to marginalise the moderate, 'social democratic' wing of the Labour party. A particular complication for Wilson was that James Callaghan, seen as a possible alternative leader, also began to question EEC membership. In a speech in May 1971 he emotively announced that membership would threaten the 'language of Chaucer'. Callaghan, who (as his official biographer underlines) was not usually so chauvinistic where Europe was concerned, believed that a referendum could become a 'life raft' to keep Labour united on Europe; he also raised the possibility of *renegotiating* the terms if Labour were re-elected. Renegotiation of Heath's terms, a ploy which might keep Labour united on the issue, had first been suggested by Callaghan's son-in-law Peter Jay, the son of Douglas Jay.[16] Meanwhile pro-marketeers, now led by Roy Jenkins, another possible leadership contender, organised their own campaign. In May 1971 they persuaded most of the party leadership to sign a pro-EEC manifesto.

To the Jenkinsites (who included social democrats such as Shirley Williams and David Owen), Wilson was showing a lack of principle by not backing the EEC and was putting party before country. The fact that the common market became wrapped up in the leadership question only added to the cynicism over Wilson's policy, which the anti-Labour press was quick to exploit.[17] However for Wilson, as for people like Denis Healey and Tony Crosland, the view was reversed. They believed Labour party unity was more important than the EEC *and* that, in any case, it was still possible to save both. L. J. Robins, in his study of Labour and the EEC, concluded that Wilson's prime concern was that EEC policy 'should be fashioned, so as to cause minimum damage to the fabric of the party'. Austen Morgan considers on the other hand that 'the ultimate test of Harold Wilson's leadership was to prevent the Labour party coming out against the EEC in principle' and Philip Ziegler agrees that Wilson's greatest success was to maintain his freedom of manoeuvre for the future, when he returned to power. One Labour frontbencher, Harold Lever, has pointed out that if Wilson had fought *for* entry on the terms available in 1971 'his only real allies would have been the Jenkinsites . . . the temptation, if they had won, to discard Harold in favour of Roy would have been very strong'.[18] With detachment from the party's rivalries, political scientists see this debate as reflecting a fundamental and growing rift within Labour, between liberal, but elitist, social democrats and populists like Benn who wished to appeal to a mass working-class electorate with a more radical Socialist programme.[19]

Meanwhile, as summer passed, Heath still had difficulties with his own anti-marketeers, though their numbers were waning. Heath ideally wanted to maintain party discipline and impress the Six with a strong pro-entry vote. But the Conservative Chief Whip, Francis Pym, believed that anti-marketeers would vote 'against' even if strong pressure was put on them, and successfully argued that it was better to allow a free vote – which would put Wilson under pressure to do the same and encourage the Jenkinsites.[20] A six-day debate, the longest since the war, was finally held in late October, and the margin in favour of entry was much greater than expected: 356 votes to 244. Even with a free vote, only 38 Conservatives joined Powell in the 'no' lobby, whilst 69 Labour MPs defied their party whip to vote 'yes'. This was not the end of parliamentary debate, but it was the key to ultimate success. Heath celebrated by welcoming Maurice Schumann to London and arranged a Royal state visit to France. In Germany there were even fears of a Franco-British 'axis' being formed.

Problems over the common fisheries policy, mainly involving Norway, delayed completion of the Treaty of Accession for Britain, Eire, Denmark and Norway, until December. A dull signature ceremony took place in Brussels on 22 January 1972 and the Treaty had then to be voted into law. To make this process easier the government drew up a Bill made up of only twelve clauses, which simply accepted all past EEC regulations (a considerable number), the Treaty of Rome and Heath's entry terms. In the votes which followed the Jenkinsites decided to obey the Labour whip and preserve party unity. Thus the government's majority dropped as low as eight in some votes, but there was secret collusion between Labour pro-Europeans and the Conservatives which ensured that Heath never actually lost a vote. In the other three applicants for membership a referendum was held to decide the issue, and in March 1972 even the French government announced a referendum on widening the Community. This led pressure to rise from Labour party chairman Tony Benn for a similar vote in Britain. Although Rippon told the Commons that referenda were 'wholly contrary to our constitutional practices', a plebiscite *was* held in Northern Ireland at this time. Faced by such pressure, and probably seeing a popular vote as a way to heal his party's divisions, Wilson now moved in favour of a referendum. This was approved by the Shadow Cabinet on 29 March, but far from uniting the party it led Jenkins to quit his Shadow Cabinet post. Jenkins' move showed questionable tactical sense: he seemed to be standing out against a popular vote, had abandoned an important power base, and had damaged his chances of ever becoming party leader.[21] Anti-marketeers continued to complain that Heath's Bill made a mockery of the complex legal, financial and constitutional questions involved in entry. They became even more incensed in April when the government cut short debates by the use of 'guillotines'. In answer to such complaints it can be said that the October 1971 vote had already shown a clear Commons majority for entry, over 300 hours of debate occurred on the European Communities Bill and public opinion was largely indifferent to the debates, which ended successfully for Heath in July. Membership would take effect on 1 January 1973.

It has already been said that Heath's enthusiasm for the EEC over the US alliance was unique among post-war premiers. Heath never questioned the need for the Atlantic alliance, but he boasted that the EEC was now the world's largest trading bloc and put Britain in a group that could equal the superpowers. This of course was a long-standing British dream, which could be traced back to Bevin's day, and dovetailed with French hopes of matching US power. Stephen George has tried to argue that Heath's policy was *not* radically more pro-European than other post-war premiers and that any differences he had with Washington were largely the fault of the US. Certainly, the Prime Minister showed little enthusiasm for EMU and criticised existing EEC policies such as the CAP. However, in seeking to maximise British influence in the EEC whilst minimising the loss of independence, Heath behaved no differently to other countries: all Community members tried to secure their own agenda within the EEC. The vital point about Heath, when compared to the succeeding three Prime Ministers, was that he was *communitaire* in his behaviour: no one could doubt his deep commitment to the Community; he did not pursue the myth of the special relationship to the detriment of EEC co-operation; and he was popular with other European leaders.[22] The tragedy for Heath was that he joined the Community when his own premiership had little more than a year to run, and when persistent inflation, strike action and low growth began to dog all Western economies, ending the expansion of the 1950s and 1960s. The floating of the Deutschmark in spring 1971 and an American import surcharge in August (criticised by Heath and EEC leaders) reflected the problems. In June 1972 Sterling was floated without any attempt at joint EEC action.

In October 1972 Heath was invited to a Community summit in Paris, along with other new entrants, Ireland and Denmark. (Norway had just rejected membership in its referendum.) The summit confirmed the lofty goal of achieving EMU, planned greater co-operation in the field of foreign policy and also hoped to create a 'European Union' by 1980. But on many issues there were divisions. Brandt agreed to set up a Regional Development Fund to reduce economic imbalances in the Community – a step from which Britain could expect to benefit and which was a vital addition to EMU – but refused to pour large sums of German money into it. Pompidou and Heath rejected attempts by Italy and Holland to control the larger states by making the European Parliament stronger (through direct elections). Heath, committed to his own domestic reform programme, opposed the idea of joint EEC social and technological programmes.[23]

In April 1973, a few months after Britain entered the EEC, the country began to reduce its tariffs with other members. That same month a European Monetary Co-operation Fund was established. This had been agreed at the Paris summit as a step to EMU. However, since attempts to tie the value of EEC currencies together – in the so-called 'snake' – proved very difficult, EMU progressed no further. The 'snake' had originally been formed in March 1972, to keep EEC currencies within a certain value of each other. Britain joined soon afterwards, but left in July 1972 due to the instability of Sterling. The Treasury (which in any case lacked sufficient reserves to maintain Sterling's value) never had much faith in European efforts at currency alignment. There was some justification for this since, unless all members agreed on tough anti-inflation measures, the Germans refused to take on the daunting task (which France seemed to intend for them) of supporting the value of other EEC currencies. Soon, thanks to global currency instability, inflation and a lack of EEC agreement on economic policies, the EEC was forced to abandon its hopes of currency union as a way to boost trade, deepen economic integration and limit German independence. In January 1974 France left the 'snake' which became a small, German-dominated group.

In Britain meanwhile unemployment rose above one million and strikes were widespread. The attempt by Barber to prepare for EEC membership, by boosting domestic demand in his 1972 budget, simply produced inflation, a trade deficit and an unsustainable 'boom'. British critics of the EEC had long argued that it would push up prices and damage trade, and they now seemed correct. 'May we not have signed the Treaty of Rome just before the collapse?', asked one press commentator. The sense of disappointment soon pervaded Whitehall too: in early 1973 the Ambassador to France, Nicholas Henderson, visited London and 'found that the top civil servants . . . were hardly enthusiastic about Europe'. Heath's opinion poll ratings, and those of the 'common market' (as most Britons persisted in calling the EEC), sank together. The situation became markedly worse however, in October 1973, when an Arab-Israeli war broke out and Arab producers forced up oil prices. 'After the oil crisis of 1973–4', Heath later recalled, 'the Community lost its momentum' and the December 1973 Copenhagen Summit of EEC leaders – the first since the ambitious Paris meetings of more than a year before – 'was the worst summit that I have ever experienced', being dominated by arguments over oil.[24] These events underlined the failure of EEC membership to reverse Britain's economic fortunes. Heath himself rejected the idea of sharing Britain's newly discovered oil resources in the North Sea with the rest of the Community. This in turn confirmed Brandt in his reluctance to pay for a substantial Regional Development Fund which might have benefited Heath. Instead of the EEC strengthening Britain, and vice versa, both were now cast into the economic and political doldrums.

Wilson's Renegotiation and the Referendum, 1974–5

In February 1974, Heath lost power following a general election. The common market arguably had an important impact on the election result because, in the closing days of the campaign, Enoch Powell recommended that Conservative opponents of the EEC should vote Labour. Labour's manifesto promised to renegotiate the terms of entry, so as to reform the CAP, reduce Britain's financial contribution and secure better terms for Commonwealth countries; it also promised a popular vote on membership, though not necessarily by referendum, with the implication that Britain might decide to withdraw.[25] Wilson, who had concerted some of his speeches with those of Powell,[26] played on voters' fears of higher food prices in the EEC. Yet Wilson's position was far from easy. He led a minority government and knew that the European issue had 'the potential to destroy the government from within'. As his official biographer writes, this issue 'had to be resolved before the government could address itself properly to any ... others'.[27] In broad terms in 1974–5 he now repeated the tactics he had used in 1966–7, tortuously manoeuvring a reluctant party towards EEC membership: he himself could still see no alternative for the country to being in the Community. But in 1974 he was in a much more difficult position with Labour anti-marketeers than in 1967. As a result EEC membership became of fundamental importance to the daily course of British politics. And the corollary was that Britain's role in the EEC was at the mercy of British domestic considerations. Heath and others accused Wilson of gravely harming Britain's standing in Europe by negotiating with the EEC with the threat of withdrawal in the background. But renegotiation was used by Wilson to allow time for pro-Community sentiments to revive in the Cabinet and the country. It also allowed him to maintain his insistence on his pragmatic point – dating back to 1962 – that the *terms* of membership mattered more than the principle. His ability to manipulate arguments, in order to please all sides in the party whilst working towards a pro-Community outcome, was seen in the Cabinet on 7 March. Here it was agreed to include renegotiation in the Queen's Speech but with the understanding that, if such renegotiation were successful, Britain would play 'a full part ... in Europe'. Industry minister Tony Benn saw this as 'a complete watering down of our Manifesto' but Wilson could counter that, in order to renegotiate in good faith, the government must accept the possibility of continued membership.[28]

In similar fashion to his use of the 1966 manifesto, Wilson was able to use the party's commitment to renegotiation of the terms of entry to outflank the anti-marketeers. He was able to direct discussions at individual issues and to avoid consideration of the principle of EEC membership. He also showed his usual astuteness in appointing ministers to government posts. It was absolutely essential, if Britain was to remain 'in Europe', that a pro-market majority should be built up in the Cabinet, because the Labour party machine was 'anti-market'. Most importantly, the renegotiation was put in the hands of the person who had first championed it: Jim Callaghan, the new Foreign Secretary, who was now likely to become committed to whatever terms he secured for Britain. When Callaghan attended his first Council of Ministers in April he embarrassed his FO officials with the lecturing tones he used to explain Britain's aims in the renegotiation. The other EEC members, however, had little alternative to accepting renegotiation and some analysts see Callaghan's April statement merely as a tough opening position, which soon mellowed.[29]

It is difficult in fact to disagree with Sean Greenwood's assertion that 'renegotiation was a sham'. Certain of Callaghan's seven aims proved to have no significance whatsoever: Labour's manifesto had promised to retain a zero VAT rate on basic items, but EEC rules did *not* obstruct this; neither did the EEC prevent Britain from protecting its balance of payments by limiting capital movements with Europe; and the Labour party's criticism of EMU was pointless because EMU was no longer in the realm of practical politics. This left only four areas for genuine renegotiation: the CAP should be reformed to benefit third world producers and bring lower food prices; other steps should be taken to help third world (and, therefore, Commonwealth) exporters; Britain's regional and industrial policies should not be impeded by the Commission in Brussels; and the financial arrangements for British membership must be altered. Whilst renegotiation was underway Britain suspended certain obligations of membership. But the underlying weakness of Britain in the renegotiation was highlighted in a special Cabinet meeting on the subject at Chequers later in April. The tone here was evidently very pessimistic about Britain's future, inside Europe or out. One memorandum highlighted the fact that Germany's income per head was now twice that of the UK. Callaghan now feared 'our place in the world is shrinking' and that, inside or outside the EEC, Britain must strengthen its economy. But he also believed that EEC membership was the best base on which to build any economic improvement.[30]

A delay in negotiations was caused in May 1974 by a French Presidential election, following the death of Pompidou. The victor was Valéry Giscard d'Estaing. At the same time Germany's Willy Brandt suddenly resigned, to be succeeded by Helmut Schmidt. Later in the month pro-marketeers in London won a surprisingly easy victory when the Cabinet agreed to renegotiate EEC membership only *within* existing treaties. Anti-marketeers evidently did not realise until too late that it would have been best for them to insist on treaty amendments – which other

Community members might have rejected. When Callaghan attended his next Council of Ministers in early June he acknowledged that EMU was no longer a problem and pointed out that EEC food prices had become less of a problem because (in the unusual circumstances of the mid-1970s) world commodity prices had risen above European levels. It was now clear that the renegotiation would be limited in scale. A major row took place in Cabinet in mid-June over the make-up of the European Strategy Committee[31] but the anti-marketeers had already lost key arguments and were also losing support. One of their number, Fred Peart, for example, was back in his previous post of Agriculture Minister, but moved in favour of continued EEC membership. Tony Benn felt that Peart had fallen under the influence of his civil servants,[32] an argument which reflected the belief of many Labour members that the consensus in Whitehall was so solidly pro-EEC that 'no Government of any party could have resisted it'.[33] Similar accusations were made against Callaghan, who later rejected charges of being dominated by the FO.[34] Callaghan was criticised by Barbara Castle, trade minister Peter Shore and other anti-marketeers in July, for developing a pro-market policy without reference to the Cabinet. But Callaghan argued that he still had an open mind about membership, and that it was the heavy workload associated with renegotiation which prevented fuller Cabinet consultations.[35]

Meanwhile Tony Benn was pressing for a commitment to hold a referendum in Labour's manifesto at the next election, which was likely to be held in October. A referendum seemed far preferable to yet another general election which, in any case, could only be seen as a way to decide EEC membership if the two major parties took opposite sides. At a joint meeting of the Cabinet and Labour's National Executive Committee (NEC) on 25 July Wilson and Callaghan favoured a twelve-month renegotiation period, to be followed by a binding referendum.[36] But the relative peace which followed this discussion was largely due to the summer holidays. With opinion polls still anti-EEC, Roy Jenkins' supporters still opposed a referendum. When discussions revived in September the Cabinet and NEC agreed that, 'within twelve months of the election' there would be a chance to decide the EEC issue 'through the ballot box'.[37] In the subsequent election campaign one pro-market minister, Shirley Williams, said she would resign if there was a 'No' vote on Europe and Jenkins supported her. Overall, however, Wilson was able to prevent the common market becoming a major issue. Even strong-minded individuals like Jenkins and Benn were ready to put on a united front. Yet the end-result was only an overall majority for Labour of four seats.[38]

In the wake of the general election the renegotiation gathered pace and the EEC took up so much time that, according to Bernard Donnoughue, one of Wilson's advisers, 'other major issues were neglected'.[39] Giscard d'Estaing had decided to call a summit meeting in Paris, for December, to take the vital decisions on renegotiation. He was still apparently reluctant to make concessions to the British. In the interim, in November, Helmut Schmidt was invited by Callaghan to address Labour's annual conference. The conference passed an anti-market motion by a clear majority, but Schmidt's plea for Britain to remain 'in Europe' impressed many delegates, and was followed by a head-to-head meeting with Wilson at Chequers. Roy Jenkins believed that Schmidt confirmed Wilson in his determination to remain in the EEC, and that Schmidt in turn won Giscard d'Estaing over to a sympathetic approach to the renegotiation. Wilson assured Schmidt that, if the terms were right, he would recommend acceptance to the British people.[40] He also took up an idea of Schmidt's for a personal meeting with Giscard. This took place in early December, in Paris. Giscard proved far friendlier than his officials had recently been, but was still reluctant to accept that individual EEC members could seek a reduction in payments; France considered financial payments to be the Community's 'own resources'. Callaghan however, countered that Britain wanted a 'refund' rather than a 'reduction', and argued this left the principle of 'own resources' intact. Wilson also showed that he could play the Community game of trading-off concessions when necessary: he agreed to support a proposal from Giscard for regular meetings of EEC leaders in a European Council. (Previously leaders' meetings had been organised only irregularly.)

In the wake of the Paris visit Wilson made his position on the renegotiation public. He still claimed to be more interested in terms than in the principle of membership, and he had no time for those who accused him of putting party before country. But a public statement that he would recommend acceptance of the 'right' terms was bound to raise expectations that he would keep Britain in Europe whatever happened. It also put him in a stronger position for the Paris summit meeting which followed.[41] Here Wilson again proved ready to 'trade' concessions. Whilst reserving his position on the idea of direct elections to the European Parliament (which France, under its new, centrist President, now accepted), he approved Giscard's idea of regular European Councils and agreed that the Belgian premier, Leo Tindemanns, should carry out a study on the future of 'European Union'. The leaders agreed that the 1980 deadline for EMU was impossible in the current climate but the conference communiqué did talk of EMU as a Community aim. Wilson was pleased to win two concessions. One was the establishment, at last, of a Regional Development Fund, not as large as originally hoped, but with Britain as the second greatest beneficiary (after Italy). Second, after difficult discussions, it was agreed to introduce a 'correcting mechanism' for budget contributions. To retain the principle of 'own resources' this was to be in the form of a 'refund', as Britain had earlier suggested; to retain the principle of equality it was to apply to all members, but everyone knew Britain would gain most. The details of the mechanism had yet to be decided but Wilson had achieved a major advance.[42]

When Wilson reported to the Cabinet on 12 December, it was evident he still faced a difficult domestic situation. In Cabinet discussions since the election anti-marketeers had continued to attack the new terms. Agriculture Minister Peart, for example, had won concessions on higher imports of Commonwealth sugar and assistance to British beef producers, but Cabinet critics pointed out that the CAP was still unreformed. The key issue, however, remained that of sovereignty. Barbara Castle even remarked, after another gloomy set of economic statistics, 'I might almost be tempted to stay in' the EEC – but only if renegotiation 'succeeded in mutilating the "European idea" of the fanatics'.[43] Yet this could only be achieved by alterations in the Treaty of Rome, a step Britain had already agreed to avoid. In the discussion on 12 December Tony Benn and Michael Foot argued that the Paris Summit, with its talk of direct European elections and 'European Union', had revealed the long-term threat to national sovereignty, but Wilson minimised such fears and insisted he had been loyal to the election manifesto. He also, according to Castle, reverted to one of his tactics used in Cabinet talks on the EEC in 1966–7, by 'reduc[ing] everything to a boring ... low key'.[44] After the Cabinet, to mollify his critics further, Wilson told the Commons: 'There is not a hope in hell ... of EMU taking place *in the near future*' (my italics). It is not clear whether Wilson genuinely believed there was no *long-term* threat to British sovereignty, or whether he believed Britain had the capacity to defeat such a threat once its future in the Community was secure. It is significant that about this time Roy Jenkins shifted in favour of a referendum. Not only had public opinion polls moved in the EEC's favour, but also Jenkins realised that Wilson would recommend a 'Yes' vote.[45] Benn chose to break his public silence over Christmas, by issuing an 'open letter' to his constituents on the threat posed by the EEC to British independence. When the junior FO minister, Roy Hattersley, attacked Benn's statement, the government's divisions were plain to see.

In early January, it was clear to keen observers that Wilson and Callaghan wanted to resolve the time-consuming and divisive EEC issue in a referendum and that, during the referendum, Cabinet ministers must 'agree to differ' in public. This was a remarkable situation given the constitutional convention of Cabinet solidarity in public. Wilson argued it was justified by the unprecedented constitutional importance of the issue, but others derided it as another dubious device to preserve Labour unity. By placing the decision in the hands of the people Wilson hoped to avoid an open split between Benn and Jenkins. But he still had to show his own preference for what the referendum result should be. After talking to Wilson and Callaghan, the Canadian High Commissioner, Paul Martin, confidently predicted they 'have made up their mind that Britain will stay in'.[46] It was a surprisingly united Cabinet which, on 21 January, heard Wilson propose the referendum and the agreement to differ, 'as casually as if he had been offering us a cup of tea'. All ministers now agreed this was the best course to maintain Labour unity. Guidelines for ministerial behaviour during the referendum would be set to keep the appearance of disunity within acceptable bounds. The referendum, set for June, was publicly announced two days later. Pro-marketeers began to organise a 'Britain in Europe' campaign (chaired by Con O'Neill, who had retired from the FO) whilst anti-market groups were united in an oddly named 'National Referendum Campaign'. Meanwhile the renegotiation drew towards its close. In February an EEC ministerial meeting promised (vaguely) to 'review' the CAP and to pursue a liberal general trade policy. That same month the EEC negotiated the Lomé Convention with members' former colonies (mainly in Africa). The convention answered left-wing criticisms by providing freer access to European markets, and greater economic aid, for developing countries. Other difficulties were to be resolved in the first European Council, in Dublin, on 10–11 March.

Wilson carefully avoided Cabinet discussion on the line he would take in Dublin.[47] Once there he upset other leaders by insisting on discussing British concerns to the exclusion of other vital issues. But Wilson was desperate to achieve a defensible settlement ahead of the June referendum and, arguably, it was in the EEC's interest that he do so. Wilson won better access to EEC markets for New Zealand butter than Heath had achieved (until 1980 instead of 1977), but not on cheese or lamb. More importantly, thanks to concessions by Giscard, and the efforts at compromise by Commission President Ortoli, a complicated new system was agreed to allow a refund on any member's net financial contribution, if it fell below a certain percentage of average GDP in the Community. To placate Benn, Wilson also got a statement safeguarding Britain's ability to pursue effective regional and industrial policies.[48] Satisfied with what he had achieved, Wilson then held a two-day Cabinet meeting about Europe. He and Callaghan defended the renegotiated terms, said Community membership was now less costly than expected, and declared EMU to be a dead issue. Wilson said he was in favour of accepting these terms '51 per cent'; Callaghan argued that Britain's international role was strengthened by membership. Benn, Foot, Castle and Shore continued to insist that British sovereignty was threatened. But other, previously neutral or mildly 'anti' ministers swung behind Wilson, who won a 16 to 7 majority in favour of a government 'Yes' recommendation in the referendum.[49] The Prime Minister thereby achieved his main aim: the Labour party might be divided, most of its members might oppose the common market, but the government would now officially campaign for a 'Yes' vote.[50]

Critics on both sides of the EEC debate in Britain were unimpressed by Wilson's new terms. Labour party officials even prepared a critique which argued there had been little change to the deal secured by Heath. This paper was used to attack Callaghan in a National Executive meeting on 19 March, where it was agreed to hold a special party conference on the issue. Wilson warned the Cabinet that the collapse of the government was possible if such public humiliation continued.[51] On 25 March ministers were informed of the guidelines Wilson wished them to follow during the referendum, including the avoidance of personalised arguments and a ban on public appearances alongside members of other political parties. Neither Jenkins nor Benn felt the latter restriction to be workable. In 'a serious error of tactics' Wilson himself did *not* attend this meeting and he was shocked when the Cabinet agreed to allow anti-market ministers to vote against the government (rather than merely abstain) in the forthcoming Commons debate.[52] When the debate was held, on 7–9 April, Wilson kept to his low-key approach, and more Labour MPs voted against membership (145) than in favour (137). Pro-marketeers too condemned Wilson's renegotiation. They argued that he had achieved little of substance except to offend the EEC, by using the veiled threat of withdrawal; concessions might just as easily have been won by patient negotiation *inside* the EEC.[53] It was only thanks to Conservative and Liberal support that Wilson won the vote to stay in the EEC by 396 votes to 170. It was another vital step for him. In contrast, when the special Labour conference on the EEC voted two to one against membership later in April, Wilson dismissed it as a 'non-event'.[54]

With Cabinet government (according to Castle) having almost ceased,[55] all energies were now devoted to the referendum. The campaign has been fully discussed by David Butler and Uwe Kitzinger. Although anti-marketeers like Benn had fought hard for the referendum, it was the pro-marketeers who were better financed (mainly by businessmen), better organised and with greater press support. Equal television time, public assistance to both campaigns and the free distribution of one 'pro' and one 'anti' leaflet, could not offset such advantages, especially when the government – thanks to the Cabinet decision in March – circulated a second 'pro' leaflet of its own. The main arguments of the antis were that the EEC threatened parliamentary sovereignty, led to higher prices, and would create unemployment, especially in regions furthest from the Continent. The pros insisted British traditions were safe, that jobs would be created by membership and that there was simply 'no alternative'. The antis had already been outmanoeuvred by Wilson in the Cabinet: now they ran a shambolic campaign and never developed a realistic alternative to Community membership. They appeared as a mixture of far Leftists, such as Benn (whose dominant personality even offended many anti-marketeers), and far Rightists, such as Enoch Powell (who was disliked by Labour members and who had now quit the Conservative party). In contrast the pro-marketeers were led by such respected moderates as Jenkins and Heath. The latter proved effective as a public campaigner at last, only months after being replaced as Conservative leader by Margaret Thatcher. Wilson took a low profile, and even allowed ministers to appear on opposing platforms in the later stages of the campaign, but the Prime Minister's preference for a 'Yes' vote was clear, and carried great weight. Despite the dangers that the referendum carried for his government and for Britain's international reputation, Wilson could afford to be confident, since opinion polls predicted a two to one majority in favour throughout the campaign.[56] The actual majority on 5 June was 67 per cent. The 'No' vote was greater in areas removed from the South-East but only the Western Isles of Scotland showed a majority for the 'No's. The public evidently believed the EEC presented the best future. Wilson and Callaghan drank a toast to 'A job well done': Austen Morgan, in his biography of Wilson, considers this to have been the Prime Minister's 'finest political hour'.[57]

For all his low profile during the campaign, there is no doubt Wilson gained much from it. The man previously castigated for putting party before country had preserved Labour unity on a potentially destructive issue and could announce that the EEC issue was settled for good.

Pro-marketeers like Jenkins might rejoice at the result, but they had never wanted the referendum. The man who had wanted it – Tony Benn – had offended Wilson too often and was now unceremoniously demoted to the energy ministry. Many had expected Benn to resign – a course taken by only one anti-marketeer, the junior minister Judith Hart. Wilson now insisted that Cabinet differences must end.[58] Nevertheless in the long term, the renegotiation and referendum bore a considerable price, even for Labour unity. Benn had succeeded in dividing Jenkins' social democrats from other elements in the party with the referendum proposal; and the social democrats had discovered that they had more in common with moderates among the Conservatives and Liberals than they had with many Labour members. John Campbell, Françoise de la Serre and others see the referendum as an important staging post to the party's split in 1981–2, and the formation of the Social Democratic party.[59] The referendum was also costly to Wilson in that it absorbed so much government time that he was unable to take the tough action required to deal with Britain's economic problems. The overall effect of high inflation, negative growth and rising unemployment added to Labour's internal divisions and created the image of a party unfit to govern. Finally, the renegotiation process also weakened Britain's standing in Europe and prevented Wilson from establishing a leading role in the Community. Instead of the Franco-British combination (which seemed possible under Heath), Schmidt and Giscard reforged the Franco-German 'axis' in 1974–5. Neither did Wilson do anything to alter this situation after the referendum. As Stephen George has argued, the government continued to stand aside from the rest of the EEC. In particular, Wilson and Callaghan (unsuccessfully) resisted attempts to make them part of an EEC delegation to a world energy conference, arguing that Britain's oil resources put it in a special position.[60]

The Callaghan Government, 1976–9

In March 1976, Wilson suddenly resigned, citing the fact that he had now reached 60. His successor was the *older* Jim Callaghan, who of course was a pragmatist on the EEC. Three months later the Cabinet held a special session on Europe to plan for the first British Presidency of the Community in January–June 1977. (The Presidency, which gives members the chairmanship of ministerial meetings, rotates among members.) The wide-ranging discussion showed that the government was willing to accept such minor new intrusions on policy-making as a European passport. But there were still strong criticisms of the CAP, the budget and the (still unfinished) Common Fisheries Policy. The Cabinet was also concerned about continued talk of supranationalism and hoped that this threat could be weakened by extending EEC membership to poorer, South European countries, such as Greece, Spain and Portugal.[61] Callaghan soon faced a renewed economic crisis and was forced to accept an IMF loan only on condition he carried out cuts in government spending. In 1977–8, with Labour's overall majority lost, he was also forced into a 'Lib–Lab' voting pact with the Liberals. Yet the economic problems and the pro-Europeanism of the Liberals did not induce Callaghan to look to the EEC for salvation. Instead the Community was seen as contributing to Britain's economic problems. In 1977–8 Community food prices again rose well above world prices. Britain was also absorbing a larger quantity of manufactured imports from Europe (mainly from Germany), which worsened the country's trade difficulties. Just as important, Britain's net financial contribution to the Community rose steeply in 1977–8, even with the 1975 refund deal. In November 1978 Callaghan began to complain about this situation, but his partners replied that the British had agreed to the EEC's financial rules. By 1979 the net contribution was £780 million and this would worsen in 1980 when the transition to full membership was achieved. Britain, the third poorest member of the Community (per head of population), was the second largest contributor after Germany.

Callaghan was concerned about the electoral impact of this situation, and about its effect on the divisions in his own party, which had quickly reappeared after the referendum. In late 1975 anti-marketeers had formed a Labour 'Common Market Safeguards Committee'. Thanks to the support of Schmidt and Giscard, Jenkins became President of the EEC Commission in January 1977, and pro-marketeers in London were strengthened by the voting pact with the Liberals. Given his own attitude towards Europe, the economic situation and his government's precarious position in parliament it is unsurprising that Callaghan tried to avoid any controversies over Europe. David Owen, the Foreign Secretary after February 1977, was one of the 'pro-European' social democrats but, like many of those who had voted for EEC membership, he shared Callaghan's dislike of supranationalism. To keep the anti-marketeers quiet, Owen tried to dampen the Euro-enthusiasm of the FO. Although policy towards the EEC was co-ordinated by a section of the Cabinet

Office, the FO provided much of the advice on European policy and the Foreign Secretary chaired the Cabinet's European Committee. Tony Benn was not the only Cabinet member to see the FO as particularly responsible for the influence of EEC policy-makers on British everyday life.[62] In July 1977, at Callaghan's behest, Owen circulated a Cabinet paper which argued that the EEC should be enlarged, should have minimal central powers and should concentrate on securing the benefits of free trade above all else. This, of course, was in line with long-standing British concerns and it predictably won Cabinet approval, but it upset pro-marketeers and the European Commission (who learnt of it via Jenkins' contacts in London and via leaks to the press).[63] Further evidence of Callaghan's political difficulties came in October when he issued a policy statement on Europe for the benefit of the party conference. Although the statement ruled out withdrawal it upset other Community members by advocating CAP reform, opposing greater centralisation and supporting EEC expansion mainly as a way to weaken supranationalism.[64] Two new issues in particular caused problems for Callaghan: direct elections to the European Parliament and a renewed attempt to co-ordinate currencies.

Direct elections to the European Parliament had been agreed on in principle at the Paris Summit in 1974. They had long been favoured by Italy and the Benelux powers as a way to limit French and German power. Giscard now supported the idea as a way to improve democratic control of Community institutions, invigorate the EEC and please French pro-Europeans. Benn and others feared that a directly elected parliament was likely to grow in stature and power, threatening national independence,[65] but in December 1975 the European Council agreed to proceed. In September 1976 Callaghan accepted mid-1978 as the date for the first Euro-elections, but the Cabinet was still divided: Denis Healey believed there was little threat to the authority of Westminster, because the Strasbourg parliament had only limited powers to influence legislation, but Benn and Michael Foot strongly disagreed. The Lib–Lab pact particularly complicated the issue, because Liberals not only supported direct elections, they also favoured a proportional (PR) system of voting. Most Labour MPs were reluctant to undermine the British 'first-past-the-post' electoral system, from which they benefited. However, in February 1977, David Owen put a paper on PR in Euro-elections to the Cabinet and, to avoid a Lib–Lab rupture on the issue, Callaghan agreed to a free vote – even for ministers – on this question in the Commons.[66] In November parliament approved Euro-elections but, despite Callaghan's vote in favour, the PR option was defeated. As a result the bill had to be reintroduced. Callaghan was then unable to meet the 1978 election date. Thanks to Britain, the EEC had to set the elections back a year. By then, Labour had lost office.

In a speech in Florence on 27 October 1977 Roy Jenkins revived the idea of a currency union as a way to galvanise the EEC, provide his Presidency with a major initiative, boost trade, and thus tackle unemployment. The speech had a lukewarm response, not least from Jenkins' former Cabinet colleagues in London, but in February 1978 the currency theme was suddenly taken up (on less ambitious lines than Jenkins') by Helmut Schmidt. The German Chancellor was growing in personal popularity and confidence after four difficult years in office, but he was under considerable pressure from the US and some European governments to reflate the German economy as a way to expand trade and so restore growth to the Western economies. This he was reluctant to do because of the failure of other Western states to tackle inflation. Schmidt's personal relations with US President Jimmy Carter were far from good, and the declining value of the Dollar against the Deutschmark (DM) – now a more important trading currency than Sterling – was reducing the competitiveness of German goods. By placing the DM in a stable monetary zone Schmidt could reduce its volatility and improve Germany's trade performance. Peter Ludlow has written a revealing study of the issue which shows that the Chancellor developed his plans carefully.[67] He first won over Giscard. Then at the European Council in Copenhagen in April, Schmidt proposed that the EEC should move towards a zone of currency stability. Callaghan, who was surprised by the initiative and Giscard's support for it, showed little liking for the proposal, fearing it would upset relations with the US. However, after excluding Britain from their earlier discussions, Giscard and Schmidt now undertook to set up a study group (kept secret from other EEC members) on a Franco-German-British basis. Callaghan, reluctant to be isolated, agreed.[68]

With the economy showing some improvement, Callaghan was in the most confident phase of his premiership in mid-1978. But there were several reasons, according to Peter Ludlow and David Owen, why he did not wish to accept Schmidt's currency proposals. First, Callaghan had a friendly relationship with Carter and favoured a joint US–EEC approach to growth, trade and the energy crisis. Second, the Treasury remained sceptical about the possibility of European currency co-operation and feared that, if it were achieved, it would simply restrict Britain's ability to manage Sterling. Owen also says Callaghan feared the reaction of the Labour Left; this is true, but Ludlow convincingly argues that it only became a vital factor later in the year. As a result of these doubts, the Treasury official sent to negotiate with the Germans and French after Copenhagen soon distanced himself from the talks.[69] (There were echoes here of Britain's policy towards the Spaak Committee of 1955.) As a result it was a Franco-German proposal which formed the basis of discussion at the next European Council, in Bremen in July, when it was agreed to draft a detailed European Monetary System (EMS). Only after this break-through, which made Germany the driving force in Community devel-opments, did Schmidt agree to reflate the German economy somewhat. British officials played a full role in technical discussions over the sum-mer, but in September the Chancellor of the Exchequer, Denis Healey, made it clear Britain would not join the EMS as a full member. Callaghan had tried to keep his options open on EMS as long as possible, preventing full Cabinet discussion of the issue until late in the year. But, after failing to call an election over the summer, he was committed to holding one in 1979 and, faced by this, could not risk upsetting the trade unions and 'anti-market' ministers. Even elements in the Conservative party opposed EMS, despite Thatcher's attacks on Callaghan for failing to join. At the Brussels Economic Council in December, Britain placed Sterling in a 'basket' of currencies which defined the new European Currency Unit (ECU), which was used in EEC financial calculations in future. How-ever, Britain did not join the Exchange Rate Mechanism (ERM) – the essential element in the EMS which pegged currency values against each other. Despite doubts from France about the details of EMS, the system became operational in March 1979.[70] By then widespread strikes during the 'winter of discontent' had destroyed Callaghan's hopes of winning the 1979 election.

Once again Britain had refused to take part in an important initiative in European co-operation. Indeed in the late 1970s – with the Franco-German axis reforged and Britain close to the US – an observer could be forgiven for thinking little had changed in the previous ten years. In 1970 when Heath had determinedly set out on the road to membership it seemed the EEC would continue to foster economic growth among its members and to increase in political significance. In the 1960s many political scientists who studied European integration foresaw the grad-ual, but inevitable, development of European state institutions as co-operation between EC members became more complex. Writers such as Ernst Haas and Leon Lindberg (known as 'neo-functionalists') analysed the success of European integration since 1950 and concluded that co-operation between Community members in one area (such as freer trade) tended to 'spill over' into others (such as monetary co-operation). This process, they reasoned, was likely to continue in future, eventually creating a genuine federation.[71] But, on the political side, member states had long sought their own particular aims in the Community, the 1966 Luxembourg Compromise had already emphasised national power in the EEC, and the creation of the European Council increased the power of national governments; whilst, on the economic front, 'stagflation' simultaneously destroyed any hope of EMU and ended the high growth of EEC members. By the time Britain joined the EEC, British leaders could justifiably claim that Federation was not a prospect in the short term. The predictions of the 'neo-functionalists' had proved false. British people decided in 1975 that EEC membership was a better alternative than withdrawal, but the lukewarm attitude of Wilson and Callaghan to any idea of 'European Union' – even one far short of a federation – was widely shared, and few people in Britain were concerned about the country's exclusion from the ERM.

6

THATCHER AND THE REVIVAL
OF EUROPEAN INTEGRATION,
1979–1990

The Debate over Policy in 1979

After the indecision of Callaghan's government, many pro-marketeers welcomed Margaret Thatcher's election victory in May 1979. With a clear majority, a manifesto declaring there was no alternative to Community membership and previous statements in favour of the European Monetary System (EMS), Thatcher seemed to promise a determined but positive attitude towards the EEC. Roy Jenkins was one who believed that the new government would improve relations with the EEC although, in his first meeting with Thatcher, he found the new Prime Minister to be determined to secure British interests in such areas as the budget contribution.[1] It soon transpired however, that Thatcher, though she demonstrated the same vigour on Europe that was evident in her other policies, was no unquestioning pro-marketeer. Far from it. It is true that she saw no alternative to EEC membership, but in that she was no different to Harold Wilson, and – ironically, given her deep contempt for Wilson's pragmatic leadership style – she soon began to resemble the ex-Labour premier in her European policy. She did not threaten withdrawal as Wilson did, but she adopted a nationalist approach to EEC issues, used this to secure popular support at home and wanted to be seen 'winning' arguments rather than seeking compromises. Indeed, whatever changes she brought to domestic politics, her policy abroad was in line with traditional aspects of British foreign policy: suspicion of European commitments, a strong defence and a close alliance with America.

There were always signs that Thatcher would prove a sceptic where European unity was concerned. Those who elected her as Conservative leader in 1975 included all the party's anti-market MPs. She played only a minor role in the common market referendum, considering it 'Ted's issue'.[2] In contrast to Heath, Thatcher represented the free market, anti-state wing of Conservatism, contemptuous of 'consensus politics' and determined to make Britain an enterprise economy. Hugo Young has pointed out that when she was Opposition leader her speeches depicted the EEC simply as a way to consolidate Western Europe against Communism. On the EEC, a leading Conservative described her as 'an agnostic who continues to go to church'.[3] The only areas in which she wished to develop Community activity were defence and foreign policy, to strengthen Britain's international voice. The 1979 Conservative manifesto included such well-established British demands as a fair fisheries policy, reform of the CAP, enlargement of the Community, 'outward-looking' trade policies and a limited British budget contribution. The Conservatives had criticised Labour's failure to join the exchange rate mechanism (ERM) but, once in power, Thatcher maintained Callaghan's policy. Britain was ready to use the currency unit (ECU) where appropriate, but not to enter the all-important ERM. When pressed to join the ERM as a way to stabilise the value of Sterling and boost trade in Europe, Chancellor of the Exchequer Geoffrey Howe repeatedly said that Britain would join when conditions were 'right'. The 1979 oil price rises, high inflation and volatile interest rates produced renewed economic problems in Western Europe, and from 1979 to 1983 there were many alterations in the ERM's central rate, which thus failed to bring real currency stability until the mid-1980s. However, the real reason for Thatcher's refusal to enter the scheme seems to have been the desire to pursue monetarist economic policies in isolation from the continentals.

Thatcher's scepticism about European involvements can only have been strengthened, at the start of her government, by the popular lack of enthusiasm for the first direct elections to the European Parliament, held on 7 June 1979. Fewer people voted in Britain, as a percentage of the electorate, than anywhere else in the Community, and the results simply mirrored votes for political parties at national level (though the latter problem was common to the whole Community). EEC membership had certainly brought no great economic gains to Britain since 1973. Opinion polls showed growing dissatisfaction with the Community since the referendum, and the depression of 1979–81 could only have a further negative effect. Meanwhile, apart from EMS, the Euro-elections and negotiations on Greek entry (which took place in 1981), the EEC was still in the doldrums it had entered in 1973, with limited economic growth and divisions among the members on a host of issues. The scene was thus set for Margaret Thatcher's crusade to cut British costs in the EEC.

Thatcher's budget crusade was not the only course open to Britain in 1979. One alternative was the pro-Community policy of the FO. David Owen too, in the closing months of the Labour government, had been planning tough talks on Britain's financial contribution, and was ready to veto CAP price increases in order to put pressure on Britain's partners for concessions. According to his memoirs, Owen came to believe that 'Community membership is a continuous negotiation' and that British interests had to be constantly defended by shifting alliances with other members.[4] But Owen's policy had drawn the wrath of pro-Europeanists in the Foreign Office. One diplomat, Nicholas Henderson, used his last telegram as Ambassador to France to advocate a more positive policy. The telegram was 'leaked' and published by *The Economist* in June. It gave Thatcher clear warning of FO attitudes. Henderson traced Britain's decline relative to Germany and France since the war and complained 'we are not only no longer a world power, but we are not in the first rank even as a European one'. Centuries-old certainties had been overturned, he said (with some exaggeration of past British power), because Britain could no longer prevent any other single power dominating the Continent. He admitted Britain's decline was largely due to economic under-performance, and spent a lot of time analysing management–union difficulties in industry. But he also complained about diplomatic failures since 1945 when, he claimed (with more exaggeration) Britain 'had every Western European government ready to eat out of our hand'; Britain had failed to take the leadership of European integration, failed to prevent the EEC emerging as a rival and could not even intrude on the Franco-German partnership: 'It is sometimes said . . . that if . . . we pursued our interests in Europe as ruthlessly as the French did we would have a scoring rate as high as theirs. This is another example of how we overestimate our influence . . . [We] do not count in Europe like the French.' Unfortunately this forceful document was thin on solutions to Britain's EEC dilemma, except to argue that London should behave 'as though we were fully . . . committed to Europe'. Britain could hope for material strengthening from North Sea oil and, with astute leadership, might begin to reverse its fortunes.[5]

A more detailed alternative policy to the budget crusade was suggested by a conference of academics and experts in 1979. Held under the auspices of such bodies as the Royal Institute of International Affairs, the conference accepted that Britain was in a difficult position in the EEC. In 1973 it had been forced to accept membership of a body which had been framed without it. Heath entertained hopes of negotiating changes to the EEC from within but had not got far; Wilson had tried a full-blown renegotiation under the threat of withdrawal but won no real concessions. Many experts believed Britain was condemned by its national attitudes to a peripheral role in the EEC. The lack of dynamic economic gains from membership, the fact that most of the improvement in trade with Europe was accounted for by North Sea oil, and the high net budget contribution all added to the feeling of pessimism. Nevertheless, the conference believed that a less ambivalent policy towards the Community was necessary and possible. Britain could gain from the EEC if it pressed for progress on certain fronts.

The question was: on which fronts? Some wanted a renewed attempt to expand the Regional Fund, which was likely to benefit Britain, but a 1977 EEC report had shown that an effective regional policy could double the Community budget; this was unlikely to appeal to the new, anti-interventionist, cost-cutting Prime Minister. David Marquand of Salford University suggested Britain should take the lead in reforming the EEC by strengthening the European Parliament. Marquand, a former Labour MP, believed such reforms would galvanise the EEC, create a common political outlook and lead to the reform of the CAP (of which many Euro-MPs were critical). But this policy lacked realism: Britain was unlikely to relish the idea of a strong, federalist parliament, whilst France and others were unlikely to welcome the destruction of the CAP. A more hopeful proposal was that Britain should concentrate on promoting economic reforms which benefited it but demanded little extra spending, or any institutional changes to the Community which could threaten British independence. The 'common market' principle could be expanded to areas such as banking and insurance, where Britain had trading advantages even over Germany; Britain, with its good record on enforcing Community rules, would also gain from getting regulations enforced fairly across the EEC; and by pressing for the removal of non-tariff barriers to commerce (such as customs formalities, currency regulations and differences in national safety standards) Britain would increase trade, push the EEC in the direction of a free trade area (a British aim since the 1950s), and achieve one of the original aims of the Treaty of Rome. This idea of a more positive British policy, which simultaneously served vital national interests, came to be supported by much of the Confederation of British Industry in the early 1980s and pointed the way to developments later in the decade, in 1984–5. But an early chance to pursue such a policy was missed, as the new government concentrated on an attempt to resolve the budget issue.[6]

The British Budgetary Question, 1979–84

The Conservative Cabinet contained several keen marketeers. The Foreign Secretary, Lord Carrington, hoped for a more concerted EEC policy towards international problems. Others favourable to the FO line were the foreign affairs spokesman in the Commons, Ian Gilmour, and Defence Minister Francis Pym. However, Thatcher refused to be dominated by these foreign policy experts. According to Hugo Young, she was soon advised by a Treasury official, Peter Middleton, that EEC membership (largely because Britain received so little from the CAP) was costing £1 billion a year.[7] The Treasury of course had frequently been less favourable to the EEC than the FO, and appealed to the Prime Minister's patriotic, cost-cutting instincts. She raised the budget issue in early meetings with Helmut Schmidt and Giscard d'Estaing (neither of whom she worked with well) and in a speech in Luxembourg in October she declared 'I cannot play Sister Bountiful to the Community'. She had successfully placed the budget item on the EEC agenda at her first European Council, at Strasbourg, in June. At that meeting her behaviour seemed reasonable (she had, for example, dropped Owen's threat to veto CAP price increases) and the conference agreed to draw up a report on the budgetary problem for the next summit, in Dublin.

It was this latter meeting, in November, which really inaugurated the struggle between Thatcher and the rest of the Community. According to EEC President Roy Jenkins, she bored and offended the other leaders by discussing the budget issue at great length, by demanding 'my money' back and refusing to compromise. She showed little understanding of the characters she was dealing with, and clashed with her own FO advisers, who blamed her performance on inexperience. Giscard and his officials caustically dismissed her as 'the grocer's daughter'. The French argued that Britain had already renegotiated its financial contribution and that, if it wished to pay less into the Community, it should concentrate its trade in Europe (reducing its susceptibility to the Common External Tariff). However, one of her sympathetic biographers, Patrick Cosgrave, has blamed the FO for failing to take Thatcher seriously and for giving continentals the impression she would compromise. Christopher Tugendhat, an EEC Commissioner at the time, has argued the other leaders *forced* her to fight when they only offered her a 'derisory' £350 million reduction in Britain's budget contribution. In her memoirs, Thatcher was characteristically unapologetic about her behaviour, insisting: 'I was completely sincere when I . . . said that Britain was asking no more than its due; and my anger when such a proposition was regarded with cynical indifference was equally genuine.'[8]

After Dublin, where no progress was made, Thatcher held firm. She refused to accept that certain revenues were the EEC's 'own resources'. She also rejected FO arguments that she could win concessions by using certain bargaining chips: sharing Britain's oil wealth perhaps, compromising on the terms of EEC fishing policy or joining the ERM. In early 1980 the British Budgetary Question (BBQ) dominated the Community agenda, despite a plethora of other vital issues: oil price inflation; recession and unemployment; and the renewed Cold War after the Soviet invasion of Afghanistan. Jenkins and the Italian leader Francesco Cossiga (current President of the EC) worked for a compromise behind the scenes, and at the April 1980 summit in Luxembourg Thatcher was offered quite a generous compromise, at least in the short term. Schmidt said the British net budget contribution should be limited to the average for 1978–9, which amounted to about a £760 million rebate. The same size of refund would be given in 1981 and meanwhile a permanent settlement would be studied. To general surprise, and despite the urgings of Jenkins, Carrington and FO chief Michael Palliser, Thatcher rejected the offer and another summit ended in failure. Nevertheless attempts to rework Schmidt's proposal continued and, at a tense Council of Ministers in late May, Carrington and Gilmour came away with a slightly improved offer. Thatcher was still unimpressed, but for once Cabinet ministers successfully put strong pressure on her to accept, including threats of resignation from Carrington and Gilmour.[9]

Thatcher had agreed to a compromise, but the BBQ went on because a permanent settlement was still needed. She had succeeded in limiting Britain's deficit on EEC payments for 1980 and 1981 without having to give any important concessions, and had impressed the public. Furthermore, her bargaining position seemed to be strengthening. The EEC, thanks to the increasing cost of the CAP, was desperately short of money and wanted governments to approve higher spending. Not only did Thatcher refuse to do this, she also widened her attack on the EEC in 1982, criticising the wastefulness of the CAP and the lack of budgetary restraint. Then her Agriculture Minister, Peter Walker, did what Owen had threatened in 1979, and vetoed the annual farm price increases. The 1966 'Luxembourg Compromise' was cited in justification. In May 1982 however, the majority of the EEC overrode Walker's veto: the French argued that farm prices could not be a 'vital, national interest' under the Luxembourg Compromise. By then the two sides seemed far apart, not only on internal Community issues but also on wider foreign policy, an area where Thatcher and Carrington had earlier hoped for co-operation. Whilst Giscard and Schmidt tried to keep détente with Moscow alive in Europe in 1980–1, Thatcher took a firm anti-Soviet line and established close links with America's President Reagan. The replacement of Giscard and Schmidt by, respectively, François Mitterrand (May 1981) and Helmut Kohl (October 1982) weakened Franco-German links for a time and gave Thatcher some advantages at EEC summits, where she was the best briefed of the three leaders. However, she failed to establish any rapport with the two newcomers. True, the EEC generally stood by Thatcher during the Falklands War with Argentina. Steps were also taken to reduce agricultural overproduction under the CAP. But in June 1982 Francis Pym, who had just succeeded Carrington as Foreign Secretary, was forced to accept another one-year compromise deal on the budget contribution.

A year later little had changed. The only notable event was a deal on fishing policy (a source of arguments since 1977) which gave Britain a third of Community fishing quotas – arguably less than it deserved, given the size of its fishing grounds. In June 1983, Thatcher, her popularity boosted by the Falklands War, was re-elected Prime Minister by a handsome margin. She told the EEC's Stuttgart summit that she would not resolve any other issues until the BBQ was permanently resolved, and she replaced the 'pro-European' Pym with one of her closest allies, Geoffrey Howe. According to John Dickie, in a work based on FO sources, the patient Howe proved an ideal foil to Thatcher in EC debates. A number of books were published at this time to mark the fact that Britain had been in the EEC for a decade. However, despite contributions from ardent pro-marketeers, these collections generally admitted that Community membership had brought neither great benefits nor great losses to Britain. This was a far cry from the extreme claims of the referendum campaign. The best pro-marketeers could do was to argue that Britain's failure to expand trade, improve investment and develop new technologies was due to internal British failings.[10] Labour pro-marketeers had now formally split from the party to form the Social Democratic Party (SDP) under Roy Jenkins, who had left the EEC Presidency. But the SDP failed to make big inroads into parliament. Meanwhile Labour itself, led by Michael Foot, hardened its anti-EEC line, proposing 'negotiated withdrawal'. This was part of an 'alternative economic strategy', aiming at central national direction of trade and investment. Such policies harked back to the old Socialist utopia of nationalisation at home and non-alignment abroad, and helped to decimate the Labour vote. In 1979 voters had marginally preferred Labour's policy on Europe to that of the Conservatives, but in 1983 Thatcher's policy was, according to Peter Riddell, 'undoubtedly effective domestically in out-manoeuvring Labour . . . [The] majority view could be characterised as favouring a strong assertion of British interests and accepting that British membership was now permanent. On both sides of this equation, Thatcher won.'[11]

Despite Thatcher's confident position at home however, profound changes were afoot in Europe which complicated her position enormously and soon lost her her short-lived dominance of the EEC. In retrospect the year after her re-election can be seen to have marked the resurgence of pressures for greater integration in the European Community, which highlighted Britain's vulnerability to outside pressures, even under the strongest leader. The French historian Georges Soutou has even argued that the French government became more committed to European integration in the mid-1980s than at any time since 1952, when Robert Schuman had ceased to be foreign minister. The precise dynamics of this change in French policy have yet to be adequately explained. Paul Taylor has persuasively argued that Mitterrand used the threat of deeper integration in 1984 to put pressure on Thatcher to settle the BBQ. This is probably true, but it does not fully explain why the French President supported greater integration or why he maintained his enthusiasm *after* the BBQ was resolved. Taylor reasons that Mitterrand's strategy 'acquired momentum because of dynamics recognised in the mid-1960s by neo-functionalist theorists', the group of academics who had argued that economic monetary co-operation in one area (such as a customs union) would 'spill over' into other areas (such as greater co-operation). However, this does not explain why the neo-functionalists should have proved correct in the mid-1980s when they had proved so mistaken over the previous 20 years. The integration process perhaps had a more favourable environment in the mid-1980s, as West European

economies recovered from a decade of poor performance. But integration also required firm political backing and Mitterrand was not the only
leader to take up the cause. Stephen George and John Pridham both
argue that the revival of integration was a reaction to US and Japanese
economic competition especially in new technology.[12] But such competition was a long-standing problem (certainly identified in the 1960s) and
again does not fully explain the political will behind the new drive
towards deeper integration.

The new drive for integration probably occurred for a number of
reasons. A desire to put pressure on Thatcher, and a need to improve
EC competitiveness and technology, were two. Favourable economic
circumstances aided the process. But there were other vital factors at
work. After years of disappointment since the 1973 enlargement, supporters of greater supranationalism desperately wanted to breathe new
life into the EEC. In 1981 the German and Italian foreign ministers,
Hans-Dietrich Genscher and Emilio Colombo, had proposed a major
overhaul of EC institutions. This led to a 'Declaration on European
Union' being issued at the June 1983 Stuttgart Summit. But the Declaration was so inoffensive – dressing up existing policies in flowery
language – that even Thatcher raised no objections to it. Initially her
confidence seemed well placed. After all, the hopes of the Italian and
Benelux governments for a stronger European Parliament and the
extension of majority votes in the Council of Ministers (designed to control the Franco-German axis) had never made progress in the past.
True, in February 1984, in the European Parliament (EP) federalists led
by Italy's Altiero Spinelli pushed through a 'Draft Treaty on European
Union', to make EC central institutions stronger and more democratic.
But the EP was still largely a consultative body and the Draft Treaty
could simply be ignored by governments, even if many member governments expressed sympathy for it.

A more pressing need for action came from the proposed 'southern
enlargement' of the Community to Greece (which entered in 1981),
Spain and Portugal. Callaghan's government had hoped that a *wider*
Community would mean a *weakening* of centralist tendencies. Actually
the opposite proved to be the case. True, Greece's Socialist government
threatened to leave the EC and so outdid Thatcher in anti-Europeanism.
But Spain and Portugal were eager to develop the Community, believing
it offered economic salvation and bolstered their liberal democratic institutions. Both countries had been ruled by dictators, from before the
Second World War to the mid-1970s, and, like Germany and Italy after

1945, they wished to co-operate closely with other democracies. Further-more, in contrast to the 1973 enlargement, the new members were among the poorest in Europe, a fact which strengthened the arguments in favour of greater regional aid, to ensure even development of the EC. This meant more pressures for a larger EC budget and stronger central institutions to manage the changes. (It also meant that Britain would gain a smaller share of the Regional Fund.) It was not until June 1984 however, that the entry date (of January 1986) was confirmed for Spain and Portugal.

What was most significant in 1983–4 was the change of French policy towards integration, and the revival of Franco-German co-operation, which had always been the backbone of progress in the EC, but which had weakened since 1981. These changes can best be explained by events in France in 1981–3. West Germany, under such firm pro-Europeans as Kohl and Genscher, continued to anchor itself firmly to the EC. Chancellor Kohl after 1982 continued to support a strong ERM, the southern enlargement and, despite the potential costs to Germany, a larger EC budget. But in 1981–3 the new Socialist government in France had pursued radical policies at home which had elements in common with the 1983 Labour manifesto. Whilst other countries were pursuing Thatcher's lead, and adopting privatisation and free market economics, Mitterrand presided over nationalisation, higher social spending and wage increases in a bid to cut unemployment and maintain demand. By March 1983 however, the budgetary costs of this policy were enormous. Not only that, but such policies upset the value of the Franc, necessitating several changes in ERM rates and putting relations with Germany at risk. Mitterrand was thus forced to retreat, introducing austerity measures at home and embracing economic interdependence abroad. The President was forced to acknowledge that no modern trading power could cut itself off from the wider world in pursuit of a Marxist utopia. France gained enormously from European trade and the CAP, and the economic value of the EC was driven home at this time. So was its political significance: the danger of losing the German alliance strengthened Mitterrand in his determination to revive EC integration and to move beyond Pompidou and Giscard in his willingness to embrace far-reaching co-operation. This *did not* mean that he wished to lose power to a European federation, but he was ready to surrender more decisions to the EC Commission and to extend majority voting in the Council of Ministers.

Deeper integration had not been seen as a realistic prospect in Europe since de Gaulle's day. Wilson and Heath had brushed aside suggestions in 1967, 1971 and 1975 that it was a menace to Britain. Now, however, a renewed threat to national sovereignty seemed a real possibility, and could stir controversy in Britain. Of course, Britain could refuse to take part in any changes to the Treaty of Rome, which required unanimous agreement. But such tactics would create the danger of a 'two-tier Europe': those countries in favour of reform might simply sign a new treaty leaving Britain, Greece and other doubters behind. This could put Britain back where it was before 1973, sidelined in Europe, without direct influence on the continentals. It was not an experience Mrs Thatcher wished to repeat and many in government insisted 'there is no alternative' to following deeper integration. However, if Thatcher could not turn the tide, she might at least hope to direct it on the most acceptable course and in 1983–4, albeit with some reticence, she agreed to develop policies to achieve this. In particular the FO encouraged her to press for EC initiatives in areas which could benefit Britain, such as foreign policy co-operation, free trade in services and the end of non-tariff barriers to trade – ideas which had appealed to Francis Pym and which, of course, had been suggested in 1979. As Paul Taylor has noted, in order to protect British national interests Thatcher was now forced to make concessions to the EC, for the threat of a 'two-tier' Europe 'opened up the prospect of a more supranational inner core which the UK could only join at the expense of its sovereignty'.[13] An early sign of the government's new tendency was Geoffrey Howe's statement in November 1983 that Britain was as *communitaire* as anyone else. However, it did not seem that way to other Europeans, for the BBQ remained unresolved. At the Athens Summit, in December, Mitterrand refused all concessions to Thatcher and the European Council could not even agree on a communiqué.

In January 1984 France assumed the six-month Presidency of the EC. Mitterrand was determined to use his country's diplomatic resources to resolve the BBQ at last, but without too many concessions to Thatcher. At the Brussels Summit in March, British and French officials seemed close to a compromise. For the first time the French accepted the idea of a formula which would define when rebates should be given on budget contributions. However, this system would apply to *all* members (Britain would not be a special case), it would only include VAT payments (not EC earnings from external tariffs) and it would be accompanied by increased VAT payments overall, to resolve the EC's financial problems and pay for Spanish and Portuguese entry. But it proved impossible for the leaders to agree on exactly how much money should be returned to Britain. Thatcher proved characteristically tough and a disenchanted Kohl refused to continue the talks. After this summit, acrimony reached new heights. The British Cabinet, it was revealed, had considered ending all payments to the EC, exploiting the Community's financial vulnerability; the French talked of excluding Britain from the new EC initiatives, thus threatening a two-tier Europe.[14] Such threats, however, simply showed both sides the dangers of disagreement. Three months later at Fontaine-bleau, another summit agreed to a budget deal largely on the Brussels lines. In future (until financial arrangements were altered) members would receive a rebate of two-thirds on the difference between their VAT contributions and their receipts from the EC. Britain was also promised tighter spending controls on the CAP but VAT payments from all members were increased from 1 to 1.4 per cent.

Fontainebleau was equally notable however, for the signs of forward progress in the EC, now the BBQ was removed. Two committees were established, to report in 1985 on possible reforms. One under Italy's Pietro Adonnino produced proposals on a 'People's Europe', which eventually led to common passports and driving licences. More important was the French-inspired 'Ad Hoc Committee', under Ireland's James Dooge, to investigate institutional reform. At the time it attracted little media attention, and appeared like an attempt to frighten Thatcher. But Thatcher showed that she knew of the dangers when she circulated a paper at Fontainbleau entitled 'Europe – the Future' which advocated closer co-operation on foreign, environmental and technological policies, and a 'single market' to end all non-tariff barriers to trade. The paper was her most favourable statement on Europe to date. Although it showed no desire to take up the institutional reforms embraced by Spinelli's 'European Union', and whilst it reflected a mixture of Thatcher's free market philosophy (there was no support for European activity in the social and monetary fields) and traditional British interests, the paper did show that Britain could accept some progress in Europe. There was little chance of Greece, Denmark or neutralist Ireland taking up co-operation in the field of defence but many leaders, including Mitterrand, *were* attracted to the idea of a 'single market', which would boost growth, make Europe more competitive with America and Japan, and compensate for the fact that *global* negotiations on freer trade were currently stalled. As early as the December 1982 Copenhagen Summit, in fact, the Community leaders had discussed the desirability of freeing their internal market more fully. Even Germany, which might possibly lose out to Britain in any free competition in banking and insurance, proved ready to accept the 'single market' in order to ensure some progress in Europe.[15]

The 'Single Market' and the Challenge of Integration, 1985–8

In the early 1980s Margaret Thatcher had scotched all progress in the EEC but in June 1984 the BBQ was resolved. Geoffrey Howe later insisted that the Fontainebleau deal justified Thatcher's approach, showed the need for financial restraint in Europe, and opened the way to a more positive British policy, which put the Community on the road to the Single European Act. Other pro-Thatcher writers, such as Patrick Cosgrave, praise her patriotism and clarity of purpose in securing the budget rebate. Shirley Letwin considers Fontainebleau 'an impressive victory', and Stephen George sees it as significant that Thatcher also secured limits on the CAP budget. And Paul Sharp points out that – in contrast to the image created by both her supporters and her critics – she was really quite restrained in her tactics, never actually trying to wreck the work of the EC or threatening to withdraw from it. Paul Taylor is not impressed by her policy but has argued that the BBQ was merely one factor in the *immobilisme* which dogged the EEC between 1973 and 1984: Thatcher reinforced a tendency to stagnation which was already there.[16] Even in 1984 however, there were many strong critics of her policy. As Ali El-Agraa pointed out, the amounts of money involved in the BBQ were not that great. The *total* EC budget was only equivalent to a large British department of state, absorbing about 1 per cent of members' national income. The Fontainebleau deal did not win much more for Britain than had been available for months before, it was open to review in future and involved the concession of increased VAT payments. It did not stop the budget growing in future. Ian Gilmour insists that the FO always aimed at a two-thirds rebate and that Thatcher originally wanted more. It could easily be argued that Thatcher had done most to delay a settlement: by taking a firm line she threatened to humiliate other leaders and so forced them to resist her. Alterations to the CAP, such as the use of quotas to reduce overproduction, were only minor, leaving the Policy basically intact. (A real overhaul, with a shift to the British preferred system of income subsidies, was only agreed in 1992.) Roy Jenkins criticised Thatcher for a lack of tactical skill, for blowing the budget's importance out of all proportion, and allowing it to dominate events for five years. Carrington and Pym both criticised her for producing a difficult atmosphere in the Community and Hugo Young has argued that she missed the chance to put her own initiatives forward.

However there is another, very different, argument against Thatcher which suggests, in the words of David Reynolds, that her 'insistence on national sovereignty was unreal': her policy reinforced the popular idea that Britain could still act independently, but this masked a growing loss of power to the EC. By 1984 Britain had accepted numerous directives from the EC Commission with little parliamentary scrutiny; and the British economy was now constrained by the need to compete in the common market. Interdependence, not independence, had long been the order of the day and Thatcher's interest in a single, free market was likely to increase the trend. Paul Taylor argues that, in the end, Thatcher's behaviour helped bring the greater integration she opposed. For, at Fontainebleau, Mitterrand and Kohl learnt that she could be outflanked by the threat of a 'two-tier' Europe.[17] Over the following years the supranational threat grew, ultimately helping to destroy her premiership.

In 1985 attention shifted from the BBQ to the issue of reform, with some members ready to accept stronger central institutions, closer economic integration and higher spending. In these debates Thatcher's priorities were clear: she favoured a single free market as well as foreign policy co-operation; she wished to control spending, not only on the CAP but also on regional aid; and she opposed strengthening the European Parliament or the Commission. In following this programme David Reynolds argues that 'to some extent the British were simply more honest about their pursuit of national self-interest. All their partners were playing the same game', such as the French in defending the CAP, or the Germans in supporting the ERM.[18] Thatcher simply did not deal in the hypocrisy of pretending her policies had universal benefits akin to the Rights of Man. But she still stood out, alongside the Greeks and Danes, as being most reluctant to take a general plunge into deeper integration. At the Brussels Council of March 1985 EC leaders asked the Commission to draw up a timetable to create a genuine 'single market'. This complex job, involving hundreds of measures to end customs, capital and currency controls, was given to a British Commissioner, Lord Cockfield. The scale of this task underlines the point that Thatcher's own policies could lead to a vast increase in EC power. For the whole exercise required uniform regulations across the Community, and had to be managed by Brussels. Furthermore it was soon argued that greater common practices were needed to bring the single market into effect: Cockfield soon claimed, for example, that VAT must be equalised across the Community – a view Thatcher rejected.

At the Milan Council three months later it was agreed in principle to achieve the single market by the end of 1992, and Thatcher even agreed to abandon the use of the veto on items necessary to fulfil the 1992 deadline. It was in Milan, however, that Kohl, Mitterrand, Italy and the Benelux governments set out to tie the single market into a wider set of reforms. The summit received the report of the Dooge Committee, the ad hoc group set up to look at institutional reform in June 1984. Despite criticisms from Britain, this Committee recommended linking the single market to a new treaty, which would strengthen EC institutions and give members a common identity. The treaty would be drawn up by an Inter-Governmental Conference (IGC). Thatcher saw no need for institutional reforms, arguing that present structures were adequate. But after some ill-tempered discussions the Council chairman, Italy's Bettino Craxi, called for an unprecedented majority vote to set up the IGC. Only Britain, Greece and Denmark voted against. Howe, who increasingly came to call Thatcher's European tactics into question, believed that Craxi was tempted into using such tactics 'as a reaction above all to the sharp tone of British leadership'.

Thatcher could have refused to attend the IGC. This, however, would have brought into existence the much-feared 'two-tier' Europe. Britain was back to the dilemma of 1955 surrounding Messina: it could stand aside from the talks, be accused of obstructing progress and lose influence over future European integration; or it must join in and become implicated in the results. But by 1985 Britain was committed to a European future. British industry and financiers in the City needed EC markets, and Community membership attracted outside investment to the UK, especially from Japan. Besides, the IGC, though it threatened to strengthen EC institutions, was itself made up of *government* representatives and had to reach agreement on a unanimous basis. Drives towards greater supranationalism had failed to advance in the past, and it was doubtful whether the French and German governments were ready to surrender large areas of decision-making to any Euro-federation. In addition, several Cabinet ministers were strongly committed to the EEC. (In January 1986 the pro-European Defence Minister Michael Heseltine was to resign over the question of whether a helicopter company should be sold to an American, rather than a European, bidder.[19]) These considerations, strongly backed by the FO, led Thatcher in July to agree to attend the IGC – though without playing a leading role. The IGC met in September and produced a draft 'Single European Act' (SEA) for the next European Council, in December.

The SEA, the first major overhaul of the Treaty of Rome, was dressed in Euro-rhetoric, but largely codified policies which had already developed since 1957. For example it formally defined the Regional Fund, and made 'European Political Cooperation' (on foreign policy, which had developed since the early 1970s, and to which the British were favourable) formally part of EC activities. Its most important feature included the commitment to a single market by 1992. There were other extensions of Community activity, for example, to social, environmental and technological questions (but it was not clear this would mean much in practice). And there were institutional reforms: the powers of the European Parliament were slightly increased; the powers of the Commission were clarified; and, most significantly, the Act extended the use of majority votes in the Council of Ministers, thus restricting Britain's power of veto. It certainly came as a disappointment to the federalist movement, and to the Italian and Benelux governments. In Denmark, more sceptical about reform, a referendum approved the SEA in February 1986. And in Britain the Act was accepted by Thatcher and easily approved by parliament.

Officials argued that the SEA was no great threat to British sovereignty. It was claimed that the single market could be created without harmonising EC policies in such areas as VAT, employment law and the free movement of people across borders, points which had worried Thatcher. The concessions that were involved on the institutional side seemed justified by the commitment to a single market which Britain wanted. It was certainly better than a 'two-tier' split in the EC. Thatcher and her FO advisers had reached an uneasy truce around a policy which Paul Taylor has described as 'minimis[ing] concessions to the European centre, while obtaining specific ends'. However, the real reason why the SEA was so limited in scope was that Mitterrand and Kohl had their own specific programmes, which involved the threat of a 'two-tier' Europe but not its implementation. As Philip Budden has argued, the SEA did represent a significant turning point: the British government had been forced to accept much wider reforms than it originally wanted, the powers of the Community's institutions had undergone a real increase, and the Act included certain promises of future action whose significance was at first vastly underestimated. In particular there was a commitment to monetary union that 'provided a base from which the Commission President could launch [a] campaign in favour of a single currency'. This would soon cause Thatcher grave difficulties.[20]

In June 1987 (a month before the SEA came into force) Thatcher was re-elected Prime Minister by a clear margin. Since 1983 Labour had reluctantly abandoned the threat to leave the EC. This was partly to compete for centre votes and to allow the party to criticise Thatcher's policies, but it also reflected growing links to European Socialist parties, and an appreciation that the EC could tackle unemployment and social problems. In December 1986, as chairman of the London Summit, Thatcher had pressed the other EC leaders to reduce unemployment (then at a high level) by the use of free market methods, but most Community leaders favoured higher state spending and the redistribution of wealth, which had more in common with Labour views. Labour's wish to remain in Europe also showed that the lessons of the French experience in 1981–3 had been learnt: the world economy was interdependent and no West European state could pursue Socialist policies in isolation. Once re-elected, Thatcher set out to prepare Britain for 1992. Her Trade and Industry Minister, Lord Young, launched an 'awareness campaign' in British industry.[21] But the danger was ever present that 1992 could 'spill over' and lead to deeper integration in other areas. In June 1987, at a summit meeting in Brussels, which discussed the impact of Spanish and Portuguese entry, it was proposed to expand spending on regional aid but Thatcher opposed this, arguing that it was first necessary to decide on controls on CAP spending. It was her ambition, more than ever, in her third term, to make the Community more disciplined financially, especially where the CAP was concerned. Other members now had a useful weapon to wield against Thatcher however: if EC income was increased, then the whole 1984 budget settlement would be thrown into question, and Britain might lose the deal made at Fontainebleau. This threat helped to secure a compromise at a special summit held in Brussels in February 1988. After some tense moments, the Fontainebleau system of budget rebates was left intact and certain limits on CAP spending were agreed, but in return Britain had to accept a doubling of spending on regional and social funds to help the Mediterranean countries. Thatcher had secured budget restraints in the EC, with annual ceilings on income and expenditure, but the deal nonetheless meant higher British payments.

In June 1988, at a European Council in Hanover, another challenge to Thatcher grew more serious when, to some surprise, a majority of leaders led by Mitterrand supported a study of European economic and monetary union (EMU). This, of course, was not a new idea. It had been suggested at the Hague Summit in 1969 and was mentioned in the SEA. Once the single market was being prepared it could be argued that a currency union was a logical accompanying step. If the EC was to have a single market, why should it not have a single monetary system, which could help create a stable, thriving economy? The new study was put in the hands of a Committee of central bank governors under Jacques Delors, who had been President of the EC Commission since 1985. Delors was a French Socialist, close to Mitterrand, sympathetic to *dirigiste* economics and to supranationalism. Few backgrounds could have been less appealing to Thatcher, yet in the absence of an alternative candidate, she actually seconded his appointment to a second term as President. Delors was not the fanatical Euro-federalist which the British press depicted, but he did believe that the SEA should lead to a deepening of economic, social and political unity in Europe. EMU had the potential to bring this about, because a currency union could well lead on to a common budgetary policy (needed to stabilise the currency) and this in turn could deeply affect each member's economic and social policies. Thatcher, for whom the Pound Sterling was a symbol of national sovereignty, made her opposition to EMU clear. She contemptuously declared that she did not expect to see a European central bank in her lifetime 'nor, if I'm twanging a harp, for quite a long time afterwards' and she privately believed that the proposal would be opposed on the Delors Committee by the governors of the British and German central banks. Her Chancellor of the Exchequer, Nigel Lawson, hastily put forward a scheme which would allow members' currencies to compete against each other for use throughout the EC. Unfortunately for the Treasury, no one else thought it a serious or workable proposal, and it was all too clearly intended to steal the initiative from Delors.

Lawson himself recognised that it was becoming impossible to resist integration in Europe. In 1985 he had forced a discussion in the government about the benefits of ERM membership, which was seen as one way to stabilise the value of the Pound (at a time when it was falling against the Dollar) and provide a mechanism for controlling inflation (which the government's earlier attempts at setting monetary targets had failed to do). Howe and some other ministers were sympathetic but Thatcher was not, fearing that ERM membership could invite *greater* speculation against Sterling and believing that Britain would do better to control its own economic destiny as far as possible. Despite the outcome of the 1985 debate, Lawson 'shadowed' the value of the Deutschmark in 1987–8, both to stabilise the Pound and as a step towards entry to the ERM. The ERM had proven a success for its members in bringing inflation down in the mid-1980s and Lawson, supported by Howe, had become convinced that membership was necessary to hold down prices in Britain. But he was criticised by Thatcher (who claims she was left in the dark about the policy for several months) and her personal economic adviser, Alan Walters. In any event 'shadowing' the Deutschmark failed to prevent inflation running out of control in 1988 and a trade deficit appearing: some even argued that it contributed to these problems. Britain's economic 'miracle' of the mid-1980s turned into an unsustainable 'boom'. With a weakening economy behind her, and falling oil output, Thatcher was less well placed to take on the rest of the Community. Germany remained the dominant economic force.[22]

The strongest statement of Thatcher's alternative vision of Europe was made in Bruges on 20 September 1988. Shirley Letwin considers this 'one of the . . . great set-pieces of Thatcherism'. John Dickie has shown that the speech, though based on an FO draft, was rewritten by Thatcher's foreign policy adviser, Charles Powell. In some ways Thatcher sounded like de Gaulle, advocating a Europe built around sovereign states not 'some identikit European personality'. Like de Gaulle, she also hoped to build foreign policy and defence co-operation in the EC, though so far this had not progressed (partly, it must be said, because of her insistence on pressing her own policies on such issues as sanctions against South Africa). To an extent her themes were reminiscent of old British concerns, especially the fear of federalism, the preference for a free trade area in Europe, and the desire for a Community 'open to the world'. However the Bruges speech very much defended her own 'new Right' viewpoint, which coupled national sovereignty with free market economics. Thus, she warned Delors, 'we have not . . . rolled back the frontiers of the state in Britain only to see them re-imposed . . . [by] a European super-state'. Socialist-style interference in social and budgetary issues was unnecessary; the EC should act to help its member states, partly by creating a single market in which to compete, but it should not attack their independence. The speech also included jingoistic references to the Magna Carta! Yet, however powerful the speech, and however popular with the Conservative press, it could not sway many from the belief that her vision was impossible. Paul Taylor has drawn out the speech's key defect: it was difficult to see how the Prime Minister's dream of a single market could be achieved without *greater* powers being transferred to EC institutions in order to manage the process.[23] The best Thatcher could hope for, if Mitterrand and others were determined to proceed, was a delaying action, to slow integration down. Meanwhile, even ministers such as Howe and Lawson were beginning to doubt the wisdom of her European policy.

The Fall of Thatcher

In April 1989 the Delors Report was published. More radical than Thatcher had hoped, it proposed to bring about EMU in three phases. Phases Two and Three would involve the gradual loss of monetary independence by member states, the creation of a European central bank and perhaps a common currency. This was vital, in the French view, to prevent a German-dominated body. Once again, it was the desire to control German economic might which was at the heart of French thinking. But in Phase One all that was envisaged was the closer alignment of currency values via the ERM. A month later the EC Commission further challenged Thatcher's Bruges policy when it published a 'Social Charter' to protect people from possible adverse effects of the single market. This highlighted the difference between Thatcher's *laissez faire* doctrine and the continental belief in a 'social market', where the impact of capitalism was tempered by state intervention and social reform. The Social Charter was not a radical document in itself. It laid down minimal conditions for education, employment and social security, most of which Britain could easily fulfil. But it could lead on to more extensive social legislation in future and Thatcher adamantly opposed such 'interventionism', seeing it as a threat to British competitiveness. This view was not shared by British trade unions who, like the Labour party, were now moving in favour of the EC. Trade unions faced common problems across Europe (such as unemployment and threats from new technology) and the EC was seen as a body which could limit Thatcherism. In September 1988 TUC President Clive Jenkins – who had opposed EC membership in the 1975 referendum but now admitted 'I got it wrong' – had invited Delors to speak to the TUC conference, where he won a standing ovation after outlining his plans to protect workers' rights in the single market.[24]

By June 1989, when the Delors Report and the Social Charter came before the Madrid European Council, Thatcher's problems were also growing *within* the British government. The economy was in trouble, with increasing inflation and a massive trade deficit; the potential electoral consequences were brought home when Labour easily won most seats in that month's elections to the European Parliament. Just before Madrid, Howe and Lawson put heavy pressure on Thatcher to set a timetable for joining the ERM. They even threatened resignation, an act condemned by one Thatcher loyalist, Nicholas Ridley, as an 'ambush'. Faced by such a combination, which united the FO and Treasury behind a common European policy, Thatcher agreed to define the conditions for ERM entry more fully than before. These included lower British inflation and progress with the single market. The Prime Minister believed that this made little difference to the policy pursued since 1979, which said Britain would join the ERM 'when the time was right'. Actually, however, her new 'conditions', so formally set out, led to expectations that Britain would soon join. Such expectations were reinforced by the decision at Madrid to achieve Phase One of the Delors Plan (currency alignment via the ERM) by July 1990. But Thatcher managed to delay any timetable for Phases Two and Three, and still hoped that Germany would be unready to accept the burdens of EMU. She also refused to endorse the Social Charter. Within weeks of Madrid, Thatcher tried to take revenge for the pre-summit 'ambush' by destroying the Howe–Lawson 'axis'. In July she moved Howe from the FO and replaced him with the little known John Major, who was likely to be more amenable. Yet Major survived at the FO barely three months before becoming Chancellor of the Exchequer because Lawson, his economic policy in tatters, then decided to resign. Ironically the crisis forced Thatcher to put the FO in the hands of a long-standing pro-European, Douglas Hurd, previously close to Edward Heath. Furthermore, Hurd and Major soon formed their own 'axis'. The two agreed that London must adopt a more flexible policy, and a more positive tone, in order to exploit debates in the EC in Britain's favour. Neither was keen on EMU in the long term but both felt Britain must enter the ERM, partly to influence future developments in Europe, partly to help control inflation.[25]

In late 1989 Thatcher was criticised for being out of touch with events. At home, the economy veered towards recession and an unpopular local government 'poll tax' deepened her electoral problems. Abroad, her old ally Ronald Reagan had gone; the collapse of Communism in Eastern Europe threatened the existence of NATO and made Thatcher's Cold War outlook redundant; and she upset Bonn by showing no enthusiasm for the idea of German reunification as Europe underwent the most profound changes since the 1940s. Some commentators believed that the end of the Cold War might mean the end too of the EC, which it had helped to spawn. But if anything – as Thatcher correctly saw – German reunification made French and German leaders more determined to tie Germany down securely in supranational bodies. At the December 1989 European Council, in Strasbourg, French and German interests again combined to sideline Thatcher. The summit expressed support for German reunification and in return Mitterrand won an agreement that another Inter-Governmental Conference would meet in twelve months' time to draw up a treaty for EMU. (A second IGC eventually met at the same time to discuss institutional reform, though Thatcher also continued to oppose all thoughts of a 'political union'.) In July 1990, as reunification drew near and German power seemed set to grow, Nicholas Ridley told a journalist that the ERM was a German attempt 'to take over the whole of Europe'. This of course was an old British fear: British people never shared the French belief that the Community *controlled* German power, but instead saw the EEC as a potential route to German domination. Yet Ridley's comments were so blunt that he had to resign, further weakening Thatcher's position in government. She did try to exploit international events, by pressing for the new regimes in Eastern Europe to be allowed into the EC as soon as possible. But this suggestion, whatever its merits in safeguarding democracy, was obviously designed to weaken the cohesion of the EC, since East European economies were in a very poor state.

In June 1990 Major launched a new effort to forestall EMU, although personally he feared that the rest of the Community were determined to proceed towards a single currency. His 'hard ECU' system proposed to allow a strengthened version of the European Currency Unit to *compete* with members' currencies across the EC. In contrast to the Delors Plan, such a scheme could be launched soon, it fitted British free market attitudes, yet it raised the possibility of the ECU becoming a genuine currency. Distrust of British motivations was such that neither France nor Germany showed enthusiasm, but Britain now had an alternative to the Delors Plan. At the same time Hurd and Major maintained pressure to enter the ERM, which seemed vital if Britain were to influence the IGC on monetary union. Hurd also believed it vital to take a more positive approach to institutional reform if Britain were to influence the debate on that subject. After eleven years of prevarication, and despite Thatcher remaining doubtful until the end, Britain finally entered the ERM on 5 October 1990. But the boost this gave to the stock market proved strictly short term and within months it was clear that Sterling's value (largely decided by the British themselves, without adequate discussion with other members) had been pegged at too high a rate.

Once again Britain had joined a European institution when its best years were coming to an end: costs of German reunification, leading to higher German interest rates, soon put strain on other ERM currencies. True, Sterling was now given the protection of EMS reserves and experience elsewhere suggested that, over the long term, it helped control inflation. Also, Britain now seemed politically better placed to influence the talks on EMU. However, once it became clear that Sterling's value *was* too high, it was difficult to do much about it. A realignment of ERM currencies was theoretically possible, but the last one had been in 1987 and most members were determined to hold currency values steady. Then, at the next EC summit, in Rome in October, the new unity at the top of British government was fatally undermined. Here Mitterrand and Kohl successfully pressed a date of 1994 for achieving Phase Two of the Delors plan (a central monetary institution). They believed such a date was necessary to ensure any progress at all was made, but setting a date was bound to offend against British pragmatism. Thatcher denounced the other leaders for 'living in cloud cuckoo land' and in a statement to the Commons on 30 October she not only attacked Delors' plans but also said that Major's 'hard ECU' should never become a European currency. This declaration undermined the Hurd–Major strategy on EMU, and seemed to justify French claims that she was out to destroy EMU.[26]

There were many factors in Thatcher's fall from power in November 1990, but European policy was one of the most important. On 1 November, Geoffrey Howe quit the Cabinet and later roundly condemned her European policy in his resignation speech. Meanwhile another of her critics on Europe, Michael Heseltine, decided to challenge her in the annual leadership election. He won enough votes in the first ballot to force her to stand down. This allowed Major, a political unknown 18 months before, to step forward and defeat Heseltine. Thatcher's supporters continued to argue that hers was the only patriotic course in Europe and, indeed, the best policy for the people of the EC. According to this view, seen in the memoirs of Nicholas Ridley and her Press Secretary Bernard Ingham, she defended British independence, won a more honest EC financial system and pointed Europe towards greater competition. There are certainly plenty of indications that she *did* have a positive European policy. She never advocated withdrawal from the EC; she launched a pro-European propaganda campaign to prepare for 1992; and Nicholas Henderson has recorded her enthusiasm for the Channel Tunnel (although John Dickie has revealed her initial scepticism about the project). But – like Bevin's 40 years before – Thatcher's policy was shaped by Britain's national needs and her own outlook, and was too often expressed in arrogant, contemptuous terms. Leaving aside her difficult personality, Stephen George feels she made Britain 'a normal and skilful actor in the Community game' and Paul Sharp has argued that even her abrasive manner was not that harmful on the really significant issues: 'To suggest that the Prime Minister of country *x* would have sided with Thatcher on the sovereignty issue, but because she was so rude . . . he decided to commit his country to . . . monetary union is counter-intuitive'. It is also possible to go far beyond Ingham and Ridley, and argue that, far from preventing progress in the EC, she helped galvanise it with the single market, which in turn – ironically – seriously intruded on British independence. When she left office half Britain's trade was with the Community and withdrawal had become unthinkable. David Reynolds, however, complains that Thatcher never faced the British people with an honest appreciation of what was happening in Europe, relying instead on the mask of patriotic jingoism to hide the growing loss of power to European institutions.[27]

7

MAJOR, MAASTRICHT AND CONSERVATIVE DIVISION, 1990–1997

The Road to Maastricht, 1990–1

In his first months as Prime Minister, John Major had no more motive to educate the British public about European realities than Thatcher had done. With an election necessary by June 1992, and even deeper divisions between 'Eurosceptics' and 'Euro-enthusiasts' in the Conservative party thanks to the bitter leadership contest, he had to try to prevent EC issues upsetting domestic politics, keep his party united and put it in a position to win an unprecedented, fourth successive term in office. His position on entering Downing Street on 28 November 1990 was not an enviable one. Inflation had hit 10.9 per cent in October and unemployment, which had been rising for six months, had reached 1.8 million as Britain entered an economic depression. Furthermore, on the European front, of course, the two Inter-Governmental Conferences (IGCs) were due to start work on 15 December on institutional reform and Economic and Monetary Union (EMU). The result of these year-long discussions would be a new treaty, designed to create a revamped economic and political union, which might provoke more Conservative division. Although Major had been endorsed by Thatcher and had won the support of most Eurosceptics in the leadership contest, he had no strong group of followers within the party and was, indeed, little known outside the government. He adopted the role of a party manager, rather than a 'conviction politician' in the style of Thatcher. The new Cabinet included several prominent Euro-enthusiasts, such as Michael Heseltine (who returned to government, after his leadership challenge, as Secretary of State for the Environment) and the Party Chairman, Major's friend Chris Patten, and it had a 'pro-European' majority. But it also contained Eurosceptical Thatcherites, such as Michael Howard (at Employment) and Peter Lilley (Trade and Industry), and had to take account of scepticism among the parliamentary party and in the constituencies where, despite a warm welcome for the single market, there was growing dismay over the Delors Plan and the Social Charter. Neither was Major helped with party management by his predecessor: in 1991 Thatcher made several statements critical of moves towards a European federation.

Major did have several factors working in his favour however, not least the fact that he was not Margaret Thatcher. He ran his government in a more collegiate style, to the satisfaction of most of his Cabinet colleagues, and the fact that he was not the leader of any faction in the party helped him foster unity. While maintaining such policies as privatisation, he was able to distance himself from Thatcher's more unpopular policies, notably the 'poll tax', and he promised to take a less confrontational style in Europe, helping to engage Britain more actively in the work of the IGCs: it was partly through the fear that Thatcher would not adopt a constructive – and therefore influential – role in these talks that opposition to her had mounted. Major's apparent lack of deep ideological commitment, his managerial style and anxiety to achieve compromises between party factions, may gradually have led to exasperation among Thatcherites, but in the short term it helped cover up Conservative divisions. The Right lacked a single strong leader after Thatcher's defeat and most Conservatives were keen to demonstrate party unity because of the looming election. Certainly, the state of the economy was poor, at least from the point of view of unemployment and growth figures. In 1991, unemployment topped 2.5 million. But membership of the Exchange Rate Mechanism (ERM) helped cut inflation below 5 per cent in 1991 and, for a time at least, it was possible both to bring down interest rates (to 10.5 per cent by September 1991, though they then stuck at that rate for many months) and to maintain the value of Sterling. Besides, for almost two years the British people were prepared to give the unassuming Major 'the longest electoral honeymoon for a post-war British prime minister'[1] and whilst the Conservatives continued to lose by-elections, so that their leader put off an election to the last moment, they never fell too far behind Labour in the opinion polls.

The new government was born into a confused world. In late 1990 German reunification, the instability of the Soviet Union and the crisis caused by the Iraqi occupation of oil-rich Kuwait combined to generate an international atmosphere of great uncertainty, as the Cold War faded. But, as William Wallace asserts, it was 'Europe' which 'was the defining issue both for British foreign policy and for internal party divisions which ... Major inherited, because it had come to symbolise so many of the policy choices over which the Conservatives were split'. There were many Conservatives who, like the Home Secretary, Kenneth Baker, had favoured EC membership in the past but who 'never favoured the diminution of sovereignty and absorption into a superstate, which is what the EC institutions in Brussels seem increasingly determined to drag us into'.[2] Thatcherites saw a minimalist European policy as going hand-in-hand with a strong central government in London, free enterprise economics, a close American alliance and the assertion of British national pride, and this approach found strong support among both the 'quality' press (*The Times* and *Daily Telegraph*) and the tabloids (notably the *Sun*). But the 'One Nation' social market alternative had been vigorously set out in 1989 in a book by Heseltine. In *The Challenge of Europe* he argued that Britain should embrace Europe enthusiastically because of the opportunity provided by the single market and that the country need not fear a loss of national identity. Heseltine pressed the political and economic benefits of EC membership rather than any idealism or cultural affinity, but he was ready to accept the Social Charter, a single currency and reform of the European Parliament.[3] Major himself, despite his brief period as Foreign Secretary, had little experience of international affairs. However, whilst he had beaten the pro-European Heseltine for the premiership and visited Washington within a month of his succession, there were clear signs that he would mark a change from Thatcher's outlook on the world. Major had grown up after the Second World War, with no animosity towards Germany or particular affinity with the US; he retained the pro-European Hurd as Foreign Secretary; also, of course, as Chancellor of the Exchequer, he had already taken Britain into the ERM. Civil servants who had worked with Major in the Treasury believed him 'friendly' to Europe, 'subject to a distinct pragmatic gloss' and, despite the divisions in his party he treated it as a managerial problem, 'a test of one's handling skill'. Anthony Seldon has described him as a 'Europragmatist'.[4] Lacking his predecessor's charisma and outspokenness, he relied far more on officials and fellow ministers for advice, and it was little surprise that he adopted a more diplomatic approach to negotiations, all of which helped breed suspicion on the Right. However, studies of his policy towards the IGCs in 1990–1 contend that it 'amounted to a change in style rather than ... content ... designed both to induce concessions from Britain's negotiating partners and to minimise domestic tensions'.[5] The new government was able to play a fuller role in the IGCs than Thatcher might have done but the basic British agenda remained the same.

The shift to a less abrasive style was seen in various areas. Chris Patten was keen to develop closer links between Conservative Members of the European Parliament (MEPs) and Christian Democrats there. Douglas Hurd, in a marked step away from previous policy, agreed in February 1991 that the EC should have a security dimension, a proposal which made more sense to most member states, given all the current international uncertainties. Also the Western European Union (WEU) should act as a kind of link between the EC and NATO. In addition, after entering the ERM, Britain was able to have a greater input into the debates on EMU. For their part the other EC leaders were prepared to give Major a friendly welcome at his first EC Council, in Rome in mid-December, which he unexpectedly enjoyed. A more *communitaire* manner not only benefited Britain in the IGCs, it also better enabled the government to press other concerns. Two in particular stood out. First, London wanted an agreement with the US and other countries in the so-called 'Uruguay Round' of talks on reduced trade restrictions, through the General Agreement on Tariffs and Trade (GATT). The Uruguay Round, under way since 1986, was particularly contentious for some EC members, notably France, because part of its focus was on reducing agricultural tariffs. But it had long been a point of British policy, of course, to reduce the impact of the Common Agricultural Policy, 'open' the EC to world trade, keep food prices down and help developing countries. Second, Britain was keen to press ahead with plans to enlarge the Community, partly in the hope that this would make it more difficult to pursue deeper integration. Eventually it was hoped to bring in the ex-Communist states of Eastern Europe, helping to stabilise their democracies and tie them into the capitalist world. However, given their deep economic problems, an 'eastern enlargement' would take many years. More realistic was an attempt to extend the EC to more West European states. In early 1992 talks began on creating a 'European Economic Area' between the Community and the remaining members of EFTA, the European Free Trade Association. (Such an agreement, which Britain had first advocated when EFTA was created, eventually came into effect on 1 January 1994.) But meanwhile some of the EFTA countries believed that full EC membership would bring better rewards. The end of the Cold War and the disintegration of the USSR were also significant here because neutral countries like Sweden and Switzerland, as well as Austria (neutralised by East–West agreement in 1955) and Finland (in a special treaty relationship with the Soviet Union since 1948) now felt free to join the Community.

A key element in Major's strategy towards the IGCs was to seek reliable allies and, in particular, he and Hurd decided to work closely with the most powerful EC state, Germany. Some officials were loath to trust the Germans, believing that Chancellor Kohl, with whom Major had his first meeting during the Rome Summit, would always put relations with France first. But the obvious alternative of 'a "French strategy" was never going to work in 1991' because of solid French support for EMU and other proposed reforms.[6] Thus the anti-German tone of Thatcher's last year disappeared and in March 1991 Major, on a visit to Bonn, declared 'I want us to be where we belong. At the very heart of Europe.' These sentences were highlighted by the press even though, as Anthony Seldon has pointed out, Major had said similar things during the November leadership campaign. In any case, as some of Major's Downing Street advisers emphasised, there was much more to the Bonn speech and it was not far removed in some respects from Thatcher's famous Bruges address. Once again it was Major's change of *tone* which separated him from his predecessor. Certainly the change was significant: rather than emulate Thatcher and become sidelined in the EC, he was determined to play an active role in the IGCs and this began the process whereby he alienated convinced Eurosceptics in the party. But his overall vision of Europe was one of strong nation states, with a free market, the preservation of the American alliance and no headlong rush into EMU.[7] Despite the limits to his European commitment, and whatever other differences existed between Britain and Germany (not least over how to respond to the threatened disintegration of Yugoslavia in late 1991), Major established a good working relationship with Kohl, who became keen to see his British colleague re-elected and was particularly helpful as an ally at the Maastricht Summit of 9–10 December 1991 which completed the negotiations on EC reform. Neither was Germany the only ally Britain found at important points in the talks. As in all EC discussions, different coalitions of states would be made on different issues, but most members were surprised in October 1991 when Britain and one of the most 'pro-federalist' states, Italy, produced a joint plan for a Common Foreign and Security Policy (CFSP). The plan made the important British concession of saying that the EC should have some role in formulating defence policy, but NATO would keep its primacy in this field. Even a joint Franco-German response (proposing a rapid move to an EC defence policy) failed to prevent the Anglo-Italian scheme from largely being adopted, a success helped by the fact that it proved acceptable to the USA, which had earlier feared a weakening of NATO.

The government did not publish a White Paper setting out its aims in the IGCs because this could have provoked Conservative wrangling and, for a time, it was still possible that Major would call a 1991 election. But the general British position in the year-long talks was clear enough from the start. London, seeing no real need for reform given all the other problems in the world and certainly not welcoming such negotiations ahead of a general election, was minimalist and sometimes downright negative in its approach, but with enough positive elements to be treated as a serious player. The government wished to keep central institutions as weak as possible, to support inter-governmental co-operation rather than supranationalism where new areas of activity (such as CFSP) were concerned; but also to avoid a 'two-tier' Europe, whereby certain countries moved without Britain on a path of deeper integration, and to secure the principle of 'subsidiarity'. Subsidiarity, which had actually been first set out by Roy Jenkins as Commission President, became an important element of policy under Major and was designed to minimise the powers taken by European bodies through ensuring that policy issues were decided at the lowest level of competence: thus the European Commission would not be given responsibilities which could be fulfilled by local or national government. Specifically, in the talks, the British sought to limit the powers of the European Parliament (EP), restrict the use of Qualified Majority Voting (QMV) and avoid commitment to the Social Charter. But more positively, they were ready to see the EP investigate fraud and to allow the European Court to fine states who broke Community rules. Whatever difficulties it had with the EC, Britain had a good record of respecting the rules and the Conservatives were determined to crack down on waste and corruption in Europe, just as they had at home.

At the Maastricht Summit there were inevitable gains and losses for all member states, and not a little disagreement, with doubts down to the end about whether a deal would be possible. But Major had some justification for claiming that he had obtained much of what he wanted. It was possible to argue, for one thing, that the centralising trend of European integration had been brought to an end. So, although the final agreements covered not only CFSP but also co-operation in Justice and Home

Affairs (on such issues as immigration, asylum, border controls and policing), these two new areas did not fall under the competence of the EC itself; instead they were the second and third 'pillars' of the Treaty on European Union (TEU) agreed at Maastricht – the first pillar being the EC itself – and they were to be handled at *inter-governmental* level. The 'pillared' structure, which tempered the power of the European Commission, had been strongly supported by Britain and France since the spring and had won through despite attempts by countries such as Holland, Germany and Italy to draft a more supranational treaty. The principle of subsidiarity was written into the TEU but a federalist goal for EC was not and, in the two areas where British sovereignty was seriously threatened, Major could claim to have secured an 'opt out', allowing the country to choose in future whether to be involved or not. The first of these areas was the third stage of EMU, where all the other members agreed that (following Phase Two, the creation of a European Monetary Institute in January 1994) they would proceed with a single currency in 1999 at latest, and possibly in 1997. However, a single currency would only come into being if certain 'convergence criteria' were met, including membership of the ERM and certain levels of performance on such economic indicators as inflation, budget deficit and the ratio of public debt to GDP. Despite its 'opt out' Britain, alongside Germany, had been an important supporter of the idea of convergence criteria. In fact Major had decided not to accept an 'opt out' at an earlier date, partly because he did wish to secure a certain form of EMU – in which it was still possible Britain might take part. To the British, the use of convergence criteria seemed much better than the Delors Plan approach, of setting dates for progress regardless of whether the economies of EMU states could face the rigours of a common currency.

The second 'opt out', agreed at the last moment after some acrimonious debate, was on the Social Charter, from now on generally referred to as the 'Social Chapter' of the Maastricht Treaty. Actually, thanks to Britain's position, it was only a protocol to the treaty rather than part of the main text (and thus the term 'opt out' is something of a misnomer). The Conservative Right had made it virtually unthinkable for Major to consider signing the Chapter alongside the other eleven members. In September a group of junior ministers had made plain their opposition to any British involvement and it could have become a resignation issue for Michael Howard, the Employment Secretary, who maintained a particularly strong line against it in Cabinet. Indeed, as Alasdair Blair has highlighted, a significant feature of Cabinet government under Major was that its collegiate nature, in contrast to the Thatcher years, allowed a minister like Howard to pursue a negative policy on one aspect of the TEU while another minister, like Hurd on CFSP, could be far more constructive. Major was not necessarily happy to see Britain divided from the other members by *two* opt outs: there had been some hope of securing a general opt out on EMU, of which any member state might take advantage, but other countries, like France, wished to keep Germany firmly committed to a single currency. (There were echoes of the Schuman Plan in 1950 here, when France insisted on a prior commitment to supranationality in order to keep Germany tied down even if Britain refused to talk on this basis.) Yet, all in all the outcome of Maastricht seemed satisfying enough and pro-Conservative newspapers immediately took up the claim of the Downing Street Press Office that it was 'Game, Set and Match' to the Prime Minister. Conservative MPs were hardly less adulatory in a Commons debate on Maastricht on 18–19 December, when only seven MPs opposed the treaty and three (including Thatcher) abstained. Even a sober judge such as the Prime Minister's foreign policy adviser, Percy Cradock, felt that, given the government's aims in the Maastricht talks 'it is difficult to see what more could have been done . . . and a certain triumphalism . . . could be excused'.[8]

'Black Wednesday' and the Maastricht Ratification

The Maastricht Treaty was formally signed on 7 February 1992 and two months later Major unexpectedly won the British general election, with Europe barely raising its head as a campaign issue. Labour differed from the government in being ready to sign the Social Chapter, but the Labour leader, Neil Kinnock, had little motive to fight the election on such an issue given Major's apparent success at Maastricht and latent divisions among Labour MPs about Europe. Indeed it is against the background of this triumph that the first 18 months of the Prime Minister's European policy must be counted a success. Whatever difficulties were to follow, his diplomacy had neutralised the danger posed by the IGCs to Conservative unity and he had passed the ultimate political test at the polls. However, his very success in this early period makes it essential to explain why his government of 1992–7 was so divided over, many would say destroyed by, European issues. And one vital point is that the Maastricht outcome had been much less than 'Game, Set and Match' to Major. Indeed other leaders, as well as Jacques Delors, were pointing out 'federalist' elements which were largely overlooked in Britain at first. The (supranational) responsibilities of the community had been extended to such areas as education, culture and health, and the competency and powers of the European Parliament had also been strengthened. There was provision for a 'cohesion fund' to spend on infrastructure projects in poorer members and a 'Committee of the Regions' was established to represent regional governments in Brussels, though only on a 'consultative' basis. CFSP operated on an inter-governmental basis but there was provision for QMV to be used in *implementing* its decisions. The Maastricht Treaty also committed its members to an 'ever closer union' and – a potential time-bomb ahead of the next general election – the treaty was to be the subject of a review IGC, starting in 1996. Even the opt out on EMU had failed to remove the single currency as a problem for British policy because, if the other countries went ahead with it, the great question was whether Britain would follow. When the treaty came to be ratified by parliament after the election (a pre-election ratification having been ruled out through insufficient time) all these points became more obvious. Then again, at first, there seemed little danger of a Commons defeat on the question. Indeed, on 21 May 1992 the Maastricht ratification bill passed its second reading by 376 votes to 92, with the Prime Minister still claiming to have kept concessions in the treaty to a bare minimum.

A second important factor, however, was that Major's parliamentary situation was not as secure after the April election as it had been before. The Conservative majority had tumbled from over a hundred to a lowly 21, making it possible for small groups of rebels to threaten the government with defeat. Those sceptics who had restrained their opinions in order to win the election, became more outspoken. Ominously, 22 Conservatives voted against the Maastricht bill in May and between 40 and 70 were reckoned to be potential opponents of ratification, with many more (including a lot of new MPs) doubtful about it. Already on 21 February, one Eurosceptic, Richard Shephard, had introduced a bill to make Maastricht the subject of a popular referendum (an idea first raised by the ex-party chairman, Norman Tebbit, in November and backed by Thatcher). Although the bill was easily defeated, the referendum pro- posal became increasingly popular with sceptics, who could pose as defenders of the national will at a time when opinion polls suggested the electorate were also, on balance, 'sceptical'. The government was secure if, as on the second reading, Labour officially abstained in European votes. But a combination of rebels and opposition parties was a potential danger and over time the government majority was likely to be trimmed still further through by-election defeats. Certainly the supposed success of the Maastricht talks had done no more than dampen the Conservative divisions on Europe which had developed in the late 1980s, and the rift in the party ran straight to the top, where Major, always managerial, kept both Euro-enthusiasts and sceptics in the Cabinet. True, there were serious differences within the latter group (just as there were among the enthusiasts). A few 'diehards' had never wanted to join the EC. Most wished to remain inside but hoped to keep its activities severely restricted or objected to certain of its policies. Some were most concerned for parliamentary sovereignty, others for national independence, others for free enterprise.[9] But most agreed that the EC should concentrate on achieving free trade among its members, who should remain strong states; and, in any case, with such a small majority Major could not rely on divisions within his Eurosceptic wing to save Maastricht. This was especially the case when a crisis broke over the whole ratification process.

It was the defeat of the TEU in a referendum in Denmark, on 2 June, which unleashed Europewide doubts over the future of the project and led Britain's Eurosceptics, including some Cabinet ministers, to argue that, since it needed to be ratified by all the signatories in order to enter into force, the treaty was effectively dead. Almost a hundred Conservative MPs signed a motion calling for a 'fresh start' on Europe. The fact that the Danes had only voted 'No' by the narrowest of margins, a mere 48 000 votes, hardly seemed to matter, and overwhelming approval for Maastricht in an Irish referendum on 18 June did not stem the Eurosceptic euphoria. Nor did the insistence of EU leaders, including Major, that renegotiation of the TEU was impossible: such renegotiation, though discussed at the Lisbon Council in late June, would have meant reopening all the issues discussed in the IGCs of 1990–1. There was a public falling out between Major and Thatcher at this time, with the former insisting that Britain could only influence EU policies by playing a proper part in talks and the latter (now Lady Thatcher) again calling for a referendum on Maastricht, which she described as 'a treaty too far'. To the annoyance of other member states, especially Kohl, Major, while ruling out a referendum, had immediately decided to suspend the ratification of the TEU until the doubts surrounding it were resolved. Major still saw Maastricht as the best deal he could have won for Britain and did not want to show bad faith to his fellow leaders, but his party managers felt the bill to be in serious danger if it were pressed at this time. In contrast, France's President Mitterand decided to throw his political reputation

reaty and called his own referendum on it, for 20 September,
... at a clear 'Yes' vote would boost its prospects among other
... This proved a fateful decision for two reasons. First, the
French people themselves soon proved to have their own doubts about
the growing powers of the EC and others threatened to vote 'No' in order
to express their disapproval of Mitterand's leadership. Second, the growing evidence that the French might vote against Maastricht led to doubts
about the prospects of the EMU project, which in turn helped to upset
the money markets, undermining several European currencies which
were part of the ERM, including Sterling.

Until the spring of 1992 Sterling's position within the ERM seemed
reasonably secure, despite arguments that it had gone in at too high a
level. Membership had certainly helped drive down inflation, to levels
not seen since the mid-1960s and, although Downing Street looked at
a possible ERM 'realignment' of currency rates in late 1991, it soon
concluded there was no need to pursue this. But there were already
complaints, especially from monetarist economists and Thatcherite
Conservatives, that fixed exchange rates were keeping interest rates too
high and pushing up unemployment. By July there was also growing
concern that ERM membership was lengthening the depression. It
seemed particularly inappropriate to link Britain's economic fortunes to
a German-led currency group at a time when Germany's interest rates
were pushed to historic highs because of the costs of propping up Eastern
Germany after reunification. By early September, in the midst of general
currency turmoil ahead of the French referendum, Sterling, at DM2.79,
was one of several countries trading just above its 'floor' within the ERM.
Determined to maintain the fight against inflation yet reluctant to raise
British interest rates further the Chancellor of the Exchequer, Norman
Lamont (despite his personal Euroscepticism), borrowed over £7 billion
to prop up the currency and pressed the Germans to lower their interest
rates. A general realignment of exchange rates within the ERM was difficult because of the desire for currency stability among those states committed to a single currency. Under the Delors Plan, after all, a stable ERM
was designed to pave the way to such a currency and a realignment could
destroy the credibility of the whole EMU project. Questions of credibility
also worried the Treasury when it considered a devaluation of Sterling:
such a move need not have prevented further speculation against it at
a lower level. Downing Street agreed. 'By how much? How often?' Major
asked, when quizzed about devaluation.[10] So he and Lamont both publicly
repeated that Sterling would remain in the ERM at the current level and

the alternatives were never fully discussed in Cabinet. But on 16 September the situation became critical. The day before, the Bundesbank had lowered its interest rates, but by only one quarter of 1 per cent and its President, Helmut Schlesinger, had hinted that Sterling *should* be devalued as the Italian Lira already (on 13 September) had been. Confidence in the Pound then collapsed and an increase in British interest rates from 10% to 12%, followed by an announcement of a 15% rate, failed to save the situation. In the evening Lamont announced that Britain had 'suspended' its membership of the ERM. Four days later the French people approved the TEU by only a few per cent. It might have been better for Major if the vote had gone the other way and killed the treaty. As it was Maastricht was still alive, the French government maintained its pro-European line, and British policy was in tatters.

'Black Wednesday', as 16 September 1992 became known, was *the* turning point of the Major premiership and a numbing experience for all involved. It encouraged the Eurosceptics (who hailed the day of freedom from the ERM as 'White Wednesday'), it crippled the Conservatives' claim to be the party of sound economic management (they had stuck to a failing policy, deepened the depression and then lost the Pound anyway), it provoked grave popular dissatisfaction with Major (who recorded a disapproval rating of 77 per cent in an October poll), it brought almost all the Conservative press to question Major's leadership and it led opinion polls to turn markedly against the government (a situation from which, this time, there was no recovery). As Hugo Young later put it, 'British membership of the ERM was Chancellor Major's baby. Leaving the ERM was Prime Minister Major's catastrophe.'[11] Indeed for several days the Prime Minister considered resignation on the issue and he refused to replace Lamont as Chancellor, pointing out that Downing Street was as responsible as the Treasury in pursuing the ERM policy. For the electorate there was a 'complete absence of scapegoats'[12] for what happened on Black Wednesday: it was the government which had put Britain in the ERM, at the mercy of the money markets, and which never apologised for the decision. Yet initially Major and Lamont did try to find a scapegoat in the shape of the Bundesbank, and even the German government itself, a step which simply offended Kohl and led Schlesinger to release evidence that the Bundesbank itself had spent huge sums trying to bolster Sterling. In place of the Major–Kohl friendship of 1991, Anthony Glees has argued that the events of September 1992 'produced what was certainly the worst period in Anglo-German relations' for four decades.[13] There was a certain irony in all this because Black Wednesday actually inaugurated what Peter Jay has called 'a period of rare enlightenment' in economic policy, though one which lacked any overarching intellectual justification, such as monetarism or a fixed exchange rate had provided.[14] Sterling was effectively devalued, falling to DM2.30 by February 1993, making it easier to export and driving an economic recovery. Interest rates were rapidly lowered, inflation continued to fall (reaching 1.3% in May 1993) and the economy began to grow again, while most of the Continent remained in depression. But there was one serious problem and that was the need to increase taxes, an unpopular step and one which broke Conservatives' pledges made during the 1992 election.

The confidence of the Conservative Eurosceptics was confirmed at the October Party Conference where Norman Tebbit received a standing ovation for an attack on Maastricht. On 4 November, thanks to a rebellion by 26 MPs, the government could only muster a majority of three when it decided to revive the ratification of the TEU. This latter step made sense in view of attempts to alter the treaty, with suitable 'opt outs' for Denmark, which was to hold a second referendum. In mid-December (at the successful end of what was widely seen as an ill-starred Presidency of the EC[15]), Major presided over a summit in Edinburgh at which such a solution was agreed and in May 1993, 58% of Danes approved the TEU. But by then the Eurosceptics were determined to continue their campaign against the treaty. The early months of 1993 witnessed a virtual state of civil war among Conservative MPs with the sceptics arranging their own whipping procedure in the Commons. Although the government could usually rely on Liberal votes and was never in danger of collapse, on 8 March it was actually defeated on a Labour amendment to the Maastricht Bill. The resignation of Lamont from the Cabinet in late May simply brought another sceptical voice to the backbenches, even as it put the Treasury in the hands of a long-standing Euro-enthusiast, Kenneth Clarke. The worst moment for Major came, however, in late July when, in another concession to malcontents, a special vote was held on the Social Chapter. The government was determined, of course, not to sign up to the Chapter. But Labour, now far more confident as an Opposition, was united in approving it and some Conservative 'sceptics', whilst detesting the Chapter itself, were ready to line up with Labour and other opposition parties to approve it – in the belief that the whole TEU would then be rejected by the government. On 22 July the government was indeed defeated, by 8 votes, with 23 Conservatives voting against. Major was forced to call a vote of confidence the following day, but easily survived. In the face of electoral annihilation only one Conservative MP dared to abstain and one voted against. A few days later however, there was further evidence that divisions over Europe ran to the core of the government, when the Prime Minister was reported to have called three of his Eurosceptic Cabinet ministers 'bastards'.

Britain finally ratified the Maastricht Treaty on 2 August. Ironically, the same day saw the virtual collapse of the ERM, membership of which had cost Major so dear: following continued currency turmoil which even threatened the position of the French Franc, its exchange rate 'bands' were widened to a virtually meaningless 15 per cent. With the ratification process completed elsewhere, on 1 November the EC became the 'European Union' (EU) and there were some signs that Major's problems might now ease. After all, with the TEU out of the way, there was less reason for his backbenchers to bicker and there were some signs of British success in Europe. On 1 January 1993 the single market, much trumpeted by Thatcherites, had finally come into being. In February, following a decision by the Edinburgh Summit, talks opened with certain EFTA states on EU membership. (Although Switzerland and Norway failed to sign up because of adverse referendums, there was eventual success with Austria, Sweden and Finland.) Two months before, it had also been agreed to extend the EU in due course to four East European countries, the Czech Republic, Poland, Hungary and Slovenia. Furthermore in December 1993 the Uruguay Round of GATT talks reached an agreement. Also, throughout 1992 and 1993, the EC's failure to come to grips with the Bosnian civil war highlighted the limits of the Community's unity and effectiveness, making it appear less of a threat to British independence. One contemporary academic study even argued that 'as the dust settled from the ratification debate it did not seem that Britain stood too far from the centre of the debate on the future of Europe, nor that it was necessarily doomed to remain an awkward partner in future': a younger generation was growing up which accepted European integration more easily than its forebears; most British trade was with the EU and Britain *was* committed to the single market; and the 'special relationship' seemed virtually defunct in 1993 thanks to the differences between Major and the new US President, Bill Clinton.[16] The Prime Minister himself certainly seemed to believe that he might be able to influence the EU in the direction of further enlargement, decentralisation of power, freer world trade and improved competitiveness. In an article in *The Economist* in September 1993 he highlighted the problems caused by economic depression, the collapse of the ERM and the political doubts surrounding Maastricht, but restated his personal commitment to EU membership and called for a drive to lower labour costs as a way to reduce unemployment. Remarkably consistent with earlier speeches by himself and Thatcher, he declared: 'It is for nations to build Europe, not for Europe ... to supersede nations. I want to see ... a wide union, embracing the whole democratic Europe, in a single market and with common security arrangements firmly linked to NATO.'[17]

Yet Major's attempts to seize on Europe's current troubles to press a minimalist British agenda could be read as yet another failure to understand the realities of integration. The ERM might have been reduced to a shell, but the commitment to EMU among the political elites of France, Germany and others remained firm. And whilst Major had secured an opt out from the single currency this did not remove the old fundamental problem: *if* such a currency were created, would the British really stand aside? On this question the Conservatives were still riven. It might be true that Germany and France had their differences, and that even in unison they found it increasingly difficult to shape the Community. But at least they were bound together behind the single currency whilst Major, after the souring of his relations with Kohl in 1992, lacked a consistent, powerful ally in EU counsels. It might also be true that there were signs of second thoughts about some elements of integration; a realisation that Maastricht had, for the present, taken centralisation as far as it could go in the near future, and that there was a need to tackle the problems of poor growth, competitiveness and unemployment. The December 1993 Brussels Summit approved a number of measures to tackle the latter group of problems and they were further developed at later summits, notably Essen in December 1995. But the preferred route of advance for many EU members in the field of unemployment was different to Conservative cost-cutting, being based on an increase in spending on such infrastructure projects as pan-European transport networks. Poorer members, such as Spain, Portugal, Greece and Ireland, were receiving ever-greater 'structural funds' to strengthen their economies – expenditure upon which caused as much concern in Conservative circles as did the continuing costs of the CAP. Neither was the danger of EU intervention in British economic and social policy easy to escape. Already, in April 1992, one incident had illustrated the limited value of Major's Maastricht opt outs when the EC had decided on a maximum 48-hour week. Britain took the matter to the European Court but other measures soon followed, with the Commission seeking to limit the hours worked by children and insisting on equal treatment of men and women as regards retirement age. The Social Chapter opt out could in fact be circumvented in a number of ways: by rulings of the European Court, by measures to implement the single market and, more significantly, by 'health and safety' measures – such as the 48-hour week – allowed under the Single European Act. Over the following years, even with the Maastricht ratification behind him, Major faced continuing trouble on European issues, on both the continental and home fronts, and on several occasions found himself isolated in arguments with the other EU leaders.

Division and Defeat, 1994–7

In the second half of his premiership Major continued to press a particular vision of Europe, similar to that of his *Economist* article and designed on the one hand to influence the debate among EU governments and, on the other, to reunite the Conservatives. In the Euro-election campaign of spring 1994 he pressed the theme of 'Euro-realism' as a middle way between Euro-enthusiasm and scepticism, but moved in a distinctly sceptical direction. In his most important speech of the campaign, at Ellesmere Port on 31 May, he advocated a 'multi-track, multi-speed, multi-layered' Europe in which different countries would pick and choose which areas of co-operation they wished to take up. In a sense Europe already was 'multi-track': some EU members were in the WEU, others were not; Britain and Denmark had their opt outs on EMU; Germany, France, Spain, Portugal and the Benelux countries pressed on with the Schengen agreement (effective in March 1995) which ended passport controls between them while strengthening controls at their external borders. Major's decision to champion a decentralised, diverse system while preserving Britain's veto over any unwelcome developments pleased even Tebbit. It did not however, save the Conservatives from a drubbing in the June elections, when they lost 14 of their 32 seats and recorded their lowest share of a national vote in the twentieth century. The result continued a long trend (not broken until the 1999 Euro-elections) in which, when it came to actual votes, the electorate showed itself unimpressed by an 'anti-European' line. The 'No' campaign in the 1975 referendum, Labour in the 1979 Euro-elections and the 1983 general election, the Conservatives in the 1989 and, now, the 1994 Euro-elections had all tried supposedly populist attacks on Brussels and been rejected. But this was a point lost on Major's Eurosceptics and the Prime Minister himself. He was more impressed that the election results, however appalling, were not as bad as expected.[18]

Major's advocacy of a multi-speed Europe may have won over sceptics for a time but it did not please his French and German partners. In Germany in particular some Christian Democrats began to argue that fuller integration would only be possible without Britain and other doubters. The Christian Democrat's Parliamentary Committee on European Affairs produced a report on 1 September 1994 saying that EMU should be pursued by a 'hard core' of states, including Germany, France and the Benelux trio. Instead of a tolerant, multi-track approach the Germans seemed to prefer a 'two-tier' Europe, from which London would be sidelined. Six days later in Leiden, in the Netherlands, Major made clear that, while continuing to advocate a flexible Europe, he rejected the 'two-tier' approach: all countries should be free to choose any areas of co-operation they wanted. Through such pragmatism, Britain could have the best of both worlds, minimising its EU involvement (including an early commitment to EMU) whilst avoiding permanent exclusion from deeper integration. It should also remain free to criticise, as Major again did at Leiden, the operation of the CAP, the EP and the Commission.[19] Another theme of British diplomacy in the mid-1990s was the continuing need to extend the EU. With Austria, Finland and Sweden joining on 1 January 1995, Britain focused on an 'eastern enlargement', steps towards which were agreed at the Essen Summit the previous month. As with past enlargements, this policy had mixed motives. Douglas Hurd told a German audience in February 1995 that an eastern enlargement would help stabilise capitalism and democracy in East Central Europe, create a common Anglo-German interest (since Germany was also particularly anxious to stabilise its eastern neighbours) and force a reform of both the CAP and the structural funds (which otherwise would be overwhelmed by the demands of poorer, agricultural new members).[20]

Britain's vision of Europe's future also had to be clarified in advance of the 'review conference' on EU institutions promised at Maastricht. This IGC was opened by the Turin Summit of March 1996 and was scheduled to end in Amsterdam in mid-1997, thus running on through Britain's general election and, whilst never aiming at a marked extension of EU competences, it created a new potential minefield for Major. This time, despite some opposition from Clarke, the government did produce a White Paper on its negotiating position which was designed to quieten the sceptics. In introducing it to the Commons, Hurd's successor as

Foreign Secretary, Malcolm Rifkind, minimised the importance of the IGC, arguing that the greatest challenges to the EU were enlargement, competitiveness and reform of the two great financial burdens on the Union, the CAP and the structural funds. Where institutional reform was concerned Britain pressed its flexible, *à la carte* approach, preserving strong nation states, the importance of NATO, a separate WEU, continued inter-governmental co-operation on CFSP and home affairs, and the principle of subsidiarity.[21] These same themes were repeated in a series of speeches by Rifkind in European capitals in early 1997.[22] As Stephen George has said, Britain was 'a status quo state . . . generally satisfied with the existing Treaty' and ready to shift its alliances in the IGC to secure what it wanted.[23] Yet, while Major remained determined to play an active role in the talks, some government declarations by this time sounded like eerie echoes of Bevin and Eden in the early post-war years. Thus Major, speaking in June 1996, stated that 'Europe is not always comfortable for Britain. Our history is different . . . and so often are our instincts . . . Our twentieth century experiences are different'. And Rifkind, speaking on the fiftieth anniversary of Churchill's Zurich speech, laid emphasis on the country's pragmatic, step-by-step approach, 'based on choosing carefully the stepping-stones towards closer co-operation; not jumping blindly towards ever greater integration'.[24]

Whilst advocating a multi-speed vision of Europe in 1994–7 Major, ever the pragmatic party manager, also tried to please both Euro-enthusiasts and sceptics on specific policies. He inclined more to the sceptical camp, perhaps, than he had in 1990–2, but not enough to satisfy them fully. In March 1994 for example, initially supported by Spain, the government opposed any alteration in the number of 'blocking votes' needed to prevent action in the Council of Ministers under QMV. In view of the forthcoming enlargement to Austria, Sweden and Finland – which of course Britain favoured – it seemed reasonable to other members to raise the 'blocking vote' from the existing 23 votes or three countries (in a Council with 76 votes in all) to a new 27 votes and four countries (in a Council of 90 votes). France and Germany, who had originally seemed likely to back the status quo, decided to support the change. However Major, with the backing of the Cabinet, not only opposed it, he also derided the Labour leader, John Smith, as 'Monsieur Oui, the poodle of Brussels', for accepting this weakening of Britain's veto power. This made it all the more embarrassing when, at the end of the month, during a meeting in Ioannina, in Greece, Hurd was isolated and forced to accept the new 'blocking' level, although as a compromise, a 23-vote minority would in future lead to a 'reconsideration' of any action.[25] The perceived climb-down led one sceptic to demand Major's resignation and in the *Daily Mail* on 30 March it was the Prime Minister who was depicted as the poodle of Jacques Delors. The *Mail*, along with the *Sun* and the two right-wing broadsheets the *Daily Telegraph* and *The Times*, was now firmly Eurosceptic.

Major impressed his sceptical wing rather better, but again offended Britain's European partners, at the Corfu Summit in June 1994 when he vetoed the appointment of Belgian premier Jean-Luc Dehaene as Com-mission President in succession to the long-serving Delors. Depicted as a 'federalist' in the pro-Conservative press, Dehaene was firmly backed by Germany and France but initially opposed by Britain and the new, right-wing government of Silvio Berlusconi of Italy – with whom the British, for a time, hoped for a close partnership. But, just as the Spanish had defected at Ioannina, so Italy eventually supported Dehaene at Corfu, leaving Britain isolated once more. The death of Labour's John Smith and triumphant election of Tony Blair as his successor in July made it vital that Major should stand his ground this time. He forced an emer-gency summit to be held in Brussels and there accepted another Benelux premier, Jacques Santer of Luxembourg, as Delor's successor. Since Luxembourg had done much to achieve the 'pillared' structure of the Maastricht Treaty, Santer could be defended as preferable to Dehaene, though not all the sceptics were convinced of this and, in fact, as Commis-sion President after January 1995, Santer proved a firm supporter of the single currency.[26]

In any case, after the summer, Conservative divisions on Europe resurfaced with a vengeance when a vote had to be faced on an EU Finance Bill. Kenneth Clarke, the Chancellor, was ready to threaten the backbenchers with a general election if the Bill were not passed, but this did not deter eight diehard sceptics from voting against it on 28 Novem-ber. Major was stunned by such a revolt on an issue of confidence, and felt he had no choice but to withdraw the whip from all the rebels – despite the fact that this most extreme of political punishments lost the govern-ment its majority in the Commons. Even then, the situation did not ease. Instead the 'whipless eight' were joined, voluntarily, by a ninth MP and in December allied with Labour to defeat a VAT increase, part of Clarke's latest budget. The defeat was one of the most serious ever suffered by a twentieth-century administration.[27] The threat of further humiliations and the need to unite the party ahead of the next local elections led Major to restore the whip to the rebels in April 1996 but the continuing problems in the party, including renewed criticisms from Thatcher and divisions within the Cabinet, resulted in another extraordinary situation on 22 June when, in a further attempt to enforce discipline, the Prime Minister resigned as Conservative leader and dared his critics to run an opponent against him in the election which followed. John Redwood, one of the Cabinet sceptics, resigned his post as Welsh Secretary to take up the challenge. On 4 July Major was re-elected leader by 218 votes to 89 over Redwood, whose triumph would have completely alienated the party's Euro-enthusiasts. At the very least, Major had shown that there was no one else who could hope to hold the Conservatives together. But, with 34 absences, abstentions or spoiled papers it was hardly a ringing endorsement, a third of the parliamentary party being disaffected.[28] The Prime Minister had failed to restore his authority either by withdrawing the whip or by calling his surprise leadership ballot. And meanwhile backbench Euro-enthusiasts too were losing faith. In October 1995 one defected to the Labour party; in December another crossed to the Liberal-Democratic benches.

The principal way in which Major tried to placate his Euro-enthusiastic wing, who always retained their majority in the Cabinet, was to leave open the possibility that Britain might 'opt in' to the common currency at the outset. He pointedly declared on 16 December 1995 that the next Conservative manifesto would *not* rule out a common currency. The idea that such a currency could be launched in 1997 had become less and less likely and, with unemployment rising in France and Germany, some even doubted whether the two key EMU states would be ready for a 1999 launch. The Madrid Summit of mid-December 1995 confirmed the 1999 target and made technical arrangements for the introduction of the single currency, to be called the 'Euro'. The meeting also confirmed the Maastricht convergence criteria, which it seemed several countries might not be able to meet. The summit further agreed to begin talks on an eastern enlargement after the Maastricht review IGC was completed and saw both Kohl and France's new Gaullist President, Jacques Chirac (elected in May) criticise the Commission for financial waste and interference in national policy. Such developments lent support to Major's claims that, in the wake of the troubled Maastricht ratification, the debate in Europe was actually moving Britain's way. But the sceptics could point to other areas where British interests were being compromised, notably on the Common Fisheries Policy (CFP) where there were increasing complaints about 'quota-hopping' by Spanish fishermen, who bought parts of the fishing quota originally given to British boats. There was another backbench revolt on 18 December, over the CFP, and a two-vote defeat for the government.

Nonetheless, from December 1995 until the election in May 1997, it was largely the single currency which continued to shape the Conservative debate on Europe. Clarke's policies as Chancellor had actually put Britain into a position to meet the Maastricht convergence criteria and Clarke himself was the leading advocate of membership, both as a way to prevent a 'two-tier' Europe and because of the expected economic gains, a stable currency and low inflation. But to sceptics acceptance of the Euro promised the end of an important national symbol (the Pound), the danger of low growth and high unemployment such as France and Germany already suffered, and severe restrictions on Britain's economic independence, since taxation and public expenditure would have to be dovetailed with the requirements of the European Central Bank. Opinion polls suggested little popular support for the Euro and there were signs that, if the Conservative party did not take a sceptical stance, others would do it for them. A UK Independence party had already been formed by Alan Sked, a University lecturer and former member of the Bruges Group. And in March 1996 a millionaire businessman, James Goldsmith, launched a well-financed campaign for a referendum, not on the narrow question of a single currency but on the wider issue of 'the sort of Europe of which Britain wants to be part', either 'a family of nations' or 'a single European Superstate'.[29] How such a question could meaningfully be framed for a referendum and how the result could possibly guide future foreign policy were mysteries, but even Conservative Central Office feared that the Referendum and UK Independence parties could cost the government some marginal seats.

It is an important question, given the Conservatives' usual emphasis on party unity and the fact that they had fallen into line behind Major ahead of the 1992 election, as to why they did not end their bickering in 1996 as another election approached. The Prime Minister has been accused of failing to unite his followers through his own weakness. But, as Philip Lynch had argued, this 'underestimates the difficulty of uniting the Conservative Party across the range of European issues, does not adequately assess the influence of the Euro-sceptics over government policy and fails to appreciate the extent to which Major's balancing act for the most part held the party together.' As Steve Ludlam has pointed out, Conservative differences on European policy had a long pedigree. Macmillan and Heath had both faced opposition to their pro-European approach. Neither were intra-party splits over questions of overseas trade relationships anything new. The Conservatives had already fought two civil wars over corn law repeal (1846) and tariff reform (after 1903).

But for a quarter of a century after 1961 the Tories had managed to combine their roles as both the patriotic party and the European party, helped in the 1960s and early 1970s by the belief that EC entry would restore the country's economic fortunes and bolster its international influence. Macmillan and Heath had also successfully minimised the potential loss of sovereignty that EC membership implied. After 1975 Thatcher may have adopted a more unilateralist policy, reinvigorating the economy by a distinctly 'Anglo-Saxon' free enterprise approach and asserting herself on the world stage by force of personality. But in her first decade as leader a combination of circumstances helped her preserve party (if not always Cabinet) unity, on the basis of defending British interests in the EC whilst never questioning actual membership: the departure of the anti-EC Enoch Powell and her defeat of the ardently pro-EC Heath helped calm the intra-party debate; the 1975 referendum seemed to settle the question of membership resoundingly; the EC did not actually advance much in this period; and Thatcher's policy on the budgetary question in 1979–84 seemed a success, certainly preferable to Labour's advocacy of withdrawal in 1983. But after 1985 the drive to deeper integration in the EC – though it was spearheaded by the single market project, which the party supported – had divided the Conservatives even more, claiming a number of Cabinet victims, starting with the resignation of Heseltine and Leon Brittan over the Westland Affair in 1986, and arguably including Thatcher herself.[30]

The ideological differences within the party when Major became leader have already been discussed.[31] He was able to patch these up until the 1992 election but thereafter was increasingly buffeted between the 'sceptic' and 'enthusiast' wings of his party, each claiming the support of up to 100 MPs, their interests increasingly irreconcilable. The Maastricht debate 'fostered . . . a habit of disagreement' in the party[32] and Black Wednesday convinced the sceptics, who included Cabinet ministers, that their cause was both right and popular. Attempts to discipline those who rebelled had failed and, since – in contrast to 1992 – opinion polls never suggested that the next general election could be won, MPs seemed more interested in positioning themselves for future internal battles than for the battle with Labour. (The fact that Labour was now better disposed to European integration made it more difficult for the Prime Minister to advocate a pro-European line.) Nor, on this occasion, was Major able to neutralise Europe as an issue as the election approached. Kohl was no longer the ally of the Maastricht talks and, in February, roundly warned that in EU debates 'the slowest ship in the convoy should not be allowed to determine its speed'.[33] March saw not only the emergence of the Referendum party and the launch of the 'Maastricht II' IGC, but also a quite unexpected crisis over British beef exports. On 20 March scientists confirmed a possible link between the so-called 'Mad Cow Disease', BSE, and its human equivalent, CJD. Several countries round the world, including America and even the British colony of Hong Kong, had long since banned beef imports from Britain but when the EU quickly decided to protect consumers by following this line it provoked uproar among the Eurosceptics and their allies in the press. Once again Major tried to neutralise the sceptics by taking a tough line with the EU. On 21 May, after weeks of diplomatic attempts to ease the EU's export ban he began the 'Beef War', vetoing any EU decisions which required unanimity. The 'war' continued until the Florence Summit on 21 June, when Major agreed to end British obstructionism in return for a vague plan to relax the export ban.[34] By then Euroscepticism had reached the point that some Conservatives seriously began to question the country's very EU membership, forcing the Prime Minister to dismiss them as living in 'cloud cuckoo land'.[35]

Meanwhile, in early April, after weeks of bitter debate, the Cabinet had decided to try to heal the divisions provoked by EMU – not least among its own members – by promising a referendum before Britain adopted the Euro. This was a rather narrower question than the Referendum party wished to tackle, but it answered a long-running demand of the Eurosceptics and their press allies, and Major hoped it would undermine Goldsmith's party. Clarke was, however, only persuaded to agree to it, abandoning thought of resignation, in return for a renewed promise from Major that membership of a single currency would *not* be ruled out by the Conservatives. There was a growing belief among sceptics that, if the party ruled out such membership for the lifetime of the next parliament it would help to minimise their electoral losses. Such arguments made more sense after November when Labour too agreed to hold a referendum on the Euro, thus matching the Conservative position. But for Clarke and the Euro-enthusiasts, it became a vital principle to retain a 'wait and see' approach to the Euro. On 19 September six former Cabinet ministers, including Heath, Howe and Hurd, publicly united to say that the Euro option must be left open. Under pressure from Clarke, Major reaffirmed this policy in early December, but the intra-party controversy persisted.[36] An attempt to introduce a Referendum Bill into the Commons on 11 June, with the broad purpose of protecting British sovereignty from the EU, won the support of 74 Conservative MPs; on 22 July one

Eurosceptic junior minister resigned, complaining that the government's EU policy was confusing and unworkable; and although the Conservatives got through their annual conference in October with a show of unity, there were renewed fears over national sovereignty in mid-November, when the European Court upheld the earlier EU directive forcing Britain to accept a maximum 48-hour week.

The work directive had actually been introduced under the terms of the Treaty of Rome, as amended by the Single European Act – an amendment accepted, without controversy, by Thatcher. But it seemed, again, to threaten the introduction of social legislation to Britain by the back door, at a time when Major was trying to unite Conservatives and the business community behind a policy of opposition to the Social Chapter, which Labour were determined to accept.[37] The financial and business community, however, usually loyal to the Conservatives, were themselves increasingly divided on the vital EU questions. Whilst smaller companies, especially those concentrating on the domestic market, might be eager to reduce social costs and were indifferent about the Euro, there were larger, multinational firms who felt it realistic to accept both the Social Chapter and the single currency. The trend was confirmed by a Confederation of British Industries survey just prior to the European Court ruling. Many business leaders were now happy to work with Tony Blair's 'New' Labour party, Social Chapter or not.

On 6 December 1996 the government finally lost its Commons majority and there was some doubt whether it could survive until a spring election. A week later the Dublin Summit discussed both the Euro and the IGC and, though provoking no great embarrassments for Major, it continued to stoke up Conservative divisions. The Prime Minister and others now argued that these divisions were unnecessary because, with German unemployment at well over 4 million, the Euro was unlikely to go ahead on schedule anyway. But Kohl and Chirac seemed determined to press on, aware that any delay in the 1999 deadline might put off a single currency indefinitely. At a bitter Cabinet meeting on 19 December ministers, many rumoured to be positioning themselves for a future leadership contest, again discussed whether to rule out British membership of the Euro. Even an anonymous, moderate Euro-enthusiast like the Health Secretary, Stephen Dorrell, felt it wise to move in a sceptical direction, publicly urging on 2 January that EU institutions be entirely reformed to steer them away from centralisation. Two months later Dorrell gravely embarrassed the government by blurting out that the Conservatives definitely would not join a single currency in 1999, a statement which,

though quickly retracted, flatly contradicted the 'wait and see' compromise around which Cabinet unity hung. A week after that one backbencher
defected to the Referendum party and, as the election campaign opened
in early April, it soon became clear that indiscipline on Europe would dog
Major to the end. Even government ministers issued election material
opposing the single currency and when the Prime Minister focused on
EU questions in the middle of the month it was to address the divide in
his own party rather than to attack Labour. Ineffectively managerial to
the last, on 16 April he insisted that the 'wait and see' policy would
remain, even though Blair and Labour themselves had virtually conceded
that Britain could not sign up for the Euro at its 1999 launch. Then, the
following day, without consulting senior Cabinet colleagues, the Prime
Minister made an impromptu promise of a free vote for Conservative
MPs on the single currency in the next parliament.[38] This amounted to
an admission of complete failure to hold the party together and, as one
junior minister privately conceded, 'Nobody wants to vote for a divided
rabble'.[39] When the polls closed on 1 May, the Conservatives were set to
win only 160 seats and Labour had a majority of 179. It was the worst
Conservative performance since universal suffrage was introduced and
had primarily to be blamed on the controversies surrounding Europe,
which had left Major in a position curiously like that of Harold Wilson
two decades before: a moderate on European issues with no obvious
alternative as leader, increasingly caught between warring ideologies
and choosing a managerial approach to hold his party together, the
preservation of the party having become more important than effective
government.

8

BLAIR AND THE BIRTH OF THE EURO, 1997–1999

The 1997 Election

Labour returned to power in May 1997 after 18 years of opposition and with a mixed pedigree where attitudes towards European integration were concerned. In 1929, with the Briand Plan, and 1950, with the Schuman Plan, Labour governments can be said to have made a lukewarm, if not negative, response to proposals for co-operation with the Continent; in 1962 Gaitskell's 'thousand years of British history' speech had left Macmillan's Conservatives as the innovators in overseas policy; and in the 1983 general election Labour had promised negotiated withdrawal from the EEC, many of its 'pro-marketeers' having already quit to form the Social Democratic party. Yet, in the immediate post-war years, the Attlee administrations had also been founder-members of the Brussels Pact and the Council of Europe; in 1967 Harold Wilson had pursued EEC entry with all the manipulative cleverness he could command; and in 1975 the same premier had presided over the decisive referendum on EEC entry. Whatever its stance in 1983 (when it fared disastrously at the polls), only a year later, in the Euro-elections, Labour concentrated on demanding the reform of the European Community from within. By the time of the 1987 general election, Labour, under the reforming influence of Neil Kinnock, had accepted that EC membership was a permanent fixture of British politics, even if many of its MPs did not. Thereafter, of course, it was the Conservatives who became publicly divided over such questions as monetary union (EMU) and a social dimension to EC policy. Labour party divisions remained on such aspects as the 'surrender' of parliamentary sovereignty to the Community and, in the 1993 Maastricht vote, when the front bench abstained on the measure, 66 Labour MPs broke ranks to oppose it. But in the 1992 and 1997 elections Labour was able both to unite, and to distance itself from the government, by espousing the Social Chapter of the Maastricht Treaty. Labour's leader in 1992–4, John Smith, was particularly known as a 'pro-European', though he tempered his enthusiasm to free the party to attack the government during the Maastricht debates. His successor, Tony Blair, was not known to take strong views on Europe, was equally keen to embarrass the government and had no wish to offend patriotic opinion ahead of the 1997 election. Indeed one of his early biographers felt his European 'policy was as unsatisfactory as Major's, a rhetorical look-both-ways'.[1] Yet if Blair did not enthuse unconditionally about the EU, neither did he castigate it in order to win votes and his 1983 support of a negotiated withdrawal had long since disappeared. The Trades Union Congress had also become keener to play a positive role, in order to influence EC policies.

During the 1997 election, any residual arguments within Labour over its European policy were skilfully hidden, while the Conservatives tore themselves apart. Labour's apparent unity on this issue, in stark contrast to the behaviour of the Major government, was an important factor in Tony Blair's landslide win. Actually, the precise views of the incoming Prime Minister on such key issues as EMU were unknown in 1997 and, at the heart of the party leadership, some differences were public knowledge, with Gordon Brown, the new Chancellor of the Exchequer, keen on EMU whilst the Foreign Secretary, Robin Cook, was more sceptical, believing the Maastricht criteria to be too deflationary. (That the ministerial head of the Treasury should be more 'Euro-enthusiastic' than his counterpart at the Foreign Office was unusual in British government.) Unity on EMU had been preserved by statements that, while the single currency was to be welcomed 'in principle', it should only be entered into if the conditions were right for Britain (a position remarkably similar to that Margaret Thatcher had taken on the ERM after 1979). Cook's biographer believes that 'he accepted from around 1996 that a single currency was a virtual certainty and that Britain had to devise a strategy of dealing with it'. Also, as the election approached, Labour's representatives had been at pains to deny that it would be 'a pushover and a soft touch on Europe' or would accept a Brussels 'super-state'.[2] Neither, when it came to the Maastricht II talks, were Labour keen to see a common European defence or immigration policy. Nonetheless, not least because of the Conservatives' emphasis on the point, Labour's support for the Social Chapter seemed significant. Furthermore, Blair's party expressed a greater readiness to commit to common measures against racialism and, above all, its spokespeople attacked the Major government because of its isolationism. Thus Robin Cook declared that 'the Government's aspiration is to stand alone while ours is to find partners'. This was not just the case where Europe was concerned. Blair was clearly determined to work closely with Washington, despite the recent differences between Major and Clinton; in what was called 'the Clintonisation of Labour', Blair's modernisation of the party was modelled in part on recent Democratic experience; and Labour's Shadow Defence Secretary, David Clark, proudly reminded parliament that his party had been associated with the origins of NATO under Bevin.[3] Labour had thus underlined its determination to work with others, including the European Union, in order to satisfy national interests, rather than to pursue the xenophobic self-assertion of Major's final years, but the tension between its European and American commitments had yet to be worked out.

Amsterdam and the Blair Agenda

One of the Blair government's first actions, on taking office in May 1997, was to sign up for the Social Chapter and put special emphasis on job creation in the EU. This in itself was unsurprising – Labour would have done the same if they had been elected in 1992 – but it was also accompanied by a surprisingly positive line on Europe in government speeches, by a readiness to accept greater QMV and increased co-decision with the European Parliament in the Maastricht II talks, and by a readiness to conclude a new Union treaty at the forthcoming Amsterdam Summit. On 5 May, at an IGC meeting in Brussels, Labour's new 'Minister for Europe', Doug Henderson, promised 'a fresh start to Britain's relations with . . . the EU' and a week later his chief, Robin Cook, who was launching a 'mission statement' on foreign policy, promised 'to make Britain a leading player in Europe'.[4] Such rhetoric was welcome in Brussels, where the scale of Labour's victory after the dreary Major years made Blair the focus of considerable interest, almost all of it sympathetic. For left-wingers in particular his election was welcome and it was followed by the victories of Lionel Jospin's Socialists in France (June 1997) and Gerhard Schröder's Social Democrats in Germany (October 1998). Labour's rhetoric seemed to be borne out at Amsterdam, on 16–17 June, where an agreement was successfully signed between the EU members, with Britain appearing as relaxed as any other member about the outcome.

The new treaty disappointed those who had hoped for a comprehensive overhaul of EU institutions ahead of the planned eastern enlargement, and in some areas it was even difficult to agree on what its clauses meant. Nonetheless it included quite a wide range of changes. It extended QMV in some areas (including action against fraud), strengthened EU powers over environmental protection and anti-discrimination measures, increased the role of the Court and Parliament, stressed the need to tackle unemployment and made further preparations for EMU. Although it was always unlikely that Britain would join a single currency at the outset, Labour was also keen to leave the option open and one of Gordon Brown's early decisions was to make the Bank of England independent of government control, a step which could be seen as making EMU membership easier. Blair had such a substantial majority in parliament, most of it loyal to his reformist, 'New Labour' vision, that ratification of the Amsterdam Treaty, in contrast to the Maastricht experience, was a formality. Labour Eurosceptics still existed but, like 'Old Labour' attitudes in general, were reduced to virtual irrelevancy: they were identified with the failed policies of the past, vastly outnumbered by the 'Blairites' and could not easily question the Prime Minister's predominance given the scale of his recent election win. Meanwhile the Conservatives' divisions continued. Major had quickly decided to stand down as leader after the May defeat and in the ensuing campaign to succeed him, the experienced Europhile Kenneth Clark was defeated by a less well known right-winger and Eurosceptic, William Hague. The centrepiece of Hague's European policy became a determination to rule out membership of the single currency for the length of two parliaments; eventually, in September 1998, he had this position overwhelmingly endorsed by a ballot of party members. In one sense this policy was meaningless: the chance of the Conservatives being in power during the period in question was not great. But Hague's approach succeeded in alienating a number of experienced MPs, such as Clarke and Michael Heseltine, which made an electoral recovery for Conservatism even less likely.

However much the Conservatives might like to depict Blair as 'selling out' British interests to the EU, Labour's Europhilia was far from unlimited. In some fields, such as the completion of the single market project, its enthusiasm for an 'eastern enlargement', its emphasis on reforming the CAP and, most notably, in its belief that unemployment was best tackled

by free enterprise ideas of a 'flexible labour market', the Blair government seemed the natural successor of Margaret Thatcher. Indeed,
having signed the Social Chapter, the government showed no enthusiasm
for introducing radical social measures under its provisions. Furthermore, alongside the positive rhetoric during the Amsterdam talks Blair
was always clear that British interests must be protected. At Amsterdam
he safeguarded Britain's right to police its own borders, helped to block a
renewed Franco-German effort to merge the WEU into the EU, and
insisted on measures (outside the Amsterdam Treaty) to prevent 'quota-
hopping', the practice whereby non-British fishermen managed to buy
up the UK's fishing quotas. Once again, in all these, Blair was not too
removed from his Conservative predecessors. This is not to say that there
were no differences between them. It could be fairly pointed out that all
member states had their own agenda in EU negotiations and that the key
element in Blair's policy, as it had been in Edward Heath's, was the determination to act in a *communitaire* manner. The Prime Minister told parliament that 'at Amsterdam, . . . for the first time for many years Britain
spoke as a united government with a clear direction for Europe' and
asserted once again 'that we can get a better deal by being constructive'.[5]
But in one important way, Blair's determination to restore Britain's
international standing after the Major years jarred against his European
commitment. He had already talked at the 1996 Party Conference of
acting as a 'bridge' between Europe and the US, and in late May 1997 he
initiated such a policy by holding a particularly friendly meeting with
President Bill Clinton in London. As one critic warned, citing numerous
post-war precedents: 'A bridge is not needed, and . . . runs a real risk of
jeopardising our relations with our European partners'.[6] Nonetheless,
whatever the dangers (and in contrast to Heath) Blair persevered over
the following years in an attempt to combine a more *communitaire* policy
in Europe with a revived special relationship.

The British Presidency and Preparations for the Euro

Labour's attempt to establish a more positive policy on Europe faced a
complex dilemma in 1997 over EMU. On this issue of course the party
had, in November 1996, promised to hold a referendum ahead of a
single currency but that still left the question of whether to join in the first
wave, planned for January 1999, or at some later date. In late September

1997 the Blair government hit its first real crisis, when rumours that early membership was possible led to a fall in the value of Sterling and ministers appeared divided over their position. There were clear arguments in favour of adopting the 'Euro' as soon as possible. This would put Britain with the majority of members and give it a real say, during the all-important early years, in how the single currency worked. But the prospects for the single currency were still in doubt (largely due to Germany's continuing economic problems), Britain's currently healthy economy contrasted with the Continent's doldrums, and membership was unpopular with most of the British press and a majority of voters. By delaying until 2002 the government could both assess the viability of the Euro and minimise the risk of the issue damaging its chances of winning the next election. The party had never won a clear majority in two successive elections and Blair's main aim in office was to break this doleful record. This craving for re-election had reinforced the need to defend British interests in the Amsterdam talks. Therefore Gordon Brown moved quickly in September to deny that Labour would rush into the EMU and Britain paid the price by seeming, now, to be peripheral to the EU's most important project.[7] Indeed in December, the Luxembourg Summit was almost completely dominated by arguments between Blair and other leaders over the powers of the 'Euro-X Committee', which would oversee the single currency; with the Prime Minister keen to prevent this body from dominating all the EU's economic decisions in future.

If Britain seemed removed from the heart of Europe where EMU was concerned, the rotation of the Presidency to London in the first half of 1998 nonetheless kept Blair at the centre of European attentions. And the Presidency proved rather more successful than Major's had been five years before. In preparation for it, Cook made a number of visits to East European capitals in late 1997, underscoring Britain's support for an 'eastern enlargement', talks on which were due to begin in March 1998. The government's agenda for the Presidency as a whole was set out by the Foreign Secretary during a speech in Dublin, on 3 November, which laid the greatest emphasis on 'giving Europe back to the people' rather than remaining obsessed with institutional reform. Promoting employment, through measures such as better training, deregulation of the jobs market and the reduction of non-salary costs on businesses, was top of an agenda which also included greater EU co-operation against crime and the protection of the environment. The speech also dealt with enlargement and reform of the Common Agricultural Policy. But it was clear that the key test of British diplomatic skill would be pushing forward preparations for a single currency – even though Britain itself would not be in at the launch.[8]

The Presidency formally opened on 8 January with a meeting between Blair and the Commission President, Jacques Santer, in London, where the Prime Minister repeated the main lines of Cook's Dublin speech. Six months later the government could be reasonably satisfied with what it had achieved. No major strides forward for the EU had been expected, but talks on the eastern enlargement went ahead in mid-March (marred by disagreements with Greece over Turkish membership), a major EU–Asia summit was held in April and there were also summits with the leaders of Russia, America and Canada, all of which served to emphasise the growing significance in international diplomacy of the EU meeting as a whole. So far as the 'People's Europe' theme was concerned, measures were agreed to tackle drug trafficking, to improve air quality and lower greenhouse gas emissions. The British could also be pleased with steps towards freer trade between the EU and North America, moves to relax the ban on British beef exports (though it was only finally lifted in August 1999), the drafting of common EU guidelines on arms exports and a ban on driftnet fishing. Also the basis was successfully laid for the launch of the Euro. Despite early arguments over Italy's fitness for membership, the lax approach taken to the Maastricht 'convergence criteria' and, worst of all, an unseemly wrangle between France and the rest over who should be head of the European Central Bank (ECB), it was agreed in early May that eleven EU members (all but Britain, Denmark, Greece and Sweden) would proceed with the 'Euro' in January 1999. The ECB was formally inaugurated in Frankfurt on 30 June. Towards the end of the Presidency, Blair's increasingly positive rhetoric appeared to promise an early announcement of British membership of the single currency and he felt confident that Britain's vision of a 'third way', between laissez-faire and corporatist approaches to economic policy, was winning through: ahead of the Cardiff Summit in June he visited EU capitals and believed a consensus was emerging on a Europe which would embrace deregulation and subsidiarity more wholeheartedly. As Cook summed it up during a speech to round off the Presidency: 'A new vision of Europe is taking hold. It is not . . . Europe creeping towards . . . a super-state . . . It is a Europe . . . devolving decisions to the lowest possible level . . . whose citizens feel it . . . serves their purposes without threatening their identity.'[9]

However, in June 1998 the press debate in Britain was generally critical of a Presidency which had seen no great policy departures, had left the CAP and EU finances unreformed and had fudged its most difficult challenge, the headship of the ECB. Steps towards a 'People's Europe' had been modest, little was done to tackle the gathering economic crisis in Asia (which threatened to plunge the world into recession) and Cook had failed in his attempts to make the EU a key player in Middle East peace efforts. Neither did the British act in as *communitaire* manner as they claimed. In particular Blair upset his fellow European leaders with his continued closeness to Washington – his decision to visit Clinton in January as the British Presidency began, and his unity with America over dealing toughly with Saddam Hussein's Iraq on UN arms inspections.[10] British popular opinion remained resolutely lukewarm about European integration and a number of issues could still stir up anti-EU feeling. One potential danger was a massive reduction in EU grants to British regions, so as to help pay for the enlargement of the Union to poor, mainly agricultural, East European countries (a step which, ironically, Britain had done much to support). Other problems in late 1998 included renewed questioning of Britain's 1984 financial rebate and a Franco-German proposal to harmonise EU tax policies: neither of these was welcome to the Blair government. But the most controversial issue remained the single currency, about which opinion polls and most of the press were particularly sceptical. Speculation that Labour would soon commit itself to a date for EMU membership led Brown in July to reiterate that such a decision would only be taken in the light of Britain's economic situation at the time. However, while such an even-handed policy deflected critics at home, it did nothing to forward Blair's claims to be a full player in Europe. Indeed, Britain's peripheral role in EMU was confirmed by the fact that, by mid-1998, it was again one of only two countries (the other was Sweden) to be a non-member of the Exchange Rate Mechanism.

With the member states chosen and the ECB established, the 'Euro' was successfully launched on 1 January 1999, at which point conversion rates between the member currencies were locked and a single monetary policy began. The actual use of Euro notes and coins would not begin until 2002, and national banknotes would remain legal tender until 2003. Neither, in theory, was the process irreversible: with the gathering economic depression, and question marks over the fitness of some members for EMU, the auguries for the Euro were not perfect. Furthermore, only a few months before it had lost one of its key creators, Helmut Kohl, defeated at the polls in Germany. But the fact that the single currency went ahead at all was a remarkable achievement given all the problems it had faced since Maastricht. For Britain the latest step on the road of

European integration posed familiar dilemmas. In the short term, the impact of the decision to avoid initial membership was unpredictable. If the edifice quickly collapsed, like the European Defence Community in the early 1950s, then British caution would be vindicated; but if EMU boosted European growth rates, as the original EEC had (apparently) done in the 1960s, the decision could again be seen as yet another 'missed opportunity'. At the very least there was a danger that Sterling, left free floating outside a major new currency bloc, would fall victim to speculation and unhelpful fluctuations in value, which could damage trade. In the long term, if the Euro proved successful, then Britain would presumably find it difficult to stand aside, but any decision to join would offend patriotic opinion and timing would be all important, especially given the need for a referendum in advance. A referendum ahead of the next general election might divide the Conservatives more than ever, highlighting the rift between its sceptics and enthusiasts, but it would also risk the danger of a 'No' vote. However, to delay could leave Britain vulnerable to monetary instability and unable to play a full role in the Union. For all its insistence on playing a positive role in Europe, the Blair Cabinet presided over a situation of semi-detachment from Europe which was not too far removed from most other post-war administrations. Pragmatism, a desire to be seen defending British interests, and a sense of separateness from the rest of Europe still took their toll on the government's ambitions to be a leader in European debates.

CONCLUSIONS

In his study of Britain's international policy David Reynolds considered membership of the EEC to be 'perhaps the most profound revolution in British foreign policy in the twentieth century'. Yet in his book on Britain's role in the EEC since 1973 Stephen George continually emphasised that, whether inside or outside the Community, 'Britain was pursuing its consistent view of how Europe ought to relate to the rest of the world. There was no conversion to the ideal of European union.' Anyone who studies British attitudes towards European unity over recent decades is faced by the apparent contradiction between the 'revolutionary' change in Britain's international policy represented by Community membership, and the persistence of long-standing British aims, including the wish to maximise Britain's own influence in world affairs, the determination to retain national control over decision-making, and to oppose all manifestations of federalism, and the desire to promote free trade and avoid a 'closed' European trade system.

An important element in this paradox was highlighted by Paul Sharp in a study of Britain's attempts to enter Europe between 1961 and 1971. He noted that Britain's post-war policy is often seen 'as a reasonably clear-cut case of the governments of a country which is experiencing a steady decline ... searching out a new orientation'. But this cannot explain why 'British governments persist in seeing the EEC ... as a means to ... a very old end, Britain's world role'. Thus Macmillan hoped EEC membership would strengthen Britain's economy and reinforce Western unity, by allowing Britain to direct the EEC towards an 'open' trade policy. He denied federalism was a threat and assumed Britain would become a leading force in the Community. Harold Wilson was faced by a narrowing of British options, and felt Britain had no alternative to membership, but he too wished to preserve Britain's independence, to make economic (and especially technological) gains from membership and was concerned with the precise terms of entry to the EEC. Edward

Heath was less interested in detailed terms of entry and believed the Community was stronger than any individual national actor, including Britain, but argued that the gains of entry would outstrip the costs by boosting British growth and allowing Britain to join a potential third superpower. In Sharp's view there *was* a shift in policy over the decade, Britain being far weaker in 1971 than it was in 1961, and the Commonwealth far less vital; but 'the notion of a world role had itself become an eternal interest' and, in order to justify membership of an organisation with supranational ambitions, all British premiers had to argue that the potential economic and political gains were enormous, the supranational threat minimal.[1]

It may be argued that Sharp's argument, though an interesting one, does not answer the main point: whatever British leaders said they were doing, the reality was that EEC membership was a reaction to decline. With the Empire lost, naval predominance ended, and the Commonwealth ineffective, Britain was forced, however reluctantly, to become a European power. In 1866 Benjamin Disraeli had declared 'England has outgrown the continent of Europe . . . she is the metropolis of a great maritime empire . . . she is really more an Asiatic Power than a European' and a century later Harold Wilson could assert that 'our frontiers are in the Himalayas',[2] but by 1973 Britain's role 'East of Suez' had come to an end. Britain remained one of the six largest industrial economies but her economic decline relative to others was hard to deny and no one could provide a persuasive alternative to EEC entry. However, these points do not necessarily invalidate Sharp's argument that British leaders supported the EEC, not as a retreat by a once-great power, but as a way to restore national fortunes by providing a new outlet for national ambitions and compensating for certain national failings. Britain is not alone in this. All members try to use the EEC to compensate for national failings: West German leaders after 1949 favoured European integration as a way to safeguard democracy from a revival of Nazism and militarism; France saw it as a way to control the German menace; Italy found it easy to identify with a European future because the Italian state could hardly be counted as a success since unification in 1860; Ireland and Greece, on the underdeveloped periphery of Europe, gained economic aid from the EEC; whilst Spain and Portugal (like Germany) sought to safeguard their new democracies via membership in the 1980s.

This point can be taken further. It is a contention of international relations theorists that all international organisations are designed to protect their members from the forces of interdependence. Better communications and the coming of the world economy (together with the ravages of total war) have threatened the power of the nation state in the twentieth century, but rather than being at the mercy of such forces, states have joined in organisations which give some protection from the threat of war and allow them to 'manage' international trade and contacts. The logic of this approach has been adopted by historians studying the development of European integration, notably in Alan Milward's 1992 work, *The European Rescue of the Nation State*. The argument provides a general explanation for the apparent contradiction in Britain's move towards Europe whilst retaining traditional aims. Britain was unable to escape the pressures of interdependence and so joined the EEC to help control them. This was a new departure but it did not imply any desire to abandon well-established policies. The point can only be fully understood however, by looking in greater detail, over a wider period, at long-term British policies and interests, at how they were challenged after 1945, and at how (and how far) the EEC provided a suitable alternative departure. Throughout most of this book attention has concentrated on governments and the policies they followed. In the conclusion the focus will be on the underlying forces which limited all British leaders in their policy options.

There is considerable room for debate about how far Britain diverges from its continental neighbours in its attitude to European integration. Many writers take it for granted that British policy has differed from other European states in the post-war period with its reluctance to get involved in the integration process at an early date and its subsequent difficulties, once inside the EEC, with any deepening of integration. Stephen George, one of the best known writers in the field, has become identified with the 'awkward partner' approach, which sees Britain as having been persistently ungainly in its European policies because of such factors as its island position, political traditions and late arrival in the Community.[3] This view has been criticised on a number of grounds, sometimes by distorting what George actually says. Thus Jim Buller talks of an awkward partner 'thesis' and criticises George for not defining the concept rigorously enough. But, as Stuart Wilks points out, 'the term "awkward" has been used by George and others to describe a tendency (not a rigid negotiating stance) which is especially characteristic of ... British relations with the institutions of the EU and its other member states'. William Patterson and Wolfram Kaiser have also been critical of what they see (in the 'awkward partner' and 'missed bus' approaches) as an 'exceptionalist' thesis on Britain and European integration, one which argues that the country took 'a historically unique departure from the apparently normal path of democratic virtue'. Patterson and Kaiser point out that Britain was far from being the only West European state to remain outside the original EEC; that the integrationist path was neither more natural than, nor morally superior to, British policy; and that Britain always had much in common with its continental neighbours. Kaiser even doubts the importance of Britain's island position in separating it from the Continent, arguing that Ireland – another island – has found it quite easy to adapt to a European future.[4]

The position taken in this book is that, in many important ways, Britain is similar to the other EU states in terms of its attitude to European integration: as said above, from the outset all the members have used European integration as a means to achieve *national* ends and there are limits on the Euro-idealism even of such key states as France and Germany. Britain is not unique in this. Furthermore, from the Second World War onwards Britain did have a European policy, it was not indifferent to co-operation with the Continent and it did decide (earlier than some other West European democracies) that its interests were best served by Community membership, joining in the first enlargement. But it is also the case that all countries have their own, individual histories, interests and customs – that all in a sense are 'exceptional' – and that the particular course steered by Britain, one of the largest members, is worthy of separate study. It may be true that only six states formed the original EEC, but Britain was easily the most significant non-member (in terms of its economic, military and diplomatic importance) in the 1950s and 1960s. Many other European countries found it impossible to join the EEC at this time, not because of choice but because of their international position: most Eastern European states were Communist, of course; Finland and Austria were in a special treaty position regarding the USSR; Switzerland (which in any case had its own particular brand of insularity) and Sweden were studiously neutral; Spain and Portugal (and, for a time, Greece) were under dictatorships; whilst for Denmark and, more particularly, Ireland the question of membership largely relied on the path taken by Britain. Thus Britain's decision not to join in the process of integration at an early point was significant in *European* as well as national terms. And the catalogue of British 'awkwardness' towards Europe, even if it has sometimes been shared by others, is a long one: non-involvement in the ECSC, EDC and original EEC were followed, once inside the Community, by budgetary hassles, opt outs and non-membership of both the original ERM group and, in 1999, the single currency.

The reasons why Britain has been so reluctant to commit itself to integration with Europe are not difficult to understand, considering the country's historical development. To an extent of course Britain is 'different' from Europe simply because it is an island: this basic geographical fact has had a profound effect on national outlook. It may be true that Ireland is also an island, and yet has found it possible to embrace integration. But Ireland is a comparatively recent creation as a state which in some ways had failed, before entering the Community, to fulfil the material expectations of its people; and it has made use of European institutions partly in order to limit the influence of its larger British neighbour (just as the Benelux countries try to limit the power of France and Germany). Great Britain, in contrast, has had nearly three centuries as an island power, strong enough to resist foreign domination and able to project its power across the oceans. It is the combination of island position and great power status which has created a stronger sense of separateness from the rest of Europe than Ireland possesses. Whereas continental countries have been forced over centuries to deal with each other every day to settle border disputes, reach common solutions to problems such as river navigation and border controls, and have suffered frequent invasions during wars, Britain has often been able to adopt an insular policy, has avoided *permanent* involvement in continental affairs and has escaped successful invasion for nearly a thousand years. British national identity, however much challenged since the 1950s, is arguably stronger because of this and the country has been able gradually to develop its unique, unwritten constitution, with an institutional continuity which is unique in the European Union. Both this strong national identity and the unwritten constitution make participation in supranational institutions difficult: continental states are more used to permanent involvements and to ornate, written constitutions. The sense of 'difference' from the Continent was further heightened after 1750 by the Industrial Revolution and the peaceful development of constitutional government in Britain, and then by the acquisition of the world's largest colonial empire, including the large Anglo-Saxon settlements in Canada, Australia and South Africa, which led to Disraeli's contention that Britain had 'outgrown' Europe.

Traditionally Britain *was* ready to involve itself in European diplomacy, to help maintain the balance of power on the Continent and to try to prevent any state gaining hegemony – as in the wars against Louis XIV, Napoleon, Hitler and finally in the Cold War against the Soviet Union. It could not have defeated any of these threats unaided by strong allies. Though an island, Britain was too geographically proximate to Europe to cut itself off from the Continent completely. It could always be menaced by a strong naval power (such as Philip II's Spain or eighteenth-century France) and in the twentieth century became vulnerable to air attack from Europe. Britain always had a 'European policy' and commercial and financial links strengthened ties to the Continent, giving Britain a greater interest in preserving European peace so that trade could thrive. However, Britain's European policy generally sought to preserve the balance of power from the *outside*, avoiding long-term commitments and entering into conflicts only in exceptional circumstances. Only in the First and Second World Wars did Britain create a large land army to fight on the Continent, but even after 1919, she tried to withdraw from the Continent, to concentrate on Imperial affairs, hoping for a balance of power between Germany and France.

However, after 1945 Britain had a more sophisticated European policy than is often realised, designed not only to unite the Continent against Soviet Communism, but also to create a British-European combination which could stand up to both superpowers. But Joseph Frankel, in his study of post-war British foreign policy, considered that: 'The sustained British efforts to establish a post-war balance could be interpreted as being ... the preparations of conditions for ... a withdrawal, a parallel for which could be found in the past after every major European war.'[5] It was of course the experience of the second 'total war' in Europe in a generation which gave the greatest impetus to European integration. Britain was not immune from this. After all, its vulnerability to attack from the Continent was now greater than ever. But the Second World War also confirmed Britain's sense of separateness from the Continent. France, Germany, Italy and others faced defeat and occupation; their political institutions – many in any case of recent origin – faced simultaneous upheaval; their military power was shattered; and they were left facing superpower domination and economic reconstruction. Britain in contrast (despite Dunkirk and Singapore) emerged victorious, one of the 'Big Three', its national institutions and the Commonwealth-Empire intact. In the immediate aftermath of the war Britain did overestimate its power in Europe, but the Labour government was flexible and *did* develop new policies. Independence for India, leadership of the Marshall Plan, and the acceptance of a permanent security alliance via NATO were all dramatic actions compared to past practice, showing that British pragmatism could accept major changes in policy.

However, it is another contention of this study that those who argue Britain could have had the leadership of Europe *on its own terms* at this time are naïve: such claims simply reflect a national obsession with 'leading' others. Robert Holland, in his study of Britain's world role in the twentieth century, also has no time for these claims, and quotes several reasons why Britain could not 'lead' Western Europe: British leaders hoped to find independent solutions to their economic problems; France distrusted Britain, wanted to lead Europe itself and specifically sought co-operation with Germany.[6] The present study is rather different. Again Britain *did* have a European policy in 1945–55, when it was the strongest West European state in economic and military terms, but it was based on inter-governmental co-operation via such bodies as the Brussels Pact and OEEC. It did not involve the pooling of sovereignty in supranational bodies, and it had to fit in with the US alliance and the development of the Commonwealth. This policy had something to do with a lack of vision on Britain's part. Certainly the pragmatic British government had little liking for federalist ideas after the war, and undoubtedly exaggerated their significance in shaping policy in France, Belgium, Italy and Germany. Monnet's insistence on an open-ended commitment to pool sovereignty in the Schuman Plan had a particularly detrimental impact on the chances of British participation. But it soon became clear that the Six Community powers had not engaged in a wholesale surrender of sovereignty to central institutions and that, if anything, they advanced in a pragmatic, practical way which kept key decisions in the hands of member governments.

The vital point here is that policy was shaped according to *national* interests, as interpreted by governments at the time. What Britain did not realise was that a degree of pooled sovereignty – whereby governments handed powers in certain limited areas to common institutions – could actually be in the national interest of member states. This was particularly significant for Franco-German relations because it was largely in order to prevent a new Franco-German war that France developed the Schuman Plan in the first place, and it was mainly to avoid a resurgence of nationalism and militarism that Konrad Adenauer backed the policy. For both states a certain loss of sovereignty was a price worth paying in order to achieve a highly desirable end: security for France, democracy for Germany. The Benelux states (also insecure after the events of 1940 and keen to develop markets in Germany) and Italy (also keen to preserve its democracy and modernise its economy) joined the supranational group. Yet Britain had no such overwhelming national need to pool its sovereignty and no leading political figure (not even supposed 'pro-Europeans' like Churchill and Macmillan) was ready to merge Britain's future with Europe whilst abandoning the Commonwealth.

In particular Britain did not share the French and German obsession with limiting German independence in a supranational grouping. In addition, Britain was distrustful of the political instability and economic weakness of continental states into the 1950s. British priorities became based around tackling Soviet Communism (which did *not* demand a loss of sovereignty) and matching US economic power (for which a European customs union seemed no solution around 1950). Both these national priorities seemed to be better served by closer co-operation with America and the Commonwealth, though Europe was included in the policy of 'three circles'.

Therefore, events in the years 1939–55 tended to consolidate existing trends. Britain did not find its international posture, its constitutional development and its industrial-financial policies called fundamentally into question by the war. The German menace and the Cold War showed that Britain could not divorce itself from the Continent but neither did they suggest that a merger of sovereignty with the Continent was necessary. Nor has any subsequent single event served to overturn many traditional British attitudes to international affairs. Many of the reasons for British reticence in European affairs simply reflect the fact that Britain is still trying to satisfy well-established policy aims in a new context. This book has argued that British policy in 1955–7, when the EEC was founded, deserves criticism on several counts. If there was a 'missed opportunity' for Britain to 'enter Europe' at an early date it came at this time. By the mid-1950s the menace posed to British influence by decolonisation, the rise of the superpowers and the West European revival was already becoming clear. The Six at that point had already created the Coal–Steel Community, but this was limited in scope and Britain was an associate member. It was already clear that 'pooled sovereignty' was not the same as federalism. By failing to join the EEC at the outset Britain lost the opportunity to help shape the original organisation, lost control of subsequent developments in the EEC, and put the French in a position where they could defeat subsequent British initiatives such as the Free Trade Area. Yet much of this only became clear in retrospect and the 'window of opportunity' for Britain to join the EEC talks was only a narrow one, if it opened at all. In the mid-1950s the Sterling Area still seemed valuable, Britain was still the wealthiest European state, and the Suez Crisis drove Britain away from France. By 1961, only a short time later, Macmillan was ready to adjust his policy and, but for de Gaulle's vetoes, Britain might have joined the EEC five or ten years earlier than it eventually did. Such are the chances, accidents and coincidences of history.

The fact that Britain did not join the EEC until after it was established should not arouse much surprise when one understands the challenge it represented to national preconceptions about external policy. It is worth restating several powerful elements which provoked British doubts. First, EEC membership was not in line with Britain's traditional defence policy and European diplomacy, which was based on naval power and saw direct involvement in continental affairs as an exceptional occurrence, not as a daily event. Second, membership upset Britain's traditional commercial and financial policy, which was built around investment in world trade, low tariffs and cheap food: the EEC meant a regional customs union and the CAP. Many pragmatic arguments against membership in the 1960s and 1970s concentrated on the costs of these policies in higher food prices. Third, membership challenged Britain's evolutionary, unwritten constitution and the sovereignty of the Mother of Parliaments, built up over centuries, with the prospect of pooled sovereignty and acceptance of the Treaty of Rome. Fourth, membership also impeded British political parties in their attempts to pursue a national economic policy: for Labour European integration seemed to threaten Socialist policies at home; for right-wing Conservatives in the 1990s the EEC impeded monetarism and 'market forces'. Fundamentally, EEC membership offended against the basic fact of British geography as an island power which has, to a large extent, developed separately from the Continent. Diplomacy, commerce, the constitution, and geography – all these are fundamental to a nation's identity. Add to them the point that Britain had less interest in controlling German power than did continental states, and it is clear why Britain's relations with the EEC have been uneasy. The fact that Britain did not join in the EEC at the outset reinforced this alienation because policies (such as the CAP) were developed without it and did not suit its interests.

However, having stated the underlying reasons for British reticence, it cannot be doubted either that by about 1960 powerful forces were at work to drive Britain towards Europe. Britain's 'separateness' from the Continent – the notion of 'exceptionalism' which many opponents of Eoropean integration have both fostered and tried to exploit – must not be exaggerated. It has already been said that Britain has long had a 'European' policy and (at least in retrospect) it can be seen to have long shared a common civilisation with Western Europe. From time to time, since the Roman period, British rulers have also been continental rulers and the English Channel was never wide enough to allow the country to ignore developments on the other side. Industrialisation, the rise of liberalism, the growth of social reforms – these and many other factors in modern history exist throughout Europe and the West, whatever Britain's significance in their early development. Britain has maintained its individual identity of course, and has often defined its national identity in terms of enmity towards its near neighbours, not least during the Second World War. But in the post-war world many trends in Britain have been paralleled in Western Europe: industrial reforms, nationalisation and the welfare state were widely developed in the 1940s; Conservative parties established their predominance in the 1950s, in the era of economic growth; the mid-1960s saw widespread discontent (notably in 1968) and working-class militancy as growth levelled off and inflation increased; whilst the 1980s saw a resurgence of market economics, spending controls and privatisation.

These common trends reflected the fact that, although the nation state continues to command considerable loyalty, no modern Western country can withstand the forces of interdependence; and it is important to note that the British and European experiences were converging long before Britain joined the Community. As suggested above, the EEC provides its members with the way to 'manage' such interdependence, and in the early 1960s it became clear that, in order to survive in a modern, interdependent Europe Britain had to come to terms with the EEC. But this situation only came about because alternative policies had failed and the weaknesses of the 'three circles' approach were being exposed. The US did not treat Britain as an equal but instead supported supranationalism among the Six and encouraged Britain to join; the Empire was disintegrating, the Commonwealth had failed to become a powerful body (even if it retained a strong hold on many British minds beyond the mid-1960s). The British did try to create their own European trading group with the 1957 Free Trade Area proposal, but this did not answer the national interests of France, and was also disliked by the US. The best Britain could do was to create the quite inadequate EFTA. Under the Wilson government, at least in 1967, many concluded there was 'no alternative' to Community membership.

An important point is that, by the late 1960s, many traditional British policies had been fatally undermined anyway. Entry to the EEC did not mean the abandonment of traditional policies, it was a reaction to their threatened demise. The disintegration of the Empire, under pressures of decolonisation, and the limits to the special relationship (as the US far outstripped British power) were two obvious developments in post-war geopolitics. But there were others. Britain's economic policy was no longer

a success, and it failed to keep up with US, Japanese and German technological progress after 1945. After 1958 Britain was in danger of being
caught between the American and EEC trade blocs. The Sterling Area
was becoming less valuable and attempts to hold up the value of Sterling
proved costly. Since 1958 there had been grave concern about Britain's
failure to match continental growth rates. Also, as Donald Maclean (the
Soviet spy) pointed out in a book written after he fled to Moscow, Britain
faced a challenge to its traditional diplomatic policy: in the first half of the
century London was able to act as the arbiter between France and
Germany; but the EEC destroyed this policy and created a Franco-
German combination whose political and economic power dominated
Western Europe.[7]

This argument can be taken further. Historically, as outlined above,
Britain has tried to maintain a balance of power on the Continent and has
opposed bids for hegemony. But after 1945 the country was faced by a
dual challenge. In Europe as a whole the bid for hegemony came from
the Soviets, and Britain took a lead in opposing them, at least in a military
sense, even agreeing to maintain a fixed number of divisions on the Continent in 1954 – another departure from tradition. In Western Europe
however, a new type of challenge emerged in the EEC, whose power was
primarily economic, which combined the three major powers (France,
Germany and Italy) and which was a voluntary organisation – not a single
state seeking domination. The EEC threatened to reduce British exports
and to become Western Europe's leading political force. The emergence
of this novel phenomenon presented a major challenge to the British.
They could not divide the EEC (though there was, arguably, an attempt
to do so in 1955–6). They could not match its economic power given
the weakness of the British economy, of the Commonwealth and of the
Sterling Area. They could not claim that it was a menace to the peace
although, in 1959–60, Macmillan accused the EEC of dividing the OEEC
and NATO. Nor could they persuade the US to oppose the EEC: Americans wanted Britain to join the EEC and only began to see the EEC as a
trade rival in the late 1960s. By 1961 Macmillan believed he must come to
terms with the new type of continental power and even hoped Britain
might become the leader of it. Thus it can be argued that, by the time
Britain negotiated EEC entry in 1971–2, the country already faced new
diplomatic, military and economic realities. It can be added that, in the
mid-1970s, faith was even undermined in Britain's much trumpeted
political stability as strikes, stagflation and calls for the devolution of
power led to claims that the country had become 'ungovernable'.

Devolution was also a reminder that Britain itself was a union of English, Scottish, Welsh and Irish identities, and that its future survival was by no means inevitable. (Indeed, by the 1990s it could be argued that membership of the European Union encouraged the devolution trend, by allowing Scottish nationalists in particular to believe that they could emulate the Irish experience, by seeking independence from London whilst retaining the economic and political security offered by European institutions – which now included the Committee of the Regions.)

The argument that traditional policies were breaking down *regardless* of EEC membership helps to explain the paradox, discussed at the start of this chapter, between the revolutionary nature of membership and the continuity of traditional concerns. Building on the idea that international organisations are the protectors of the nation state in an interdependent world it is possible to see the EEC not as a last retreat for British power, but as a means of safeguarding old interests. Undoubtedly EEC entry meant dramatic changes in British policy. Trade and investment patterns would have to change; the CAP was alien to British practice; EEC legislation would have to be accepted with precedence over British law; and there was still the danger that the Community would veer towards greater supranationalism. But the British were nothing if not pragmatic; they were unable to construct a viable alternative to membership and they could see a number of gains from the EEC, which fitted their traditional concerns. Furthermore, once inside the EEC Britain could hope to shape its policies in line with British interests. Both 'pro' and 'anti-Europeans' could agree that Britain must pursue its own interests in the EEC. On the commercial and financial side, Europe could offer a large market supposedly based on free international trade, which would provide a basis for economic and political resurgence; once inside Britain could press for genuine free trade in investment and services as well as goods, seen in the Single European Act. It could also work for a reform of the CAP (achieved to some extent after 1992), and for an 'outward-looking' community, which helped third world producers (as in the Lomé convention), reached an agreement with EFTA (finally signed in 1992) and pursued freer trade within GATT (in the Uruguay Round).

Politically Britain would be combining with states which shared its own values – liberal-democratic and anti-Communist, with wide-ranging social reforms – and by 1961 of course it was already evident that the Six pooled their sovereignty in specific areas and were not, at least in the short term, bent on establishing a federation. Indeed France, Germany and the others successfully used the EEC to *strengthen* their international role: the France of General de Gaulle could hardly be said to lack influence and independence, rather it seemed a resurgent power. This was a highly significant point for Macmillan. Militarily Britain had already committed itself to European defence through NATO (of which many EEC states were members) and the EEC was slow to take on any security dimension, development on this front being concentrated in the Western European Union, of which Britain was a founder member. Diplomatically the EEC could provide Britain with a basis for international action which allowed it to influence world affairs, compensated for the weakness of the Commonwealth and provided the possibility of matching US power (which is often underestimated as a post-war British aim). It also ensured an end to Franco-German enmity, removing the danger of war in Western Europe which had been so costly early in the century. In addition it opened up the possibility, once Britain was inside, of again playing the arbiter between France and Germany, something which seemed a possibility in 1972–3 at least, when Heath worked closely with Pompidou and the French were suspicious of Germany's *Ostpolitik* and the power of the Deutschmark. Once inside Britain could also help preserve links between the EEC and the US.

Yet if EEC membership could be seen as a way for Britain to achieve consistent interests – diplomatic, commercial, political, military – and if no realistic alternative presented itself, there can be no doubt that as a policy option it had imperfections. The EEC represented a narrowing of Britain's world role to that of a regional one, even if Britain continued to trade with many powers outside the EEC. The fact remained that Britain had not founded the EEC and that many elements within it which Britain disliked could not easily be changed. In 1992 the Community budget was three times its 1971 size in terms of GDP, and the CAP, despite some reforms, took up two-thirds of spending. Trade relations with the US and GATT were poor. National governments might still be the prime force in the Community but the Commission had extensive powers and the Maastricht Treaty (whatever its future and despite the important, if vague, principle of 'subsidiarity') showed that the loss of national independence was a real possibility. Whatever had been claimed when Britain entered the Community, the 'Community method' of co-operation led to an incremental growth in the power of Brussels; qualified majority votes were extended and national parliaments could not properly scrutinise Community actions. Thus entry had considerable political and economic costs. Neither can the EEC be said to have brought all the gains that many of its supporters expected. In particular the economic gains promised by Macmillan, Wilson and Heath had not emerged. To some extent this was because Britain joined the Community when the 'boom' years had ended. But the unrest on Conservative backbenches after the 1992 election arguably had some justification.

However, many would argue that EEC membership *in itself* was not an economic panacea. The EEC provided Britain with certain opportunities, but the very fact that it was made up of nation states meant that those states had to pursue their own economic policies, albeit in a 'managed' environment. British government and industrial leaders were well aware of the need to compete, indeed they welcomed it, but it cannot be said that they fared very well. Tony Benn, in arguing in favour of a nationally based Socialist programme of recovery for Britain in the 1970s, insisted that the EEC would *impede* rather than assist British growth in future, and he complained, 'The myth of Empire has been replaced by the myth of Europe' as a way to escape domestic troubles. Average British growth rates since 1973 have still lagged behind most of the original Six. In particular Britain suffered throughout the post-war period from a lack of industrial and technological investment, a problem which needed to be tackled whether inside or outside the Community.[8] The fact that EC membership has had such profound effects on British identity also means that it has tended to cut across party lines and, at times, could have divided either of the main political parties down the middle. Arguably it did have an important role in leading Labour pro-Europeans to form the Social Democratic party. Such party divisions have greatly increased the tendency of pragmatists, both Labour and Conservative, to play down their commitment to European Union, even if they see no alternative to EEC membership.

This is not to say of course that Britain has gained nothing from EEC membership. In a sense it has gained as much as any other member. Despite frequent condemnations of EEC policies, Britain has as many representatives in European institutions as other leading countries. It also has access to a large, competitive market, is able to attract investment from countries such as Japan, and has joined a peaceful, democratic grouping which can help to control nationalist ambitions in Germany. The benefits of belonging to a peaceful and economically successful regional grouping have been highlighted since 1989 by events in the former USSR and Yugoslavia. But the costs of EEC membership are perhaps greater than Britain was led to expect in the 1975 referendum and the benefits not so great. The problem is of course that a cost-benefit analysis is itself too pragmatic a way to look at the EEC. Arguably it is because Britain was 'sold' EEC membership as a pragmatic step, and because the British people judge the results in these terms, that Britain has *not* become a leading player in the Community. It does not share the idealism of other members, and this has an important effect on how it fares.

In 1974 Fred Northedge warned that if Britain wished to avoid being overwhelmed by world events 'that can only be done from a basis of economic power which . . . only Europe can now provide'; but to be effective in the EEC, Britain 'must act from national interest plus . . . concern for the Community', and he doubted it could achieve this. Two decades later Northedge's fear seems to have been borne out. As David Reynolds writes, 'the Community is frequently depicted in Britain as a centralised autocracy . . . That is to underestimate its diversity . . . in which national governments . . . are constantly manoeuvring . . . but success depends on being regarded as a full player'.[9] The present study has little sympathy with those who argue that Britain is unable to share the enthusiasm for European Union for philosophical reasons – that Britain is somehow too 'practical' and 'realistic' to indulge in any form of idealism. Britain has been quite ready to demonstrate idealism in the past, not least in its inflated hopes for the Commonwealth and the special relationship. Nor can it be said that France and Germany have always demonstrated idealistic faith in European unity. It has been repeated throughout this study that they generally looked to their *national* interests even within the EEC context. It is actually possible to argue, from a *pragmatic* viewpoint, that British interests would be served by *deeper* European integration. Fuller union could lead to a redistribution of wealth in the Community from which Britain, as the fifth poorest member, might benefit; a stronger European Parliament would reduce the 'democratic deficit', encourage greater public interest in the Community and limit the power of the Franco-German combination; full monetary union might enable all members to control Germany and destroy the power of the Bundesbank. However, the chances of Britain pursuing such a policy are nil.

To understand British reluctance one needs to consider again the historical experience of Britain and the attitudes to Europe which this has created. An island power, with a strong national identity and a strong parliament, will never find it easy to accept the ideal of 'closer union' and a powerful European parliament. The recent leader of a global Empire finds it hard to accept a secondary role to France and Germany in a regional union. Neither are British ministers used to sharing power with members of other parties, still less with members of other national governments: the British 'first-past-the-post' electoral system instead creates a 'winner-takes-all' result, where coalition government is a rarity; and in the days of the Empire (although, ironically, Britain was at the forefront of organising international conferences) London was the undisputed 'leader' of its most significant group of overseas partners. Stuart Wilks sees the heavily centralised structure of the British state as being particularly responsible for the country's 'awkwardness' in Europe. Unused to permanent involvement in continental affairs, Britain has found it difficult to adjust to the 'continuous renegotiation' demanded by Community membership, and often treats the European Community as something 'alien'. Certainly the EU, with its unique method of tying states together into a voluntary union, is a novel development for all its members, and in all the member states there is frequent resentment at the 'meddling' of Brussels 'Eurocrats' in national affairs: Community policy seems to be in the hands of an unelected elite who frequently appear to cause unnecessary, and unsettling, changes in everyday life. In all EU states citizens have a mutiplicity of identities – local, regional and national, as well as European. The European identity, partly because it has become important most recently, still has trouble competing with the others, especially with national identity. All the member states too have their particular histories, myths of national identity and sense of exceptionalism (often fostered by rivalries with their neighbours) which make European integration, though not impossible, difficult to pursue quickly. But in Britain indifference to Europe goes much deeper than in most other members and the sense of a European identity is comparatively shallow. Federalists, defined in the British sense, are very few. Only a third of British voters turn out for the Euro-elections; the Community average can be up to 60 per cent. The basic problem of an island power adjusting to 'continuous negotiation' was compounded by the way Britain felt forced, by the threat posed by the EEC and by a lack of alternatives, into membership. British politicians have seldom involved the country in a national debate about Europe and even the more responsible ones find it easy to appeal to patriotic sentiment in order to win popularity. As Stephen George writes, 'for the British people European integration was at best a necessity, not . . . an ideal'; and as Jeremy Black argues 'while Britain has bought membership' of the European Union 'it has not bought the myth' of a European identity.[10] Britain may have seen the EEC as a way to bolster its flagging power and provide a new basis for political and economic strength, but the very logic of this was that the Community should strengthen *British* power, not destroy its independence.

The Thatcherite approach of course was that the EEC should, as with the single market, manage freer competition between *nation* states. Both main parties have eventually come to accept EEC membership but the approach of British governments since 1961 (with the possible exception of Heath's and Blair's) has been a minimalist one, a logic Margaret Thatcher simply applied more vigorously: the EEC should compensate for national weaknesses, but should make nation states stronger not weaker.

Britain's insular background and minimalist approach explains why Britain is generally seen as being on the European periphery, even though – in the view of this book – *all* Community members pursue their own national agendas, and compromises between nation states continue to have the major role in shaping Community policy. It is not that continental states have an idealism about Europe which British pragmatism can never share: rather, Britain's historical experience and attitudes towards external affairs do not fit in well with European integration. Greece (geographically separate from the rest of the EEC) and Denmark (which shares some of Britain's evolutionary constitutional development) may also be described as 'reluctant' Europeans but, as discussed above, most members have strong national reasons for seeking closer integration: the Second World War helped weaken their faith in nationalism, and all continental states are used to dealing with each other on a permanent basis. Particular differences continue to arise between Britain and the original Six signatories of the Treaty of Rome, some of whom might welcome a 'two-tier' Europe, with themselves progressing to a deeper union. However, it is the Franco-German combination which continues to cause Britain the gravest problems, because it forms the engine of any drive to deeper integration. As seen with the European Defence Community and with de Gaulle's policies, if France objects to a particular European development, it is unlikely to proceed. There is always the danger that a resurgence of French and German nationalism will end their partnership (though a resurgence of German nationalism would be in no one's interests). But when France and Germany agree on an initiative, as with the widening of the Community after 1969 or the European Monetary System a decade later, it provides the foundation for progress. The trouble is that such progress is usually defined in terms of French and German national needs, a point which makes even Italy and the Benelux states resentful.

The problem for Britain here is that it has never managed to play the arbiter between France and Germany (despite a few attempts to do so) and, because of its lack of enthusiasm for the Community, has not been able to build a tripartite combination with them either. As a result Britain's influence in the Community has been limited. This has been another great failure of British hopes from the time they joined the EEC: the country has not been able to take control of developments in the Community; instead, at best, it has simply been able to delay and dilute initiatives. It was the Franco-German combination which, of course, put an end to British obstructionism in the mid-1980s, and later set the EEC on the road to Maastricht. Alone, Britain now lacks the economic power to act as a balance between France and Germany and as Nicholas Henderson so pointedly stated in 1979, Britain simply does not matter as much as France. This rules out any idea that British obstructionism (in the style of de Gaulle) can have lasting effect. The factors which led to the Schuman Plan in 1950 still hold good 45 years later. France's deep desire to control German power in a European framework is matched by the German government's desire – so long as it remains liberal-democratic – to tie itself to other liberal democracies. German reunification has only made these urges stronger because France, always weaker than Germany in material terms, fears a more assertive Germany after reunification. Britain is consequently faced by another drive for deeper union. Britain has an interest, of course, in controlling Germany and avoiding Franco-German conflict, but has never seen a loss of sovereignty as the ideal way to achieve this. One possible way to match the French and Germans would be for Britain to ally itself with other EEC members, but Italy, Spain and the Benelux states all favour deeper integration than Britain does.

To return to the contradiction raised at the outset. British policy has faced a revolution by 'joining Europe': an independent, insular but world power, committed to free trade, evolutionary political development and a strong parliament, and until recently the head of a vast Empire, has committed its future to a regional grouping, which includes an element of pooled sovereignty, its own elected parliament and executive, a closed agricultural system and common external tariff. Nonetheless, alongside such a profound change in orientation there is also a good deal of continuity in British interests, attitudes and ambitions, shaped over centuries. Britain continues to favour a freer trade system, both inside and outside the EEC; it wishes to minimise the loss of sovereignty to centralised institutions, and to use the Community to strengthen its national impact on world affairs. This is because Britain remains influenced by its background as an island power, its parliamentary tradition and its need for overseas trade. EEC membership was seen by its leading political advocates as a way to restore national strength at a time when other policies – the Sterling Area, Empire, US alliance – were losing their value. But the commitment to the EEC was not Britain's preferred option in the late 1950s and the organisation was framed without Britain's aims in mind. Britain joined the Community because the Community seemed an economic and political threat, hardly a good basis for easy relations once the country was inside. In a sense Britain is no different from other countries in its pursuit of a national agenda within the Community, but its particular historical development makes it a poor player of the Community game. An attempt by British leaders to educate the country about European affairs might force popular attitudes to evolve more rapidly in favour of greater co-operation, but too often it is easier to win votes by posing as the defender of national interest from a supposed 'foreign' intruder, and European policy remains largely in the hands of a Westminster and Whitehall elite. The result is that Britain is left committed to a European future but with little relish for the task, as summed up in the term 'there is no alternative'. Whilst some of its leaders may want Britain to be at the heart of Europe, the country often seems to lie on the periphery of the Continent in more than a geographical sense.

NOTES

All places of publication are London except where otherwise stated.

1   The Birth of European Unity, 1929–1949

1. Public Record Office (PRO), FO 371/49069/9595 (13 August); Alexander Cadogan diaries, Churchill College, Cambridge, 1/15 (13 August).
2. Standard critical accounts of British policy include: N. Beloff, *The General Says No* (1963); M. Charlton, *The Price of Victory* (1983); A. Nutting, *Europe Will Not Wait* (1960); R. Mayne, *The Recovery of Europe* (1970). To these may now be added R. Denman, *Missed Chances: Britain and Europe in the twentieth century* (1996).
3. R. W. D. Boyce, 'Britain's First "No" to Europe: Britain and the Briand Plan, 1929–30', *European Studies Review*, 10 (1980), 17–45; Robert Boyce, 'British Capitalism and the Idea of European Unity between the Wars', in P. Stirk (ed.), *European Unity in Context* (1989), pp. 65–83 (Tyrell quoted on p. 66); P. J. V. Rollo, *Britain and the Briand Plan: the Common Market that never was* (Keele, 1972); R. White, 'Cordial Caution: the British Response to the French Proposal for European Federal Union', in A. Bosco (ed.), *The Federal Idea: the History of Federalism from Enlightenment to 1945* (1991), pp. 237–62; M. Burgess, *The British Tradition of Federalism* (1995). For evidence that British reluctance over European commercial integration had a long pedigree see J. Galston, 'The Free Trade Diplomacy Debate and the Victorian European Common Market Initiative', *Canadian Journal of History*, 22 (1987), 59–82.
4. A. Bullock, *The Life and Times of Ernest Bevin*, Vol. I: *Trade Union Leader* (1960), pp. 356–63, 369–71, 386–8, 440–7, 622–3, 630–4, 648–9.
5. R. A. Wilford, 'The Federal Union Campaign', *European Studies Review*, 10 (1980), 102–4; A. Bosco, 'Federal Union, Chatham House . . . and the Anglo-French Union', in Bosco (ed.), *Federal Idea*, pp. 291–325.
6. A. Shlaim, 'Prelude to Downfall: the British Offer of Union to France, June 1940', *Journal of Contemporary History*, IX (1972), 27–63.
7. H. B. Ryan, *The Vision of Anglo-America: the US–UK alliance and the emerging Cold War, 1943–6* (Cambridge, 1987); see also, for example, R. B. Woods, *A Changing of the Guard: Anglo-America 1941–6* (Chapel Hill, North Carolina, 1990) or, more generally: H. G. Nicholas, *The US and Britain* (Chicago, 1975); and the collection of essays from D. C. Watt, *Succeeding John Bull* (1979).

8. See especially, C. Thorne, *Allies of a Kind: the US, Britain and the war against Japan, 1941–5* (Oxford, 1978); also W. R. Louis, *Imperialism at Bay, 1941–5: the US and the decolonisation of the British Empire* (Oxford, 1977).

9. In general see M. Kitchen, *British Policy toward the Soviet Union during the Second World War* (1986).

10. Public Record Office (PRO), CAB 66/21, WP 4(42) 8. On the wartime evolution of the Western bloc proposal see J. Baylis, *The Diplomacy of Pragmatism: Britain and the formation of NATO* (1993), ch. 1.

11. CAB 66/30, WP (42) 480; P. H. Spaak, *The Continuing Battle* (1971), pp. 76–8; O. Riste, 'The Genesis of North Atlantic Defence Cooperation', *NATO Review*, 29, No. 2 (April 1981), 22–9.

12. Sir L. Woodward, *British Foreign Policy in the Second World War*, Vol. V (1976), pp. 181–97; J. Baylis, 'British Wartime Thinking about a Post-war European Security Group', *Review of International Studies*, 9 (1983), 265–81; A. Shlaim, *Britain and the Origins of European Unity, 1940–51* (Reading, 1978), pp. 54–85.

13. Reproduced in R. Butler and M. E. Pelly (eds), *Documents on British Policy Overseas* (hereafter *DBPO*), Series 1, Vol. 1 (1984), document 102.

14. On these aspects see S. Greenwood, 'Ernest Bevin, France and "Western Union", 1945–6', *European History Quarterly*, 14 (1984), esp. 322–6.

15. *DBPO*, Series 1, Vol. 1, record of meeting of 25 July 1945.

16. J. W. Young, *Britain, France and the Unity of Europe, 1945–51* (Leicester, 1984), p. 26.

17. See especially, F. Kersaudy, *Churchill and de Gaulle* (1983).

18. Woodward, *Second World War*, Vol. III (1974), pp. 95–103; J. W. Young, *France, the Cold War and the Western Alliance, 1944–9* (1990), pp. 32, 45–6.

19. C. de Gaulle, *War Memoirs*, Vol. III: *1944–6* (1960), p. 192.

20. For a fuller account see Young, *Unity of Europe*, pp. 14–25.

21. Greenwood, 'Ernest Bevin and Western Union', p. 334; PRO, FO 371/67670/25.

22. Young, *Unity of Europe*, pp. 29–33.

23. FO 371/59955/8895, 8989; quote from Hugh Dalton's diary, British Library of Political and Economic Science, 10 September 1946.

24. Young, *Unity of Europe*, pp. 39–41.

25. A. S. Milward, *The Reconstruction of Western Europe, 1945–57* (1984), p. 235; F. Lynch, 'A Missed Opportunity to Plan the Reconstruction of Europe?', in M. Dumoulin (ed.), *Wartime Plans for Postwar Europe* (1995), pp. 459–67.

26. For the debate on these issues: J. Charmley, 'Duff Cooper and Western European Union, 1944–7', *Review of International Studies*, II (1985), 53–63; J. Charmley, *Duff Cooper* (1986); and J. W. Young, 'Duff Cooper as Ambassador to France', in J. Zametica (ed.), *British Officials and British Foreign Policy, 1945–50* (1990). See also Cooper's memoirs, *Old Men Forget* (1954).

27. J. Baylis, 'Britain and the Dunkirk Treaty: the Origins of NATO', *Journal of Strategic Studies*, 5 (1982), 236–47; S. Greenwood, 'Return to Dunkirk: the Origins of the Anglo-French Treaty of March 1947', *Journal of Strategic Studies*, 6 (1983), 49–65; Young, *Unity of Europe*, pp. 44–51; B. Zeeman, 'Britain and the Cold War: an alternative approach. The Treaty of Dunkirk example', *European History Quarterly*, 16 (1986), 343–67. But on Baylis's later views see his *Diplomacy of Pragmatism*, ch. 4.

28. On the changes in French policy see Young, *France and the Western Alliance*, pp. 142–7.
29. Young, *Unity of Europe*, pp. 55–6, 60–1.
30. *Foreign Relations of the United States, 1945*, Vol. II (hereafter *FRUS*) (Washington, 1972), p. 629.
31. M. J. Hogan, *The Marshall Plan: America, Britain and the Reconstruction of Western Europe, 1947–52* (Cambridge, 1987), pp. 48–51; Milward, *Reconstruction*, pp. 62–3.
32. A. Bullock, *Ernest Bevin*, Vol. III: *Foreign Secretary* (1983), pp. 404–6.
33. Ibid., passim; Charmley, 'Duff Cooper'; D. Dilks, 'The British View of Security', in O. Riste (ed.), *Western Security: the formative years* (New York, 1985), pp. 25–55, esp. p. 51; F. K. Roberts, 'Ernest Bevin as Foreign Secretary', in R. Ovendale (ed.), *The Foreign Policy of the Labour Governments, 1945–51* (Leicester, 1984). This approach is also usual in general histories such as: K. Middlemas, *Power, Competition and the State*, Vol. I: *Britain in Search of Balance, 1940–61* (1986), p. 160; A. Sked and C. Cook, *Post-war Britain* (1982), pp. 54–6; K. O. Morgan, *Labour in Power* (Oxford, 1985), esp. p. 276.
34. A. Adamthwaite, 'Britain and the World, 1945–9: the view from the Foreign Office', *International Affairs*, 61 (1985), 223–35, esp. 228; M. Howard, Introduction to Riste (ed.), *Western Security: the formative years*, pp. 12, 17. Milward, *Reconstruction*, pp. 235–6, also sees Bevin's interest in European co-operation merely as 'a step towards his greater vision of a transatlantic Western Union'.
35. K. Larres, 'Britain and the Origins of a Western European Union', in B. Brivati and H. Jones (eds), *From Reconstruction to Integration* (1993), p. 85; Lord Beloff, *Britain and European Union* (1996), p. 53; R. Ovendale, *The English-Speaking Alliance: Great Britain, the US, the Dominions and the Cold War* (1985), p. 45, and see pp. 83–4.
36. F. Williams, *Ernest Bevin* (1952), p. 262.
37. Shlaim, *Britain and the Origins of European Unity*, pp. 115–42; G. Warner, 'The Labour Governments and the Unity of Western Europe', in R. Ovendale (ed.), *The Foreign Policy of the British Labour Governments 1945–51* (Leicester, 1984), esp. pp. 64–5, 79–80; and see also Warner, 'Britain and Europe in 1948', in J. Becker and F. Knipping (eds), *Power in Europe? France, Great Britain, Germany and Italy in a post-war world, 1945–50* (New York, 1986), esp. pp. 34–7; Baylis, *Diplomacy of Pragmatism*, pp. 73–74.
38. J. L. Gaddis, 'The US and the Question of a Sphere of Influence in Europe', in Riste (ed.), *Western Security*, p. 78.
39. R. Holland, *The Pursuit of Greatness, 1900–70* (1991), p. 225; J. Kent, 'Bevin's Imperialism, and the Idea of Euro-Africa', in M. Dockrill and J. W. Young (eds), *British Foreign Policy, 1945–56* (1989); J. Kent, 'The British Empire and the Origins of the Cold War', in A. Deighton (ed.), *Britain and the First Cold War* (1990). But see especially Kent, *British Imperial Strategy and the Origins of the Cold War 1944–9* (1993); S. Greenwood, *The Alternative Alliance: Anglo-French relations before the coming of NATO* (1996).
40. *TUC Congress Report* (1947), pp. 420–2; CAB 128/10, CM (47) 77. The British customs union study set up in January 1947 had made a negative decision but Bevin brushed this aside, arguing that a new situation had arisen.

41. Young, *Unity of Europe*, pp. 68–70; Milward, *Reconstruction*, pp. 239–43;
     Hogan, *Marshall Plan*, pp. 66–7, 109–10.
42. Milward, ibid., pp. 236–7, 242–4; Hogan, ibid., pp. 110–11.
43. See for example E. Barker, *The British between the Superpowers, 1945–50*
     (1983), p. 127; N. Beloff, *The General Says No*, pp. 52–3.
44. CAB 129/23, CP (48) 6.
45. *The Times*, 5 January 1948, p. 4.
46. See for example Bullock, *Bevin*, pp. 395–8; J. Schneer, 'Hopes Deferred or
     Shattered; the British Labour Left and the Third Force Movement, 1945–9',
     Journal of Modern History, 56 (June 1984), 197–226.
47. CAB 129/23, CP (48) 8.
48. FO 371/62555/12502 (22 December–10 January).
49. House of Commons debates, Hansard (*H. C. Deb. 5s*), Vol. 446, Cols. 387–409
     (Bevin) and 418–28 (Eden).
50. *The Times*, 23 January 1948, editorial. The arguments in favour of a Labour
     'third force' policy are developed further in J. Kent and J. W. Young, 'The
     Third Force and the Origins of NATO', in B. Heuser and R. O'Neill (eds),
     Securing Peace in Europe, 1945–62 (1992), pp. 41–61.
51. *H. C. Deb. 5s.*, Vol. 456, cols 96–107.
52. R. S. Churchill (ed.), *The Sinews of Peace* (1948), pp. 198–202; M. Gilbert,
     Never Despair: Winston S. Churchill, 1945–63 (1988), pp. 171, 265–7, 278–
     321, 329–30; and on Conservative views, see S. Onslow, *Backbench Debate
     within the Conservative Party and its Influence on British Foreign Policy* (1997),
     chs 1 and 2.
53. Lord Strang, *Home and Abroad* (1956), p. 290.
54. This is the title, and underlying theme, of M. Carlton's 1983 book, based on
     a number of interviews.
55. See note 51 above. On policy over The Hague see: J. T. Grantham, 'British
     Labour and the Hague Congress', *Historical Journal*, 24 (1981), 443–52.
56. On French policy see Young, *France and the Western Alliance*, pp. 186–7, 193,
     205–7, 209 and esp. 211–13.
57. For a fuller discussion see Young, *Unity of Europe*, pp. 110–17.
58. Ibid., pp. 129–31.
59. Ibid., pp. 118–24; J. Black, *Convergence or Divergence* (1994), pp. 4–5.
60. For example, Warner, 'Unity of Western Europe', 70; Hogan, *Marshall Plan*,
     pp. 212–13. On the November discussion see R. Woodhouse, *British Policy
     towards France, 1945–51* (1995), pp. 130–1. On the Monnet–Plowden talks see:
     J. Monnet, *Memoirs* (1978), pp. 277–81; Mayne, *Recovery of Europe*, pp. 175–6;
     Beloff, *The General Says No*, pp. 53–4.
61. See G. C. Peden, 'Economic Aspects of British Perceptions of Power', in
     Becker and Knipping (eds), *Power in Europe?*, pp. 256–9; Milward, *Recon-
     struction*, pp. 335–61; Kent, 'Bevin's Imperialism', passim.
62. R. S. Churchill (ed.), *In the Balance* (1950), pp. 151–4.
63. For a fuller discussion about military aspects of European co-operation:
     J. Kent and J. W. Young, 'The Western Union Concept and British Defence
     Planning', in R. Aldrich (ed.), *British Intelligence, Strategy and the Cold War* (1992),
     ch. 7; on the reluctance of the British to commit to European defence see
     P. Cornish, 'The British Military View of European Security', in A. Deighton

(ed.), *Building Postwar Europe* (1995), pp. 70–86. On Britain and the negotiation of the Atlantic Pact see Baylis, *Diplomacy of Pragmatism*, chs 7–9.
64. FO 371/76384/3114 (9 May); CAB 129/37, CP (49) 208.
65. S. Newton: 'Britain, the Sterling Area and European Integration, 1945–50', *Journal of Imperial and Commonwealth History*, 13 (1985), 163–82; 'The 1949 Sterling Crisis and British Policy towards European Integration', *Review of International Studies*, 11 (1985), 169–82.
66. Acheson to Schuman, 30 October, reproduced in H. Beyer (ed.), *Robert Schuman* (Lausanne, 1986).
67. P. Weiler, 'British Labour and the Cold War', *Journal of British Studies*, 26 (1987), 75–7, 80–1.
68. Mayne, *Recovery of Europe*, p. 131; Beloff, *The General Says No*, pp. 50–1; Nutting, *Europe will not Wait*, pp. 1–27, esp. pp. 4–5.
69. Other discussions on the debate surrounding Bevin's European policy include: J. Melissen and B. Zeeman, 'Britain and Western Europe, 1945–51: opportunities lost?', *International Affairs*, 63 (1987), 81–95; C. A. Wurm, 'Grossbritannien, Westeuropa und die Anfänge der europäischen integration, 1945–51', in G. Schmidt (ed.), *Grossbritannien und Europa – Grossbritannien in Europa* (Bochum, 1989), pp. 57–88.

2 The Schuman Plan, the European Army and the Treaties of Rome, 1950–1957

1. On the principles behind British policy see R. Bullen, 'Britain and "Europe", 1950–7', in E. Serra (ed.), *The Relaunching of Europe and the Treaties of Rome* (Brussels, 1989). Also published in E. di Nolfo (ed.), *Power in Europe? Vol. II: Britain, France, Germany and Italy, and the Origins of the EEC, 1952–7* (New York, 1992).
2. J. W. Young, *France, the Cold War and the Western Alliance, 1944–9* (1990), p. 209; and on the antecedents see also J. W. Young, *Britain, France and the Unity of Europe* (Leicester, 1984), pp. 145–6.
3. On the background to the Plan, see: J. Monnet, *Memoirs* (1978), pp. 288–304; A. Milward, *The Reconstruction of Western Europe, 1945–51* (1984), pp. 380–96.
4. R. Massigli, *Une Comédie des Erreurs* (Paris, 1978), pp. 180–1.
5. M. J. Hogan, *The Marshall Plan: America, Britain and the Reconstruction of Western Europe, 1947–52* (Cambridge, 1987), pp. 368–72.
6. A. Cairncross (ed.), *The Robert Hall Diaries, 1947–53* (1989), pp. 112–13.
7. This account is based on Young, *Unity of Europe*, pp. 150–7.
8. Milward, *Reconstruction*, pp. 400, 405, and see pp. 400–6 in general; J. Monnet, *Memoirs* (1978), pp. 311–14; R. Mayne, *The Recovery of Europe* (1970), has a fair account on pp. 180–9; A. Nutting, *Europe will not Wait* (1960), pp. 28–9, 31 and 34.
9. G. Warner, 'The Labour Governments and the Unity of Western Europe', in R. Ovendale (ed.), *The Foreign Policy of the British Labour Governments, 1945–51* (Leicester, 1984), pp. 72–4; R. Bullen (ed.), *Documents on British Policy Overseas* (*DBPO*), Series II, Vol. I (1986), pp. xii–xviii; and on Henderson's views see his 'leaked' final despatch from Paris, *The Economist*, 2 June 1979.

10. Public Record Office (PRO), CAB 128/17, CM (50) 34 and CAB 129/40, CP (50) 120.
11. D. Jay, *Change and Fortune* (1980), pp. 198–200.
12. Massigli, *Comédie*, pp. 203–7; P. Calvocoressi, *World Politics since 1945* (1982), p. 164.
13. B. Donnoughue and G. W. Jones, *Herbert Morrison* (1973), p. 481; R. Woodhouse, *British Policy towards France, 1945–51* (1995), p. 139; E. Dell, *The Schuman Plan and the British Abdication of Leadership in Europe* (1995), quote from p. 294; C. Lord, *Absent at the Creation* (1996), esp. pp. 90–2 and 151–2, quote from p. 165.
14. Jowitt quote from Hugh Dalton's diary, British Library of Political and Economic Science, entry of 27 June. In general again this account is based on Young, *Unity of Europe*, pp. 158–64. On Monnet's reaction to Macmillan see also Monnet, *Memoirs*, pp. 315–17. On Churchill and the Conservatives see: M. Gilbert, *Never Despair: Winston S. Churchill, 1945–64* (1988), pp. 535–7; S. Onslow, *Backbench Debate within the Conservative Party and its Influence on British Foreign Policy* (1997), pp. 57–72.
15. The standard account used to be R. McGeehan, *The German Rearmament Question* (Urbana, IL, 1971), but French policy is better traced through J. Moch, *Histoire du Réarmement Allemand* (Paris, 1965), and the story of The European Defence Community is told by E. Fursdon's book of that title (1980). The best account, using British and US archives, is now S. Dockrill, *Britain's Policy for West German Rearmament, 1950–5* (1991).
16. Full documentation of the 'Atlantic Army' episode can only be found in R. Bullen and M. E. Pelly (eds), *DBPO*, Series II, Vol. III (1989), pp. 217–20, 230–2, 255–8, 289–96, and 301–4. On British policy in October–January see Dockrill, *German Rearmament*, pp. 41–58, and on Bevin's attitude Bullen, 'Britain and Europe', pp. 327–8.
17. Donnoughue and Jones, *Morrison*, pp. 480–3; Young, *Unity of Europe*, pp. 115–16, and 177–8.
18. Young, ibid., pp. 180–2.
19. *DBPO*, Series II, Vol. I, pp. 723–4. And on Britain's endorsement of the Pleven Plan see Dockrill, *German Rearmament*, pp. 59–79.
20. Boothby later wrote regular letters about the 'missed opportunity' to *The Times*. See R. R. James, *Bob Boothby* (1991), pp. 363–6.
21. Lord Boothby, *My Yesterday, Your Tomorrow* (1962), p. 83; Earl of Kilmuir, *Political Adventure* (1964), p. 187; H. Macmillan, *Tides of Fortune, 1945–55* (1969), pp. 461–3; and see A. Eden, *Full Circle* (1960), pp. 31–3.
22. P. H. Spaak, *The Continuing Battle* (1971), pp. 219–25.
23. For example: M. Ceadel, 'British Parties and the European Situation, 1950–7', *Storia Delle Relazioni Internazzonale*, 4, 1 (1988), 183–7; Dockrill, *German Rearmament*, pp. 80–8; A. Seldon, *Churchill's Indian Summer, 1951–5* (1981), pp. 413–14; and J. W. Young, 'Churchill's "No" to Europe', *Historical Journal*, 28 (1985), 923–37. A. Horne's *Macmillan, 1894–1956*. Vol. I of the Official Biography (1988), pp. 348–51 fails to resolve the contradictions in Macmillan's position at this time.
24. CAB. 129/48, C (51) 32.

25. J. Wheeler-Bennett, *Action This Day: Working with Churchill* (1968), p. 41; Young, 'Churchill's "No" to Europe', pp. 930–1; Ceadel, 'British Parties', pp. 185–6.

26. Bullen, 'Britain and Europe', pp. 324–5; *DBPO*, Series II, Vol. II, pp. 742–4; D.Dutton, *Anthony Eden* (1997), p. 312; and on Eden's attitude to the EDC see S. Mawby, *Containing Germany: Britain and the arming of the Federal Republic* (forthcoming), chs 3–6.

27. D. Folliot (ed.), *Documents on International Affairs, 1952* (1955), pp. 41–6.

28. D. Carlton, *Anthony Eden* (1981), pp. 312–13; but see Dockrill, *German Rearmament*, pp. 98–9, 102–3; and J. W. Young, 'German Rearmament and the European Defence Community', in J. W. Young (ed.), *The Foreign Policy of Churchill's Peacetime Administration, 1951–5* (1988), pp. 85–7.

29. Nutting, *Europe will not Wait*, pp. 41–6; Young, 'Churchill's "No" to Europe', pp. 932–6; J. W. Young, 'The Schuman Plan and British Association', in Young (ed.), *Churchill's Peacetime Administration*, pp. 113–17.

30. R. Ranieri, 'The Italian and British steel industries face . . . the European Coal and Steel Community', in A. Milward et al., *The Frontier of National Sovereignty* (1993), pp. 129–52; see also Young, 'Schuman Plan and British Association', pp. 117–30.

31. K. Larres, 'Integrating Europe or Ending the Cold War? Churchill's postwar foreign policy', *Journal of European Integration History*, 2 (1996), 15–49; and in general on Churchill and détente see J. W. Young, *Winston Churchill's Last Campaign: Britain and the Cold War, 1951–5* (1996).

32. Spaak, *Continuing Battle*, p. 188; R. R. James, *Anthony Eden*, p. 389. For full accounts of British policy in 1952–4, see: Dockrill, *German Rearmament*, pp. 105–50; Young, 'German Rearmament', pp. 87–101.

33. Mayne, *Recovery of Europe*, p. 216; A. Deighton, 'The Last Piece of the Jigsaw: Britain and the creation of the Western European Union', *Contemporary European History*, 7 (1998), 182.

34. PRO FO 371/73096/5782 (15 July, 1948) Jebb quoted in J. W. Young, 'Britain, the Messina Conference and the Spaak Committee', in M. Dockrill and J. W. Young (eds), *British Foreign Policy, 1945–56* (1989), pp. 201–2. Among those who claim that the 'UK sent an emissary to the Messina conference' see R. Leach, *Europe: a concise encyclopedia* (1998), p. 150.

35. For a fuller account see Young, ibid., pp. 201–4 including views of the Mutual Aid Committee; also S. Burgess and G. Edwards, 'The Six Plus One: British policy-making and the question of European economic integration, 1955', *International Affairs*, 64 (1988), 396–9.

36. PRO, T.232/431 (4 Aug.).

37. M. Charlton, *The Price of Victory* (1983), p. 195.

38. T.232/433 (14 Oct.).

39. The above account of events, in July 1955–February 1956, is based on: Bullen, 'Britain and Europe', pp. 333–7; Burgess and Edwards, 'The Six Plus One', pp. 399–41; M. Camps, *Britain and the European Community 1955–63* (1964), pp. 29–53; Küsters, *Fondements*, pp. 105–13; and Young, 'Britain . . . and the Spaak Committee', pp. 204–16. See also H. Macmillan, *Riding the Storm, 1956–9* (1971), pp. 66–71.

Quotes from: E. Kane, 'The Myth of Sabotage' in E. du Reau (ed.), *Europe des Elites? Europe des Peuples?* (Paris, 1998), p. 295; S. Greenwood, *Britain and European Co-operation since 1945* (1992), p. 76; J. Ellison, *British Policy towards European Integration: the proposal for a Free Trade Area* (PhD, Christ Church College, Canterbury, 1997), p. 25. On British policy towards the formation of Euratom see M. O'Driscoll, 'Missing the Nuclear Boat?', *Diplomacy and Statecraft*, 9 (1998), 135–62.

40. This is a major theme of Küsters, *Fondements*.

41. The key Cabinet discussions were CAB 128/30, CM (56) 65 and 66 in September (which discussed memoranda CAB. 129/83, CP (56) 207 and 208) and CM (56) on 13 November; 'Plan G', is reproduced in Macmillan, *Riding the Storm*, pp. 753–4, and see the discussion on pp. 73–88; Camps, *Britain and the European Community*, pp. 95–119, quote from p. 510; Kane, 'Myth of Sabotage', p. 300. On Selwyn Lloyd's scheme see CAB 128/30, CM (57) 3 (8 January 1957); and on British industry see R. J. Lieber, *British Politics and European Unity* (1970), pp. 56–60.

42. Bullock, *Bevin*, p. 784; Nutting, *Europe will not Wait*, pp. 34–5; Lord, *Absent at the Creation*, pp. 165–6.

43. Nutting, ibid., p. 3; Boothby quoted in Ceadel, 'British Parties', p. 186, from 555 *H. C. deb. 5s.*, col. 1674; Camps, *Britain and the European Community*, p. 506.

44. Boothby letter to Lord Beaverbrook, Beaverbrook Papers, House of Lords Record Office, file C/47; Nutting, ibid., p. 46; and in general see M. Camps, 'Missing the Boat at Messina and Other Times?', in B. Brivati and H. Jones (eds), *From Reconstruction to Integration* (1993), pp. 134–43.

45. CAB 134/1004 (7–20 Oct. 1955).

46. Ibid. (section on political considerations).

47. See G. Warner, 'Aspects of the Suez Canal', in E. di Nolfo (ed.), *Power in Europe?*, pp. 64–5.

48. J. Barnes, 'From Eden to Macmillan', in P. Hennessy and A. Seldon (eds), *Ruling Performance: British governments from Attlee to Thatcher* (1987), p. 131; A. Milward, *The European Rescue of the Nation State* (1992), p. 433.

3   Macmillan, the Free Trade Area and the First Application, 1957–1963

1. H. Macmillan, *Riding the Storm, 1956–9* (1971), p. 435.

2. P. Gore-Booth, *With Great Truth and Respect* (1974), p. 247; R. J. Lieber, *British Politics and European Unity* (1970), pp. 52–4; W. Kaiser, *Using Europe, Abusing the Europeans* (1996), pp. 80–3 and 88–9.

3. R. Lamb, *The Macmillan Years: the emerging truth* (1995), p. 108 and see ch. 7 generally on the FTA talks in 1956–8. M. Camps, *Britain and the European Community, 1955–63* (1964), is still very useful on this period but British policy during the Free Trade Area is now the subject of two detailed doctoral studies:

J. Ellison, *British Policy towards European Integration: the Proposal for a European Free Trade Area* (PhD, Christ Church College, Canterbury, 1997); and E. Kane, *Tilting to Europe: British policy towards developments in European Integration, 1955–8* (DPhil, University of Oxford, 1996).

4. Camps, ibid., p. 509. G. Peden, 'Economic Aspects of British Perceptions of Power, in E. di Nolfo (ed.), *Power in Europe?* Vol. II: *1952–7* (1992), pp. 139–59, quote from p. 158; Public Record Office (PRO), CAB 134/153. Report on 'Position of the UK in World Affairs', July 1958.

5. See, for example, PRO, PREM 11/1841, telegram of 17 April and minute of 28 April.

6. Gladwyn Jebb, *The Memoirs of Lord Gladwyn* (1972), pp. 292–9; Macmillan, *Riding the Storm*, pp. 435–6; PREM 11/1844 (18 April and 3 June 1957).

7. R. Maudling, *Memoirs* (1978), pp. 67–72; A. Horne, *Macmillan*, Vol. II: *1957–86* (1990), pp. 34–5; quote from Macmillan, ibid., pp. 436–8. On the 2 May Cabinet: CAB 128/31, C (57), 37th.

8. Camps, *Britain and the European Community*, pp. 143–4; Lamb, *Macmillan Years*, p. 116; Lieber, *British Politics*, pp. 68–71.

9. J. Chauvel, *Commentaire: de Berne à Paris* (1973), pp. 275–8.

10. Macmillan, *Riding the Storm*, pp. 446–61.

11. PREM 11/2315, minute of 24 June.

12. Camps, *Britain and the European Community*, pp. 508–9; Macmillan, *Riding the Storm*, pp. 455–7.

13. Quotes from: Gore-Booth, *Great Truth*, pp. 250–53; H. Macmillan, *Pointing the Way, 1959–61* (1972), pp. 49–50. On the breakdown see: CAB. 128/32, C (58), 86th (18 Dec.) and 88th (23 Dec.).

14. On the work in Whitehall at this point see especially: CAB 130/154, Gen. 670 (ministerial committee) meetings; and CAB 129/96, C (59) 27 (Feb. 1959 Treasury paper).

15. Macmillan, *Pointing the Way*, pp. 50–4. On pressure groups see Lieber, *British Politics*, pp. 61–8 and 72–90. Key Cabinet meeting was CAB 128/33, C (59) 30th (7 May).

16. Macmillan, ibid., pp. 57–9; quote from Maudling, *Memoirs*, p. 78; Jebb, *Memoirs*, pp. 302–3; CAB 128/33, CM (59) 63rd (15 Dec.) and CAB 129/99, C (59) 188 (14 Dec.).

17. On the Moscow visit see Horne, *Macmillan*, pp. 129–35. On Adenauer's criticisms of Britain: R. H. Ferrell (ed.), *The Eisenhower Diaries* (1981), p. 363; quote from T. Prittie, *Konrad Adenauer* (1971), pp. 263–4; P. H. Spaak, *Continuing Battle* (1971), pp. 335–6.

18. On Macmillan's views see: Steering Committee paper SC(59) 40 (27 Oct.) and memorandum drafted by Philip de Zulueta (22 Oct.) in PREM 11/2985; Macmillan; *Pointing the Way*, pp. 54–6. Preparation of the Steering Committee paper is in FO371/143697, ZP15/24.

19. Macmillan, ibid., pp. 112–14; see also Horne, *Macmillan*, p. 222.

20. CAB/134/1822; J. Tratt, *The Macmillan Government and Europe* (1996), pp. 95–101 (quote from p. 95); N. Beloff, *The General Says No* (1963), pp. 84–90.

21. PREM 11/2998 (15 Feb.); K. Middlemas, *Power, Competition and the State*, Vol. II: *1961–74* (1990), p. 33.

212 Notes

 22. On the Macmillan–de Gaulle meetings see: Horne, *Macmillan*, pp. 222–3; Macmillan, *Pointing the Way*, pp. 313–15; PREM 11/2998.
23. CAB 128/34, CM (60), 31st (13 July), looking at memorandum CAB 129/102, C (60) 107; Tratt, *Macmillan Government*, pp. 122–6; Lamb, *Macmillan Years*, p. 139.
24. Papers in PREM 11/3311 and 3325 (esp. 3 Jan. 1961); Horne, *Macmillan*, pp. 284–5; Macmillan, *Pointing the Way*, pp. 312–13, 323–6.
25. On the US see: G. Ball, *The Discipline of Power* (1968), pp. 66–8 and 90–117; H. Macmillan, *At the End of the Day, 1961–3* (1973), p. 111. On the Rambouillet talks: PREM 11/3322 includes Macmillan's plans for winning de Gaulle over.
26. Tratt, *Macmillan Government*, ch. 12; Lamb, *Macmillan Years*, p. 143; L. Butler, 'Britain, Europe and the Commonwealth, 1959–61' in B. Brivati and H. Jones (eds), *From Reconstruction to Integration* (1993), pp. 157–65; Camps, *Britain and the European Community*, pp. 511–14. On the Commonwealth see also S. Ward, 'The Problem of the Old Dominions', in G. Wilkes (ed.), *Britain's Failure to Enter the European Community, 1961–3* (1997), ch. 5.
27. CAB 128/35, CM (61), 42nd (21 July), and 43rd (24 July); CAB 129/106, C (61), 103, 104, 108, 111 and 124 (including results of Commonwealth consultation).
28. Macmillan, *End of the Day*, pp. 16–17.
29. Beloff, *General Says No*, pp. 108–10; A. Howard, *'Rab': the Life of R. A. Butler* (1987), pp. 286–7, 295; H. Evans, *Downing Street Diary* (1975), pp. 150–1, 165. On pressure groups see Lieber, *British Politics*, pp. 92–105, and 116–32.
30. Lieber, *British Politics*, p. 207.
31. A. Roth, *Heath and the Heathmen* (1972), pp. 154–5, gives the details on Heath's travels. On his speech see: M. Couve de Murville, *Une Politique d'Etrangère* (Paris, 1971), pp. 398–9; P. H. Spaak; *The Continuing Battle* (1971), pp. 474–5.
32. Horne, *Macmillan*, pp. 314–19; Macmillan, *Pointing the Way*, pp. 426–8, and *End of the Day*, p. 32; PREM 11/3338, telegram of 28 Nov.
33. Roth, *Heath*, p. 162; P. Dixon, *Double Diploma* (1968), pp. 282–3; Macmillan, *End of the Day*, pp. 114–15, 118–19.
34. Macmillan, *End of the Day*, pp. 119–23; Horne, *Macmillan*, pp. 326–30; Roth, *Heath*, p. 162; Couve, *Politique*, pp. 403–4; H. Alphand, *L'Etonnement d'Etre* (1977), pp. 379–80; P. Ludlow, *Dealing with Britain: the Six and the first UK application to the EEC* (Cambridge, 1997), p. 122; C. Pagedas, 'Harold Macmillan and the 1962 Champs meeting', *Diplomacy and Statecraft*, 9 (1998), 225–42; Kaiser, *Using Europe*, pp. 186–91.
35. On this phase of talks, see especially Dixon, *Pierson Dixon*, pp. 283–92.
36. On Gaitskell see especially: P. M. Williams (ed.), *The Diary of Hugh Gaitskell* (1983) ch. 25 and Appendix III, document 24; L. J. Robins, *The Reluctant Party: Labour and the EEC, 1961–75* (Ormskirk, 1979), pp. 11–43, quote from p. 41; and Lieber, *British Politics*, pp. 166–85 (with 185–206 on the Conservative party). But see also: G. Catlin, *For God's Sake Go* (1972), p. 413; G. Brown, *In My Way* (1971), pp. 218–19; and D. Donnely, *Gaderene '68* (1968), pp. 77–8. On the Commonwealth conference see Horne, *Macmillan*, pp. 355–7; Macmillan, *End of the Day*, pp. 129–38.

37. Macmillan, ibid., pp. 140–1.
38. Ibid., pp. 336–8; Dixon, *Double Diploma*, p. 296; Ball, *Discipline of Power*, p. 83.
39. Macmillan, *End of the Day*, pp. 340–55; Horne, *Macmillan*, pp. 428–36; Dixon, ibid., pp. 299–301.
40. Macmillan, ibid., pp. 355–62; Horne, ibid., pp. 437–44; Dixon, ibid., p. 301.
41. Macmillan, ibid., pp. 363–8; Dixon, ibid., pp. 302–4; Couve, *Politique*, pp. 408–14; Spaak, *Continuing Battle*, pp. 475–6; but the fullest account is Beloff, *General Says No*, pp. 11–17; 165–71. On de Gaulle's reaction to Nassau, see also F. Catigliola, *France and the United States* (1992), pp. 132–3. And on the post-veto period see R. Steininger, 'Great Britain's First EEC Failure in January 1963', *Diplomacy and Statecraft*, 7 (1996), 404–35.
42. Macmillan, ibid., pp. 368–72; Spaak, ibid., p. 477; Evans, *Downing Street*, p. 250.
43. Macmillan, *End of the Day*, p. 366.
44. Dixon, *Double Diploma*, pp. 299–300; Kaiser, *Abusing Europe*, pp. 192–3; E. Heath, *The Course of My Life* (1998), p. 226.
45. Steininger, 'EEC failure', p. 432; Tratt, *Macmillan Government*, pp. 198–200; Ludlow, *Dealing with Britain*, see esp. pp. 244–9; and see A. Deighton and P. Ludlow, 'A Conditional Application', in A. Deighton (ed.), *Building Post-war Europe* (1995), pp. 107–26. Lamb, *Macmillan Years*, p. 202 also criticises Macmillan's dithering.
46. O. Bange, 'Grand Designs and the Diplomatic Breakdown', in Wilkes (ed.), *Britain's Failure*, p. 193; Tratt, ibid., pp. 188–9; Kaiser, *Using Europe*, pp. 166–73 and 202–3, quote from p. 108; K. Middlemas, *Power, Competition and the State*, Vol. II: *1961–74* (1990), p. 16, see also pp. 8–9, 33–4; Beloff, *General Says No*, pp. 172–8; A. Deighton, 'Harold Macmillan, Whitehall and the Defence of Europe' in E. du Reau (ed.), *Europe des Elites? Europe des Peuples?* (Paris, 1998), p. 245; Horne, *Macmillan*, p. 436.

4 Wilson's Entry Bid, 1964–1970

1. D. E. Butler and A. King, *The British General Election of 1964* (1965), p. 131. On the Labour government of 1964–70 see especially C. Ponting, *Breach of Promise* (1989). On EEC entry U. Kitzinger, *The Second Try* (1968), is a valuable collection of documents, especially on the public debate.
2. L. J. Robins, *The Reluctant Party: Labour and the EEC, 1961–75* (Ormskirk, 1979), p. 45; R. Holland, *The Pursuit of Greatness, 1900–70* (1991), p. 321; Gordon-Walker papers, Churchill College, Cambridge, 3/4 (Memorandum of August, 1964). Gordon-Walker expressed similar views in an article in *Foreign Affairs*, 42, No. 3.
3. M. Stewart, *Life and Labour* (1980), p. 144.
4. B. Ledwidge, *De Gaulle* (1982), pp. 297–6.
5. G. Brown, *In My Way* (1971), pp. 207–12, 214–15; E. Roll, *Crowded Hours* (1985), p. 172.

6.   P. Gore-Booth, *With Great Truth and Respect* (1974), p. 350; G. Moorhouse, *The Diplomats* (1977), p. 372; Stewart, *Life and Labour*, pp. 146, 162–3.

7.   Castle, *The Castle Diaries, 1964–70* (1984), pp. 18, 20, 33.

8.   J. Morgan (ed.), *The Backbench Diaries of Richard Crossman, 1951–64* (1981), pp. 74–5.

9.   Public Record Office (PRO), PREM 13/904 (15 June, 10 and 28 Dec. 1965, and 18 Jan. 1966); PREM 13/905 (21 January and 3 February 1966); D. Jay, *Change and Fortune* (1980), p. 361; R. Crossman, *Diaries of a Cabinet Minister*, Vol. I: *Minister of Housing, 1964–6* (1975), entries of 31 Jan. and 2 Feb. 1966.

10. See the Gallup Poll evidence in U. Kitzinger, *The Second Try* (1968), pp. 172–3. Quote from P. Ziegler, *Wilson: the authorised life* (1993), pp. 130–1.

11. Crossman, *Diaries*, 9 February 1966.

12. C. King, *The Cecil King Diary 1965–70* (1972), p. 67, and see pp. 55–8; Ziegler, *Wilson*, pp. 240–2 and 331–2; B. Pimlott, *Harold Wilson* (1992), pp. 433–5; A. Morgan, *Harold Wilson* (1992), p. 295; J. Dickie, *Inside the Foreign Office* (1992), p. 98.

13. D. E. Butler and A. King, *The British General Election of 1966* (1966), pp. 110–14; A. Roth, *Heath and the Heathmen* (1972), pp. 198–9; H. Wilson, *The Labour Government, 1964–70* (1974), pp. 283–4; Morgan, ibid., p. 295.

14. PRO, CAB 134/2705 (9 May); Crossman, *Diaries*, 9 May 1966; and see the initial Roll Committee report in PREM 13/905 (5 April).

15. On the Foreign Office see Gore-Booth, *Great Truth*, p. 350; on the influence of Palliser see M. Williams, *Inside Number 10* (1972), p. 180.

16. PREM 13/907 (8 and 27 July); Gore-Booth, *Great Truth*, p. 351; Roll, *Crowded Hours*, pp. 172–3; M. Couve de Murville, *Une Politique d'Etrangére* (Part 3, 1971), pp. 416–19.

17. Castle, *Diaries*, p. 145.

18. Lord Wigg, *George Wigg* (1972), pp. 338–9.

19. Wilson, *Labour Government*, p. 380; Brown, *In My Way*, pp. 205–6.

20. CAB 134/2705 (22 Oct.); quote from Wilson, *Labour Government*, p. 381. On the meeting see also: T. Benn, *Out of the Wilderness: Diaries 1963–7* (1987), p. 480; Castle, *Diaries*, pp. 177–9; Crossman, *Diaries*, Vol. II: *Lord President of the Council and Leader of the House of Commons, 1966–8* (1976), pp. 22 and 23 Oct.; Jay, *Fortune*, pp. 365–6.

21. R. Marsh, *Off the Rails* (1978), p. 96; D. Healey, *The Time of My Life* (1989), pp. 329–30.

22. King, *Diary*, pp. 95–6; and on changing Labour attitudes see Robins, *The Reluctant Party*, pp. 47–54 and 62–9.

23. PREM 13/1475 (16 and 22 Dec.); Brown, *My Way*, pp. 219–20.

24. R. J. Lieber, *British Politics and European Unity: parties, elites and pressure groups* (Berkeley, CA, 1970), ch. 9, quote from p. 261.

25. Crossman, *Diaries*, Vol. II, 9 January 1967; Castle, *Diaries*, pp. 210–11; and on Rome see: records of meetings (16–17 Jan.) in PREM 13/1475; Wilson, *Labour Government*, pp. 419–27.

26. Records of the meetings are in PREM 13/1476; quote from a French source in B. Reed and G. Williams, *Denis Healey and the Politics of Power* (1971), pp. 127–8, 184–6; Wilson, *Labour Government*, pp. 428–36.

27. Wilson, ibid., pp. 437–41, 470–7; and among the official records there is a 'master' version of records on all the probe visits in PREM 13/ 1478.
28. H. Alphand, *L'Etonnement d'Etre* (Paris, 1977), p. 484.
29. Wilson, *Labour Government*, pp. 477–7, 495–7; Jay, *Fortune*, pp. 381–4.
30. Castle, *Diaries*, pp. 235–7; Crossman, *Diaries*, Vol. II, 21 March; Jay, ibid., pp. 381–4, 406.
31. On the meetings generally see: Castle, *Diaries*, pp. 239–47; Crossman, *Diaries*, Vol. II, 6–27 April; Jay, *Fortune*, pp. 386–6, 406; Wilson, *Labour Government*, pp. 497–8. Records of all the Cabinet meetings are in PRO, CAB 128/ 42.
32. Benn, *Out of the Wilderness*, p. 496; Castle, ibid., pp. 247–51; Crossman, ibid., 29 and 30 April and 2 May; Jay, ibid., pp. 387–93; Wilson, ibid., pp. 498–9.
33. PREM 13/1482 (20 May); King, *Diary*, p. 123.
34. PREM 13/1483 (19 June); Wilson, *Labour Government*, pp. 515–29 esp. pp. 522–6.
35. Castle, *Diaries*, pp. 275–6; and on the 'Chalfont Affair' see documents in PREM 13/1498, plus Dickie, *Foreign Office*, pp. 171–5.
36. W. Brandt, *People and Policies* (1978), pp. 162–3.
37. Wigg, *George Wigg*, pp. 338–9.
38. Castle, *Diaries*, p. 247.
39. Crossman, *Diaries*, Vol. II, 1 January 1967.
40. See especially Castle, *Diaries*, pp. 364, 378–9, and T. Benn, *Office Without Power: Diaries, 1968–72* (1988), pp. 20–1.
41. R. Nixon, *Memoirs* (1978), pp. 370–5.
42. In general on the Soames Affair: U. Kitzinger, *Diplomacy and Persuasion: How Britain joined the Common Market* (1973), pp. 45–58; J. Haines, *The Politics of Power* (1977), pp. 74–81; Ledwidge, *De Gaulle*, ch. 22; Stewart, *Life and Labour*, pp. 224–7; Dickie, *Foreign Office*, pp. 166–71. Interesting details are added by: Benn, *Office Without Power*, pp. 149–50, 152, Castle, *Diaries*, pp. 605–6, 610. On the French reaction: Couve, *Une Politique*, pp. 427–9; Alphand, *L'Etonnement*, pp. 517–19.
43. Jay, *Change and Fortune*, pp. 440–2.
44. Alphand, *L'Etonnement*, pp. 524, 528.
45. For a fuller discussion on the Hague Summit and French diplomacy see: Kitzinger, *Diplomacy*, pp. 59–76.
46. Wilson, *Labour Government*, pp. 960–1; Roth, *Heath*, p. 208; Ziegler, *Wilson*, pp. 337–8.
47. Castle, *Diaries*, pp. 782–3.

5   Entry, Renegotiation and the Referendum, 1970–1979

1. Whitehead, *The Writing on the Wall: Britain in the Seventies* (1985), pp. 52–4.
2. C. Lord, *British Entry to the European Community under the Heath Government* (Aldershot, 1993), pp. 99–103. On Powell's views see: P. Cosgrave, *The Lives of Enoch Powell* (1990), pp. 265–9; D. E. Schoen, *Enoch Powell and the Powellites* (1977), pp. 74–9.

3.   N. Tebbit, *Upwardly Mobile* (1988), pp. 106 and 117.
4.   See: H. Kissinger, *The White House Years* (1979), pp. 87–9 and 932–5; C. Hill and C. Lord, 'The Foreign Policy of the Heath Government', in S. Ball and A. Seldon (eds), *The Heath Government, 1970–74* (1996), pp. 302–9.
5.   D. Butler and M. Pinto-Duschinsky (eds), *The British General Election of 1970* (1971), p. 105.
6.   Whitehead, *Writing*, pp. 59–60. On the Luxembourg meeting see S. Z. Young, *Terms of Entry: Britain's negotiations with the EC, 1970–2* (1973), pp. 1–21.
7.   Young, ibid.; U. Kitzinger, *Diplomacy and Persuasion* (1973), pp. 78–112; Lord, *British Entry* (note 2 above).
8.   D. C. Watt and J. Mayall, *Current British Foreign Policy, 1970* (1971), pp. 498–503.
9.   Kitzinger, *Diplomacy*, pp. 102–3, 105–8; W. Brandt, *People and Policies* (1978), pp. 249–50; and on the experts' talks see Young, *Terms of Entry*, pp. 21–209.
10. The best secondary account is still Kitzinger, ibid., pp. 114–23, 126–7 but important details are added by E. Heath, *The Course of My Life* (1998), pp. 364–72 and D. Hurd, *An End to Promises* (1979), pp. 61–4; whilst on the Sterling problem see Young, ibid., pp. 199–207.
11. See Rippon's statement of 24 June in House of Commons debates, vol. 819, cols 1603–28. Final details in the talks were settled at a meeting on 12 July.
12. Command Paper 4715, *The UK and the European Communities* (1971); E. Heath, *Old Worlds, New Horizons* (1970), pp. 34 and 56–7; E. Heath, 'European Integration over the Next Ten Years', *International Affairs*, 64 (1988), 199.
13. Cosgrave, *Powell*, pp. 305–22.
14. M. Falkender, *Downing Street in Perspective* (1983), p. 35; B. Pimlott, *Harold Wilson* (1992), p. 602.
15. See D. E. Butler and U. Kitzinger, *The 1975 Referendum* (Basingstoke, 1976), pp. 8–11; D. Jay, *Change and Fortune* (1980), pp. 451–2. On the revival of anti-market attitudes in the Labour party see L. J. Robins, *The Reluctant Party: Labour and the EEC, 1961–75* (Ormskirk, 1979), pp. 77–121.
16. J. Adams, *Tony Benn* (1992), p. 330; K. Morgan, *Callaghan: a life* (1997), p. 395, but in general see pp. 392–7 on Callaghan's European outlook; P. Kellner and C. Hitchens, *Callaghan: the Road to Number 10* (1976), pp. 115–19.
17. See, for example, R. Jenkins, *A Life at the Centre* (1991), pp. 315–26; J. Campbell, *Roy Jenkins* (1983), pp. 138–43.
18. Robins, *The Reluctant Party*, p. 119; A. Morgan, *Harold Wilson* (1992), p. 396; Lever quoted in Whitehead, *Writing*, p. 65; P. Ziegler, *Wilson: the authorised life* (1993), pp. 387 and 380–7 in general; see also S. Crosland, *Tony Crosland* (1982), pp. 218–25.
19. An early statement of the analysis is: H. Lazer, 'British Populism: the Labour Party and the Common Market Parliamentary Debate', *Political Science Quarterly*, 91 (1976), 259–77.
20. Heath, *Course of My Life*, pp. 378–80; Hurd, *Promises*, pp. 67–9.
21. Jenkins, *Life at the Centre*, pp. 388–49; Campbell, *Jenkins*, pp. 143–6.
22. S. George, *Britain and European Integration since 1945* (1991), pp. 50–3 but see also his *An Awkward Partner: Britain in the EC* (1990), pp. 60–70.

23. On the Paris Summit see George, *Awkward Partner*, pp. 56–60; Heath, *Course of My Life*, pp. 387–92.

24. King, *Diary*, p. 255; N. Henderson, *Mandarin* (1994), p. 51; Heath, *Course of My Life*, pp. 393 and 395.

25. D. Butler and D. Kavanagh, *The British General Election of February 1974* (1975), pp. 55–6, 89–91 and 103–5.

26. Cosgrave, *Powell*, pp. 342–7; B. Donnoughue, *Prime Minister: the conduct of policy under Harold Wilson and James Callaghan* (1987), p. 42; Falkender, *Downing Street*, pp. 69–70.

27. J. Haines, *The Politics of Power* (1977), pp. 69 and 132; Ziegler, *Wilson*, p. 422.

28. T. Benn, *Against the Tide: diaries, 1973–6* (1989), p. 116, and see pp. 128, 134–5. B. Castle, *The Castle Diaries, 1974–6* (1980), p. 39.

29. Morgan, *Callaghan*, pp. 414–17; Kellner and Hitchens, *Callaghan*, pp. 152–3.

30. S. Greenwood, *Britain and European Cooperation since 1945* (1992), pp. 100–1. On the Chequers meeting: Benn, *Against the Tide*, pp. 142–3; J. Callaghan, *Time and Chance* (1987), p. 326.

31. Castle, *Diaries*, pp. 111–13.

32. Benn, *Against the Tide*, p. 165.

33. Haines, *Politics of Power*, p. 71.

34. Callaghan, *Time and Chance*, p. 315.

35. Ibid., pp. 302–5, 310, 319; Castle, *Diaries*, pp. 125–6, 128, 143–4.

36. Benn, *Against the Tide*, pp. 192–3, 206–7; Castle, ibid., pp. 154–5.

37. Castle, ibid., pp. 182–3.

38. D. Butler and D. Kavanagh, *The British General Election of October 1974* (1975), pp. 30–1, 58, 76–7, 119–21.

39. Donnoughue, *Prime Minister*, p. 59.

40. Jenkins, *Life at the Centre*, pp. 399–400; Callaghan, *Time and Chance*, p. 314, and see p. 302 on previous reassurances to the Germans.

41. H. Wilson, *Final Term* (1979), pp. 88–91; Callaghan, ibid., pp. 311–13; Morgan, *Callaghan*, pp. 421–2.

42. Wilson, ibid., pp. 92–7; Callaghan, ibid., pp. 314–17.

43. Castle, *Diaries*, pp. 211–12, 219–25, 229–30 (quote from pp. 212 and 225).

44. Ibid., pp. 248–50; Benn, *Against the Tide*, pp. 282–3.

45. Wilson, *Final Term*, p. 97; Jenkins, *Life at the Centre*, pp. 399–401.

46. P. Martin, *The London Diaries, 1975–9* (Ottawa, 1988), pp. 1–7, quote from pp. 6–7; and on the precedent for an agreement to differ, see P. Goodhart, *Full-hearted Consent: The Story of the Referendum Campaign* (1976), pp. 219–26.

47. According to Castle, *Diaries*, pp. 333–4.

48. Wilson, *Final Term*, pp. 101–3; Callaghan, *Time and Chance*, pp. 322–4; Butler and Kitzinger, *Referendum*, pp. 40–3; Morgan, *Callaghan*, pp. 423–4.

49. Benn, *Against the Tide*, pp. 341–9; Castle, *Diaries*, pp. 340–3; Jenkins, *Life at the Centre*, pp. 403–4; and see Wilson, ibid., p. 103.

50. On Wilson's tactics see Whitehead, *Writing*, p. 136.

51. Kellner and Hitchens, *Callaghan*, pp. 159–63; Benn, *Against the Tide*, pp. 350–5; and for a defence of the terms secured by Callaghan see Morgan, *Callaghan*, pp. 427–9.

52. Castle, *Diaries*, pp. 351–2; Jenkins, *Life at the Centre*, pp. 406–7; quote from Wilson, *Final Term*, pp. 103–4.
53. See, for example, J. Pinder, 'Renegotiation: Britain's costly lesson', *International Affairs*, 51, 2 (April 1975), 153–65.
54. Wilson, *Final Term.*, pp. 106–7.
55. Castle, *Diaries*, pp. 357, 376–7.
56. Butler and Kitzinger, *Referendum;* see also P. Goodhart, *Full-hearted Consent*; and on voting behaviour see also R. Jowell and G. Hoinville (eds), *Britain into Europe: public opinion and the EEC, 1961–74* (1976).
57. Falkender, *Downing Street*, p. 183; A. Morgan, *Harold Wilson* (1992), p. 469.
58. Castle, *Diaries*, pp. 409–10.
59. J. Campbell, *Roy Jenkins* (1983), p. 171; F. de la Serre, *La Grande-Bretagne et la Communauté Européenne* (Paris, 1987), p. 101.
60. George, *Awkward Partner*, pp. 96–104.
61. Benn, *Against the Tide*, pp. 578–9.
62. D. Owen, *Time to Declare* (1992), pp. 245–8 and 262–3. And on FO influence see P. Hennessy, *Whitehall* (1989), pp. 402–5; F. E. C. Gregory, *Dilemmas of Government: Britain and the European Community* (Oxford, 1983), pp. 127–9.
63. R. Jenkins, *European Diary, 1977–81* (1989), pp. 133–4; Owen, ibid., pp. 329–31.
64. Jenkins, ibid., pp. 147–8; Owen, ibid., pp. 333–4.
65. See, for example, Benn, *Against the Tide*, pp. 462–3.
66. But ministers could not speak against the government's bill. D. Healey, *The Time of My Life* (1989), p. 459; Owen, *Time to Declare*, pp. 275–6; and see Benn, ibid., pp. 516–17.
67. P. Ludlow, *The Making of the European Monetary System: a case study of the politics of the EC* (1982), pp. 37–55, 63–80. On the origins of EMS see also Jenkins, *Life at the Centre*, pp. 463–75.
68. Ludlow, ibid., pp. 88–94; Jenkins, ibid., pp. 475–8 and *European Diary*, pp. 244–9.
69. Ludlow, ibid., pp. 104–6 and see pp. 81–2; Owen, *Time to Declare*, p. 367.
70. Ludlow, ibid., especially pp. 122–32, 144–5, 185–7, 217–25, 244–6; and on opposition in the Labour party and Cabinet see T. Benn, *Conflicts of Interest: Diaries, 1977–80* (1990), pp. 365, 376, 380, 384, 395–8 and 411.
71. E. Haas, *The Uniting of Europe* (Stanford, CA, 1963); L. Lindberg, *The Political Dynamics of European Economic Integration* (1963). The best analysis of the neo-functionalists and the failure of their predictions in the 1970s is: P. Taylor, *The Limits of European Integration* (1983). For a shorter discussion see S. George, *Politics and Policy in the European Community* (2nd edn, 1991), ch. 2.

6   Thatcher and the Revival of European Integration, 1979–1990

1. R. Jenkins, *European Diary, 1977–81* (1989), pp. 374, 400 and *A Life at the Centre* (1991), p. 493.
2. P. Cosgrave, *The Lives of Enoch Powell* (1990), p. 399.

3. H. Young, *One of Us* (1990), pp. 184–5.
4. D. Owen, *Time to Declare* (1991), pp. 277–8; on the 1979 Euro-elections see F. de la Serre, *La Grande Bretagne et la Communauté Européenne* (Paris, 1987), ch. 6.
5. *The Economist*, 2 June 1979; reproduced in N. Henderson, *Channels and Tunnels* (1987), pp. 143–58.
6. W. Wallace (ed.), *Britain in Europe* (1980) contains the proceedings of the conference, with a valuable summary on pp. 1–17; on D. Marquand's views see also his *Parliament for Europe* (1979).
7. Young, *One of Us*, pp. 185–7; on Carrington's views see his memoirs, *Reflect on Things Past* (1988), pp. 322–4.
8. Jenkins, *Diary*, pp. 464–6, 528–31 and *Life at the Centre*, pp. 494–500; P. Cosgrave, *Thatcher: the First Term* (1985), pp. 87–8; M. Thatcher, *The Downing Street Years* (1993), p. 81; Young, ibid., pp. 187–8.
9. Jenkins, *Diary*, pp. 545–6, 592–3, 604–7 and *Life at the Centre*, pp. 501–8; Young, ibid., pp. 189–90 says ministers threatened resignation on the issue; Carrington, *Reflect*, p. 319 is disappointingly short on detail; but I. Gilmour, *Dancing with Dogma* (1992), pp. 236–41 confirms the threat. Thatcher, ibid., pp. 85–6 admits to being 'far from favourable' to the deal initially but says she accepted it because it gave most of what Britain wanted.
10. J. Dickie, *Inside the Foreign Office* (1992), p. 121; R. Bailey, *The European Connection* (Oxford, 1983), C. D. Cohen (ed.), *The Common Market· ten years after* (1983); A. M. El-Agraa, *Britain within the European Community* (1983); R. Jenkins (ed.), *Britain and the EEC* (1983).
11. P. Riddell, *The Thatcher Government* (Oxford, 1983), pp. 214–15.
12. G. Soutou, Paper presented to the Conference on 'Power in Europe, 1938–68', King's College, London, March 1992; P. Taylor, 'The New Dynamics of EC Integration in the 1980s', in J. Lodge (ed.), *The European Community and the Challenge of the Future* (1989), pp. 3–24, quote from p. 23; J. Pinder, 'The Single Market', in the same collection, 74; S. George, *An Awkward Partner: Britain in the EC* (1990), p. 164.
13. Taylor, ibid., pp. 3–4, 7 and passim; F. Pym, *The Politics of Consent* (1984), pp. 75–6.
14. On the summit see: Taylor, ibid., pp. 4–8; Young, *One of Us*, pp. 383–5; Thatcher, *Downing Street*, pp. 537–9.
15. On Fontainebleau see: Taylor, ibid., pp. 5–7; Young, ibid., 385–7; Thatcher, ibid., pp. 541–5; G. Howe, *Conflict of Loyalty* (1994), pp. 399–402; D. Reynolds, *Britannia Overruled* (1991), pp. 266–8.
16. De la Serre, *Grande Bretagne*, p. 181; Young, ibid., pp. 387–8 (on Howe); Cosgrave, *Thatcher*, pp. 90–1; D. Elles, 'The Foreign Policy of the Thatcher Government', in K. Minogue and M. Biddiss (eds), *Thatcherism: personality and politics* (1987), pp. 100–3; S. R. Letwin, *The Anatomy of Thatcherism* (1992), p. 281; George, *Awkward Partner*, pp. 159–62; P. Taylor, *The Limits of European Integration* (1983), ch. 8.
17. A. M. El-Agraa, 'Mrs Thatcher's EC Policy', in D. S. Bell (ed.), *The Conservative Government, 1979–84* (1985), pp. 166 and 174–82; Jenkins, *European Diary*, p. 375; Carrington, *Reflect*, pp. 318–19; Pym, Politics of Consent, pp. 70–1; Young, ibid., pp. 386–7 and 190–1; Reynolds, *Britannia*, pp. 266–7 and 273;

Taylor, 'EC Integration', pp. 7–8; Gilmour, *Dancing with Dogma*, p. 235. On the question of 'who won?' the BBQ see also P. Sharp, *Thatcher's Diplomacy* (1997), pp. 155–9.

18. Reynolds, ibid., p. 267.
19. On the origins of the IGC see Howe, *Conflict*, p. 409; Thatcher, *Downing Street*, pp. 548–51; P. Budden, *The Making of the Single European Act* (DPhil, Oxford, 1994), chs 2–4. On the Westland case see: M. Linklater and D. Leigh, *Not with Honour: the inside story of the Westland scandal* (1986); L. Freedman, 'The Case of Westland and the Bias to Europe', *International Affairs*, 63 (1986), 1–19.
20. Taylor, 'EC integration', 12; Budden, ibid., chs 5 and 6, quote from p. 404; Thatcher, ibid., pp. 551–7; Howe, ibid., pp. 453–8.
21. J. Grail and C. Teague, 'The British Labour Party and the EC', *Political Quarterly*, 59 (1988), 72–85; Lord Young, *The Enterprise Years* (1990), pp. 258, 380–3.
22. On the origins of EMU and British monetary policy in the mid-1980s see especially: P. Stephens, *Politics and the Pound* (1997), pp. 39–51; Thatcher, *Downing Street*, pp. 693–707 and 740–2; N. Lawson, *The View from Number 11* (1992), chs 39, 40, 52, 59, 63, 64, 71 and 72; Howe, *Conflict*, pp. 448–52; and H. Thompson, *The British Conservative Government and the Exchange Rate Mechanism* (1996), chs 2 and 3.
23. Letwin, *Thatcherism*, p. 301; Dickie, *Foreign Office*, pp. 280–3; Taylor, 'EC Integration', pp. 22–4.
24. C. Jenkins, *All Against the Collar* (1990), pp. 130, 137–40. And on changing TUC attitudes see D. MacShane, 'Trades Unions and Europe', *Political Quarterly*, 62 (1991), 351–64.
25. N. Ridley, *'My Style of Government': The Thatcher Years* (1991), pp. 207–11; Thatcher, *Downing Street*, pp. 709–18 and 750–8; Lawson, *View*, chs 73 and 74; Howe, *Conflict*, pp. 578–86.
26. On ERM entry and Thatcher's growing problems see especially: Stephens, *Politics*, pp. 112–20; Thompson, *Conservative Government*, chs 4 and 5.
27. Ridley, *Style*, ch. 7; B. Ingham, *Kill the Messenger* (1991), pp. 264–5; Henderson, *Channels and Tunnels*, ch. 1; George, *Awkward Partner*, p. 206; Sharp, *Thatcher's Diplomacy*, p. 179; Reynolds, *Britannia*, pp. 274–5; Dickie, *Foreign Office*, pp. 73–4.

7 Major, Maastricht and Conservative Division, 1990–1997

1. I. Crewe, 'Electoral Behaviour', in D. Kavanagh and A. Seldon (eds), *The Major Effect* (1994), p. 99.
2. W. Wallace, 'Foreign Policy', in ibid., p. 284, and in general see pp. 283–7; K. Baker, *The Turbulent Years* (1993), pp. 441–2.
3. M. Heseltine, *The Challenge of Europe* (1989); and see M. Crick, *Michael Heseltine: a biography* (1997), pp. 309–13, for an analysis.
4. E. Pearce, *The Quiet Rise of John Major* (1991), p. 130; A. Seldon, *Major: a political life* (1997), pp. 163–4.

5. A. Forster, *Empowerment and Constraint: Britain and the Negotiation of the Treaty on European Union* (Oxford, DPhil thesis, 1995), p. 55. See also another excellent doctoral thesis, A. Blair, *The UK and the Negotiation of the Maastricht Treaty, 1990–91* (Leicester, PhD thesis, 1998), passim; and the second edition of S. George, *An Awkward Partner* (1994), which argues, p. 236, that Major had tried to change the tone of policy as Chancellor and, p. 253, that the lack of a change on substance did not prevent Major winning real results.

6. S. Hogg and J. Hill, *Too Close to Call: power and politics – John Major in No 10* (1995), p. 76.

7. See the discussion in ibid., pp. 77–9; Seldon, *Major*, pp. 134 and 164–8.

8. P. Cradock, *In Pursuit of British Interests* (1997), p. 139; and on Major's collegiate Cabinet and the Hurd–Howard differences see especially Blair, *UK and the Maastricht Treaty*, pp. 296–9.

9. On the rebels, their subgroups and problems of disciplining them see: D. Baker, A. Gamble and S. Ludlam, 'Whips or Scorpions? The Maastricht Vote and the Conservative Party, *Parliamentary Affairs*, 46 (1993), 147–65.

10. P. Junor, *The Major Enigma* (1993), p. 266, and see pp. 258–66 on 'Black Wednesday'. But the fullest discussion of the Pound's troubles in 1992 is in P. Stephens, *Politics and the Pound: the Tories, the economy and Europe* (1997), chs 9 and 10.

11. H. Young, 'The Prime Minister', in Kavanagh and Seldon, *Major Effect*, p. 23; and see also Stephens, ibid., ch. 11.

12. I. Crewe, 'Electoral Behaviour' in Kavanagh and Seldon, *Major Effects*, p. 116.

13. A. Glees, 'The Diplomacy of Anglo-German Relations: a study of the ERM crisis of September 1992', *German Politics*, 3(1994), 76.

14. P. Jay, 'The Economy', in Kavanagh and Seldon, *Major Effect*, p. 188; and see P. Sinclair's essay on 'The Financial Sector' in the same volume, especially pp. 224–6 and 232–4.

15. See S. George, *An Awkward Partner: Britain in the European Community* (2nd edn, Oxford, 1994), pp. 248–50, for a more optimistic view of the British Presidency; and on the Edinburgh Summit, Seldon, *Major*, pp. 348–51.

16. Seldon, ibid., p. 254, and see pp. 255–61.

17. J. Major, 'Raise your Eyes, there is a Land Beyond', *The Economist* (25 September 1993), pp. 23–7.

18. Seldon, *Major*, pp. 463–70.

19. Ibid., pp. 485–6.

20. D. Hurd, 'The Future in Europe', German Society for Foreign Affairs, Berlin, 28 February 1995, Foreign and Commonwealth Office (FCO), Website http://www.fco.gov.uk.

21. M. Rifkind, Speech opening the IGC debate, ibid.

22. Speeches of 3 Feb. (Stockholm), 19 Feb. (Bonn), 3 March (Paris) and 19 March 1997 (The Hague), ibid.

23. S. George, 'Britain and the IGC', in G. Edwards and A. Pijpers (eds.), *The Politics of European Treaty Reform* (1997), pp. 100–17, quote from p. 108.

24. J. Major, 'The Future of Europe', Goldsmith's Hall, London, 19 June 1996; and M. Rifkind, Churchill Commemoration, Zurich, 18 September – both on FCO website.

25.   Seldon, *Major*, pp. 448–55.
26.   Ibid., pp. 470–4 and 476–7.
27.   Ibid., pp. 507–12 and 514–15. For a strong statement of the rebels' case see
      T. Gorman, *The Bastards* (1993).
28.   Seldon, *Major*, pp. 560–3 and 568–87; and on Thatcher's criticisms see her
      The Path to Power (1995), published in June as a supposed memoir of her
      early life but with lengthy criticism of Major and the EU (pp. 470–507).
29.   *Guardian*, 11 March 1996 and see 29 Nov. 1996 for the eventual framing of a
      Referendum party question (the choice between 'a federal Europe' or 'an
      association of sovereign nations').
30.   P. Lynch, *The Politics of Nationhood* (1998), pp. 99; S. Ludlam, 'The Spectre
      Haunting Conservatinism: Europe and backbench rebellion', in S. Ludlam
      and M. Smith (eds.), *Contemporary British Conservatinism* (1995), pp. 98–120.
31.   Above, pp.152–3.
32.   Young, in Kavanagh and Seldon, *Major Effect*, p. 25. The same point is made
      in Hogg and Hill, *Too Close*, p. 265.
33.   H. Kohl, speech at Louvain University, 2 Feb. 1996, quoted in the *Guardian*,
      3 Feb. 1996.
34.   Seldon, *Major*, pp. 639–43 and 648–53.
35.   J. Major, speech to the Institute of Directors, 24 April 1996, quoted in the
      Guardian, 25 April. For a summary of the arguments in favour of quitting the
      EU, see the editorial in the *Sunday Times*, 5 May 1996.
36.   M. Crick, *Michael Heseltine* (1997), pp. 431–3; Seldon, *Major*, pp. 635–9, 685–91,
      also 697–8; and on the March–April Cabinet debate, Stephens, *Politics and
      the Pound*, pp. 337–44.
37.   Major argued that, even if the Social Chapter itself was vague and the
      amount of legislation introduced under it was as yet limited, it could *in future*
      become much more significant: speech of 24 April 1996 (note 35 above); and
      speech in Brussels, 4 Feb. 1997, FCO website.
38.   On the election and EU issues see Seldon, *Major*, pp. 721–4.
39.   P. Oppenheim, 'Diary of an Underdog', entry of 19 April, published in the
      Sunday Times, 4 May 1997.

8   The Blair Government and the Birth of the Euro, 1997–1999

1.   J. Rentoul, *Tony Blair* (1995), p. 441.
2.   See House of Commons debates (*H.C. Deb.*), *6s.*,Vol. 287, cols 497–452 for a
     December 1996 statement by a party spokesperson; and on Cook see J. Kempf-
     ner, *Robin Cook* (1998), p. 180.
3.   *H. C. Deb*, Vol. 267, cols 148 and 217. On 'Clintonisation' see J. Sopel, *Tony
     Blair: the moderniser* (1995), pp. 142–3. On Labour's European policy in the
     years 1992–5 see W. Patterson et al., *The European Policies of Labour and Conser-
     vative Parties in Great Britain* (Sankt Augustin, Germany, 1993), pp. 26–50.
4.   FCO website (http://www.fco.gov.uk/). Speeches of 5 and 12 May 1997.
5.   *H. C. Deb.*, Vol. 296, cols 313–16 (18 June 1997).

6. Geoffrey Warner, 'Foreign, Defence and European Affairs: commentary', in
    B. Brivati and T. Bale (eds), *New Labour in Power* (1997), p. 157.
7. H. Pym and N. Kochan, *Gardon Brown: The first year in power* (1998), ch. 11.
8. FCO website, speech of 3 November 1997. See also the speech by Blair on 5
    December at Waterloo Station and a further speech by Cook, on 14 January
    1998, to the European Parliament.
9. Ibid., Chatham House speech, 25 June 1998.
10. For two similar, downbeat appreciations of the Presidency from different
    sides of the press spectrum see 'Analysis': *Guardian*, 9 June 1998, and 'Pres-
    ident Blair's Euro flop', *Sunday Times*, 14 June 1998.

Conclusions

1. D. Reynolds, *Britannia Overruled* (1991), p. 238; S. George, *An Awkward Part-
    ner* (1990), p. 40; P. Sharp, 'The Place of the EC in the Foreign Policy of Brit-
    ish Governments, 1961–71', *Millennium*, 11 (1982), 155–71, quotes from 155
    and 164.
2. Disraeli quoted in the introduction to K. Wilson (ed.), *British Foreign Secretaries
    and Foreign Policy* (1987), p. 5; Wilson quoted in Reynolds, ibid., p. 228.
3. In addition to George's *Awkward Partner* see also 'The Awkward Partner: an
    overview', in B. Brivati and H. Jones (eds), *From Reconstruction to Integration*
    (1993), ch. 15.
4. J. Buller, 'Britain as an Awkward Partner' and S. George, 'A Reply to Buller',
    Politics, 15 (1995), 33–47; S. Wilks, 'An Awkward Partner or an Awkward
    State?', *Politics*, 16 (1996), 160; W. Patterson, 'Britain and the European
    Union Revisited', *Scottish Affairs*, 9 (1994), 1–12; W. Kaiser, *Using Europe,
    Abusing the Europeans* (1996), esp. pp. xvi–xvii.
5. J. Frankel, *British Foreign Policy, 1945–73* (1975), pp. 234–5 and see pp. 236–19.
6. R. Holland, *The Pursuit of Greatness, 1900–70* (1991), pp. 258, 349–50.
7. D. Maclean, *British Foreign Policy Since Suez, 1956–68* (1970), pp. 76–7, and
    see pp. 75–81.
8. This was a point made at the time of Britain's first application: see A. Lamfa-
    lussy, *The UK and the Six: an essay on economic growth in Western Europe* (1963).
    On Benn see T. Benn, *Against the Tide: diaries 1973–6* (1989), pp. 142–3.
9. F. S. Northedge, *Descent from Power: British Foreign Policy, 1945–73* (1974),
    p. 362; Reynolds, *Britannia Overruled*, p. 298.
10. Wilks, 'Awkward Partner', pp. 159–65; George, *Awkward Partner*, p. 66;
    J. Black, *Convergence or Divergence?* (1994), p. 267.

SELECT BIBLIOGRAPHY

All places of publication are London except where otherwise stated.

Memoirs and Diaries

Acheson, D., *Present at the Creation* (1970).
Benn, T., *Out of the Wilderness: diaries, 1963–7* (1987).
——, *Office Without Power: diaries, 1968–72* (1988).
——, *Against the Tide: diaries, 1973–6* (1989).
——, *Conflicts of Interest: diaries, 1977–80* (1990).
Boothby, Lord, *My Yesterday, Your Tomorrow* (1964).
Brandt, W., *People and Policies* (1978).
Brown, G., *In My Way* (1971).
Cairncross, A. (ed.), *The Robert Hall Diaries, 1973* (1989).
Callaghan, J., *Time and Chance* (1987).
Carrington, Lord, *Reflect on Things Past* (1988).
Castle, B., *The Castle Diaries, 1964–70* (1984).
——, *The Castle Diaries, 1974–6* (1980).
——, *Fighting All The Way* (1993).
Cooper, A. Duff, *Old Men Forget* (1954).
Crossman, R., *The Backbench Diaries of Richard Crossman, 1951–64* (1981).
——, *Diaries of a Cabinet Minister*, Vols I *1964–6*, II *1966–8* and III *1968–70, 1975–7*.
Donnoughue, B., *Prime Minister: the conduct of policy under Harold Wilson and James Callaghan* (1982).
Eden, A., *Memoirs: Full Circle* (1960).
Falkender, M., *Downing Street in Perspective* (1983).
Gilmour, I., *Dancing with Dogma* (1992).
Gladwyn, Lord, *The Memoirs of Lord Gladwyn* (1972).
Gore-Booth, P., *With Great Truth and Respect* (1974).
Haines, J., *The Politics of Power* (1977).
Healey, D., *The Time of My Life* (1989).
Heath, E., *Old Worlds, New Horizons* (1970).
——, *The Course of my Life* (1998).
Henderson, N., *Channels and Tunnels* (1987).
——, *Mandarin: diaries* (1994).

Hogg, S. and Hill, J., *Too Close to Call: John Major in Number Ten* (1995).
Howe, G., *Conflict of Loyalty* (1994).
Hurd, D., *An End to Promises: sketch of a government, 1970–74* (1979).
Ingham, B., *Kill the Messenger* (1991).
Jay, D., *Change and Fortune* (1980).
Jenkins, R., *European Diary, 1977–81* (1989).
——, *A Life at the Centre* (1991).
Kilmuir, Earl of, *Political Adventure* (1964).
King, C., *The Cecil King Diary, 1965–70* (1972).
——, *The Cecil King Diary, 1970–74* (1975).
Kissinger, H., *The White House Years* (1979).
Lawson, N., *The View from Number Eleven: memoirs of a Tory radical* (1992).
Macmillan, H., *Tides of Fortune, 1945–55* (1969).
——, *Riding the Storm, 1956–9* (1971).
——, *Pointing the Way, 1959–61* (1972).
——, *At the End of the Day, 1961–3* (1974).
Martin, P., *The London Diaries, 1975–9* (Ottawa, 1988).
Massigli, R., *Une Comédie des Erreurs* (Paris, 1978).
Mayhew, C., *Time to Explain* (1987).
Maudling, R., *Memoirs* (1978).
Monnet, J., *Memoirs* (1978).
Owen, D., *Time to Declare* (1991).
Ridley, N., *My Style of Government: the Thatcher Years* (1991).
Roll, E., *Crowded Hours* (1985).
Spaak, P. H., *The Continuing Battle* (1971).
Stewart, M., *Life and Labour* (1980).
Tebbit, N., *Upwardly Mobile* (1988).
Thatcher, M., *The Downing Street Years* (1993).
——, *The Path to Power* (1995).
Walker, P., *Staying Power: an autobiography* (1991).
Wigg, G., *George Wigg* (1972).
Williams, M., *Inside Number 10* (1982).
Wilson, H., *The Labour Government, 1964–70* (1971).
——, *Final Term: 1974–6* (1979).

Secondary Works

Adams, J., *Tony Benn* (1992).
Aldous, R. and Lee, S. (eds), *Harold Macmillan and Britain's World Role* (1996).
Aldrich, R., *British Intelligence, Strategy and the Cold War, 1945–51* (1992).
Anderson, B., *John Major* (1991).
Ball, S. and Seldon, A. (eds), *The Heath Government, 1970–74* (1996).
Barker, E., *Britain in a Divided Europe* (1971).
——, *The British Between the Superpowers 1945–50* (1983).
Baylis, J., *The Diplomacy of Pragmatism: Britain and the Making of NATO, 1942–49* (1993).

Becker, J. and Knipping, F. (eds), *Power in Europe? France, Great Britain, Germany and Italy in a Post-war World, 1945–50* (New York, 1986).

Bell, D. S. (ed.), *The Conservative Government, 1979–84* (1985).

Bell, L., *The Throw that Failed: Britain's original application to join the common market* (1995).

Beloff, Lord, *Britain and the European Union* (1996).

Beloff, N., *The General Says No: Britain's exclusion from Europe* (1963).

Black, J., *Convergence or Divergence: Britain and the Continent* (1994).

Brivati, B., *Hugh Gaitskell* (1996).

Brivati, B. and Jones, H. (eds), *From Reconstruction to Integration: Britain and Europe since 1945* (1993).

Bullock, A., *Ernest Bevin: Foreign Secretary, 1945–51* (1983).

Burgess, M., *The British Tradition of Federalism* (1995).

Butler, D. and Kitzinger, U., *The 1975 Referendum* (1976).

Campbell, J., *Roy Jenkins* (1983).

——, *Edward Heath: a biography* (1993).

Camps, M., *Britain and the European Community 1955–63* (1964).

Carlton, D., *Anthony Eden* (1981).

Charlton, M., *The Price of Victory* (1983).

Connolly, B., *The Rotten Heart of Europe* (1994).

Cosgrave, P., *Thatcher: the First Term* (1985).

——, *The Lives of Enoch Powell* (1990).

Critchley, J., *Heseltine* (revd edn, 1994).

Crosland, S., *Tony Crosland* (1982).

Deighton, A. (ed.), *Building Postwar Europe* (1995).

Dell, E., *The Schuman Plan and the British Abdication of Leadership in Europe* (1995).

Denman, R., *Missed Chances: Britain and Europe in the twentieth century* (1996).

Dixon, P., *Double Diploma: the life of Sir Pierson Dixon, don and diplomat* (1968).

Dockrill, M. and Young, J. W. (eds), *British Foreign Policy, 1945–56* (1989).

Dockrill, S., *Britain's Policy for West German Rearmament, 1950–5* (1991).

Donnoughue, B. and Jones, G. W., *Herbert Morrison* (1973).

Dumoulin, M. (ed.), *Wartime Plans for Postwar Europe* (Brussels, 1995).

Dutton, D., *Anthony Eden: a life and reputation* (1997).

Frankel, J., *British Foreign Policy, 1945–73* (1975).

Franklin, M., *Britain's Future in Europe* (1990).

Fursdon, E., *The European Defence Community* (1980).

Gamble, A., *Britain in Decline* (1986 edn).

George, S., *Politics and Policy in the EC* (1985).

——, *An Awkward Partner: Britain in the EC* (3rd edn, 1998).

——, *Britain and European Integration Since 1945* (1991).

Goodhart, P., *Full-hearted Consent: the story of the referendum campaign* (1976).

Greenwood, S., *Britain and European Cooperation since 1945* (1992).

——, *Britain and European Integration since the Second World War: documents* (1996).

——, *The Alternative Alliance: Anglo-French relations before the coming of NATO, 1944–48* (1996).

Gregory, F. E. C., *Dilemmas of Government: Britain and the EC* (Oxford, 1983).

Hennessy, P. and Seldon, A. (eds), *Ruling Performance: British Governments from Attlee to Thatcher* (1987).

Heuser, B. and O'Neill, R. (eds), *Securing Peace in Europe, 1945–62* (1992).

Hogan, M. J., *The Marshall Plan: America, Britain and the Reconstruction of Western Europe, 1947–52* (Cambridge, 1987).

Holmes, M. (ed.), *The Eurosceptical Reader* (1996).

Holland, R., *The Pursuit of Greatness: Britain and the World Role* (1992).

Horne A., *Macmillan*, Vols I *(1894–1956)* and II *(1957–86)* (1988–1989).

Howard, A., *RAB: the life of R. A. Butler* (1987).

James, R. Rhodes, *Anthony Eden* (1986).

——, *Bob Boothby* (1991).

Jenkins, R. (ed.), *Britain and the EEC* (1983).

Jowell, R. and Hoinville, G. (eds), *Britain into Europe: public opinion and the EEC, 1961–75* (1976).

Kaiser, W., *Using Europe, Abusing the Europeans: Britain and European Integration, 1945–63* (1996).

Kampfner, J., *Robin Cook* (1998).

Kavanagh, J. and Seldon, A., *The Major Effect* (1994).

Kellner, P. and Hitchens, C., *Callaghan: the road to Number 10* (1976).

Kennedy, P., *The Realities behind Diplomacy: background influences on British external policy, 1865–1980* (1981).

Kent, J., *British Imperial Strategy and the Origins of the Cold War, 1944–49* (1993).

Kitzinger, U., *The Second Try: Labour and the EEC* (Oxford, 1968).

——, *Diplomacy and Persuasion. how Britain joined the Common Market* (1973).

Lamb, R., *The Macmillan Years: the emerging truth* (1995).

Letwin, S. R., *The Anatomy of Thatcherism* (1992).

Lieber, R. J., *British Politics and European Unity: parties, elites and pressure groups* (1970).

Lodge, J. (ed.), *The European Community and the Challenge of the Future* (1989).

Lord, C., *British Entry to the European Community under the Heath Government of 1970–4* (1993).

——, *Absent at the Creation: Britain and the formation of the European Community, 1950–2* (1996).

Ludlow, Peter, *The Making of the European Monetary System* (1982).

Ludlow, Piers, *Dealing with Britain: the Six and the first UK application to the EEC* (1997).

Lynch, P., *The Politics of Nationhood: sovereignty, Britishness and Conservative politics* (1998).

Maclean, D., *British Foreign Policy Since Suez, 1956–68* (1970).

Middlemas, K., *Power, Competition and the State* (3 vols, 1986–91).

Milward, A. S., *The Reconstruction of Western Europe, 1945–51* (1984).

——, *The European Rescue of the Nation-State* (1992).

Milward, A. S. et al., *The Frontier of National Sovereignty* (1993).

Minogue, K. and Biddiss, M. (eds), *Thatcherism: personality and politics* (1987).

Moon, J., *European Integration in British Politics, 1950–63: a study of issue change* (Aldershot, 1985).

Morgan, A., *Harold Wilson* (1992).

Morgan, K., *Callaghan: a life* (1997).

di Nolfo, E. (ed.), *Power in Europe? Vol. 1I. Great Britain, France, Germany and Italy and the Origins of the EEC, 1952–7* (1992).

Northedge, F. S., *Descent from Power: British foreign policy, 1945–73* (1974).

Nutting, A., *Europe Will Not Wait* (1960).

Onslow, S., *Backbench Debate within the Conservative Party and its influence on British foreign policy, 1948–57* (1997).

Ovendale, R. (ed.), *The Foreign Policy of the Labour Governments, 1915–51* (Leicester, 1984).

Paterson, P., *George Brown* (1993).

Pimlott, B., *Harold Wilson* (1992).

Ponting, C., *Breach of Promise* (1989).

Pym, H. and Kochan, N., *Gordon Brown: the first year in power* (1998).

Reau, E. du, *Europe des Elites? Europe des Peuples?* (Paris, 1998).

Rentoul, J., *Tony Blair* (1995).

Reynolds, D., *Britannia Overruled* (1991).

Riddell, P., *The Thatcher Government* (Oxford, 1983).

Riste, O. (ed.), *Western Security: the formative years* (New York, 1985).

Robins, L. J., *The Reluctant Party: Labour and the EEC, 1961–75* (Ormskirk, 1979).

Rollo, P. J. V., *Britain and the Briand Plan* (Keele, 1972).

Ross, G., *Jacques Delors and European Integration* (1995).

Routledge, P., *Gordon Brown: the biography* (1998).

Seldon, A., *Churchill's Indian Summer, 1951–5* (1981).

——, *Major: a political life* (1997).

Serra, E. (ed.), *The Relaunching of Europe and the Treaties of Rome* (Brussels, 1989).

de la Serre, F., *La Grande Bretagne et la Communauté Européenne* (Paris, 1987).

Sharp, P., *Thatcher's Diplomacy* (1997).

Shlaim, A., *Britain and the Origins of European Unity, 1940–51* (Reading, 1978).

Sopel, J., *Tony Blair: the moderniser* (1995).

Stephens, P., *Politics and the Pound* (1997).

Stirk, P. (ed.), *European Unity in Context: the interwar period* (1989).

Stirk, P. and Willis, D. (eds), *Shaping Postwar Europe* (1991).

Taylor, P., *The Limits of European Integration* (1983).

Thompson, H., *The British Conservative Government and the Exchange Rate Mechanism* (1996).

Tratt, J., *The Macmillan Government and Europe* (1996).

Thorpe, D. R., *Alec Douglas-Home* (1996).

Wallace, W. (ed.), *Britain in Europe* (1980).

Whitehead, P., *The Writing on the Wall: Britain in the Seventies* (1985).

Wilkes, G. (ed.), *Britain's Failure to Enter the European Community, 1961–63* (1997).

Woodhouse, R., *British Policy Towards France, 1945–51* (1995).

Woodward, L., *British Foreign Policy in the Second World War*, Vol. V (1976).

Young, H., *One of Us* (1990).

Young, J. W., *Britain, France and the Unity of Europe, 1945–51* (Leicester, 1984).

——, *Winston Churchill's Last Campaign: Britain and the Cold War, 1951–5* (1993).

——, *Britain and the World in the Twentieth Century* (1997).

Young, J. W. (ed.), *The Foreign Policy of Churchill's Peacetime Administration, 1951–5* (Leicester, 1988).

Young, S., *Terms of Entry: Britain's negotiations with the EC, 1970–72* (1973).

Ziegler, P., *Wilson: the authorised life* (1993).

Articles

Adamthwaite, A., 'Britain and the World, 1945–9', *International Affairs*, 61 (1985), 223–35.

Baker, D. et al., 'Whips or Scorpions? the Maastricht vote and the Conservative Party', *Parliamentary Affairs*, 46 (1993), 147–66.

Baylis, J., 'British wartime thinking about a post-war European security group', *Review of International Studies*, 9 (1983), 265–81.

——, Britain and the Dunkirk Treaty: the origins of NATO', *Journal of Strategic Studies*, 6 (1982), 236–47.

Blair, A., 'UK policy co-ordination during the 1990–91 Intergovernmental Conference', *Diplomacy and Staecraft*, 9 (1998), 160–83.

Boyce, R., ' 'Britain's first "No" to Europe: Britain and the Briand Plan, 1929–30', *European Studies Review*, 10 (1980), 17–45.

——, 'Was there a British Alternative to the Briand Plan?', in Catterall, P. and Morris, C. (eds), *Britain and the Threat to Stability in Europe, 1918–45* (1993).

Burgess, S. and Edwards, G., 'The Six Plus One: British policy-making and the question of European economic integration, 1955', *International Affairs*, 64 (1988), 393–413.

Charmley, J., 'Duff Cooper and Western European Union, 1944–7', *Review of International Studies*, II (1985), 53–63.

Deighton, A., 'The Last Piece of the Jigsaw: Britain and the Creation of the Western European Union', *Contemporary European History*, 7 (1998), 181–96.

Dutton, D., 'Anticipating Maastricht: the Conservative Party and Britain's First Application to join the European Community', *Contemporary Record*, 7 (1993), 522–40.

Freedman, L., 'The Case of Westland and the Bias to Europe', *International Affairs*, 63 (1986), 1–19.

Galston, P., 'The Free Trade diplomacy debate and the Victorian European common market initiative', *Canadian Journal of History*, 22 (1987), 59–82.

Garry, J., 'The British Conservative Party: divisions over European policy', *West European Politics*, 18 (1995), 170–90.

Geddes, A., 'Labour and the European Community, 1973–93', *Contemporary Record*, 8 (1994), 370–80.

Glees, A., 'The Diplomacy of Anglo-German Relations: a study of the ERM crisis of September 1992', *German Politics*, 3 (1994), 75–90.

Grail, J. and Teague, R., 'The British Labour Party and the EC', *Political Quarterly*, 59 (1988), 72–85.

Grantham, J. T., 'British Labour and the Hague Congress', *Historical Journal*, 24 (1981), 443–52.

Greenwood, S., 'Ernest Bevin, France and Western Union, 1945–6', *European History Quarterly*, 14 (1984), 312–26.

——, 'Return to Dunkirk: The Origins of the Anglo-French Treaty of March 1947', *Journal of Strategic Studies*, 6 (1983), 49–65.

Heath, E., 'European Integration over the next Ten Years', *International Affairs*, 64 (1998), 199–207.

Henderson, N., 'Britain's Decline', *The Economist*, 2 June 1979.

Kaiser, W., 'The Bomb and Europe: Britain, France and the EEC entry negoti-ations', *Journal of European Integration History*, 1 (1995), 65–85.

Kent, J., 'The British Empire and the Origins of the Cold War', in Deighton, A. (ed.), *Britain and the First Cold War* (1990).

Kent, J. and Young J. W., 'The Western Union concept and British defence policy, 1947–8', in Aldrich, R. (ed.), *British Intelligence, Strategy and the Cold War, 1945–51* (1992), pp. 166–92.

——, 'The Third Force and the Origins of NATO', in Heuser, B. and O'Neill, R. (eds), *Securing Peace in Europe, 1945–62* (1992).

Larres, K., 'Integrating Europe or Ending the Cold War? Churchill's postwar for-eign policy', *Journal of European Integration History*, 2 (1996), 15–49.

Lord, C., 'Sovereign or Confused? the great debate about British entry to the EC twenty years on', *Journal of Common Market Studies*, 30 (1992), 419–36.

MacShane, D., 'Trades Unions and Europe', *Political Quarterly*, 62 (1991), 351–64.

Melissen, J. and Zeeman, B., 'Britain and Western Europe, 1945–51', *International Affairs*, 63 (1987), 81–95.

Newton, S., 'Britain, the Sterling Area and European Integration 1945–50', *Journal of Imperial and Commonwealth History*, 13 (1985), 163–82.

——, 'The 1949 Sterling Crisis and British Policy towards European Integration', *Review of International Studies*, II (1985), 169–82.

Pagedas, C., 'The After-life of Blue Streak: Britain's American answer to Europe', *Journal of Strategic Studies*, 18 (1995), 1–24.

——, 'Harold Macmillan and the 1962 Champs Meeting', *Diplomacy and Statecraft*, 9 (1998), 224–42.

Patterson, W., 'Britain and the European Union Revisited', *Scottish Affairs*, 9 (1994), 1–12.

Riste, O., 'The Genesis of North Atlantic Defence Cooperation', *NATO Review*, 29 (1981), 22–9.

Schaad, M., 'Plan G – a counterblast? British policy towards the Messina coun-tries, 1956', *Contemporary European History*, 7 (1998), 39–60.

Schenk, C., 'Decolonization and European Integration: the Free Trade Area negotiations, 1956–8', *Journal of Imperial and Commonwealth History*, 24 (1996), 444–63.

Schneer, J., 'Hopes deferred or shattered: the Labour Left and the Third Force Movement, 1945–9', *Journal of Modern History*, 56 (1984), 197–226.

Sharp, P., 'The Place of the EC in the Foreign Policy of British Governments, 1961–71', *Millennium*, II (1982), 155–71.

Shlaim, A., 'Prelude to Downfall: the British offer of union to France, June 1940', *Journal of Contemporary History*, 9 (1972), 27–63.

Steininger, R., 'Great Britain's first EEC failure in January 1963', *Diplomacy and Statecraft*, 7 (1996), 404–35.

Steinnes, K., 'The European Challenge: Britain's EEC application in 1961', *Contemporary European History*, 7 (1998), 61–79.

Weiler, P., 'British Labour and the Cold War', *Journal of British Studies*, 26 (1987), 70–81.

White, R., 'Cordial Caution: the British response to the French proposal for European Federal Union, 1929–30', in Bosco, A. (ed.), *The Federal Idea* (1991).

Wilford, R., 'The Federal Union Campaign', *European Studies Review*, 10 (1980), 102–14.

Young, J. W., 'Duff Cooper as Ambassador to France', in Zametica, J. (ed.), *British Officials and British Foreign Policy*, 1945–50 (1990).

——, 'Churchill's "No" to Europe, 1951–2', *Historical Journal*, 28 (1985), 923–37.

Zeeman, B., 'Britain and the Cold War: an alternative approach. The Treaty of Dunkirk example', *European History Quarterly*, 16 (1986), 343–67.

INDEX

234

Index

European Defence Community,
33–41, 46, 49, 183, 200
European Economic Area, 153–4
European Economic Community,
passim from 45
European Free Trade Association,
62–72, 75, 79, 81–3, 91, 96,
253–4, 163, 175, 193, 195
European Parliament, 110, 115,
122–3, 127, 129, 134, 145,
152–3, 155, 158, 165, 178
European Political Cooperation,
101, 141
European Union, 163, 177,
179–82
Evans, H., 71, 77
Exchange Rate Mechanism,
123–8, 131, 135, 139, 143–8,
151–3, 156, 160–4, 176, 182

Falkender, M., 107
Faure, E., 40
Federal Union movement, 4–5
Federation (later Confederation)
of British Industry, 47, 58, 62,
64
Finland, 154, 163, 166–7
Foot, M., 116–18, 122, 133
Foreign Office, 1, 6–13, 15–16, 18,
20–1, 23, 28–30, 34, 36–7,
39–42, 44, 46, 53, 64, 66–7,
83–7, 90–1, 96–8, 102–3,
113–14, 121–2, 128, 130–1,
136, 138, 140, 145–6, 176
France, *passim*
Frankel, J., 189
Free Trade Area proposal, 43–8,
51–66, 78, 171, 191, 193
Fritalux proposal, 27

Gaddis, J., 14
Gaitskell, H., 69, 75–6, 84, 86, 175
De Gasperi, A., 28
De Gaulle, 5, 8–9, 59–99, 135, 144,
191, 196, 200
General Agreement on Tariffs and
Trade, 20, 63–5, 153, 163, 195
Genscher, H.-D., 134

George, S., 109, 120, 134, 148, 167,
184, 186–7, 199
Germany, *passim* to 81, 92–3, 95,
97–8, 101, 104–5, 108, 110–11,
113, 120–4, 129, 132, 134–5,
139–40, 146–8, 152, 154–7,
164–70, 177, 179–80, 185,
188–99, 200–1
Gilmour, I., 130, 132, 138
Giscard d'Estaing, V., 113, 115,
117, 120–3, 130, 132, 135
Glees, A., 161
Goldsmith, J., 170, 172
Gordon-Walker, P., 82
Gore-Booth, P., 53, 61, 83, 87, 90
Gouin, F., 9
Greece, 37, 121, 128, 134–7,
139–40, 164, 181, 185, 200
Greenwood, S., 7, 9, 11, 14, 45,
113
Guardian, the, 66

Haas, E., 124
Hague Congress (1948), 18–19, 26
Hague, W., 178
Haines, J., 98
Hall, R., 28–9
Hallstein, W., 58
Hart, J., 120
Harvey, O., 9
Hattersley, R., 116
Healey, D., 87, 93, 108, 121, 124
Heath, E., 67–8, 72–4, 77–8, 84,
86, 99–112, 117–20, 124, 127,
135–6, 146, 170–2, 179, 184–5,
196
Heathcoat-Amory, D., 67
Henderson, D., 177
Henderson, N., 30, 111, 128, 148,
201
Heseltine, M., 140, 148, 151–2,
171, 178
Hogan, M., 12, 28
Holland, R., 14, 82, 190
Home, A. Douglas- (later Lord),
67, 100
Horne, A., 81
Howard, M., 13, 151, 156–7